St. Helena Library
1492 Library Lane
St. Helena, CA 94574
(707) 963-5244

Praise for *The Deficit Myth*

"*The Deficit Myth* is simply the most important book I've ever read. Stephanie Kelton carefully articulates a message that obliterates economic orthodoxy about public finance, which assumes that taxes precede spending and deficits are bad. Kelton's work is on a par with the genius of DaVinci and Copernicus, heretics who proved that Earth revolves around the sun."
> —David Cay Johnston, recipient of the Pulitzer Prize, an Investigative Reporters and Editors Inc. Medal, and the George Polk Award

"A remarkable book both in content and timing. A 'must-read' that is sure to influence many aspects of policymaking going forward."
> —Mohamed El-Erian, chief economic advisor, Allianz

"In a world of epic, overlapping crises, Stephanie Kelton is an indispensable source of moral clarity. Whether you're all in for MMT, or merely MMT-curious, the truths that she teaches about money, debt, and deficits give us the tools we desperately need to build a safe future for all. Read it—then put it to use."
> —Naomi Klein, author of *On Fire: The Burning Case for a Green New Deal*

"Kelton's game-changing book on the myths around government deficits is both theoretically rigorous and empirically entertaining. It reminds us that money is not limited, only our imagination of what to do with it. After you read it you will never think of the public purse as a household economy again. Read it!"
> —Mariana Mazzucato, author of *The Value of Everything: Making and Taking in the Global Economy*

"*The Deficit Myth* is a triumph. It is absorbing, compelling, and—most important of all—empowering. Embracing a well-researched framework that focuses on how real-world economies actually operate, she lays out a realistic path to true economic prosperity. It is an approach that focuses on Main Street and not Wall Street and will permit us to not only revitalize the struggling middle class, but address critical social problems like chronic unemployment, poverty, health care, and climate change. We of course face many binding constraints on our ability to act, but Kelton argues that the intentional underemployment of our own resources that results from the pervasive influence of deficit myths should not be one. We have needed this book for a very long time. Everyone should read it, and then reread it, before it is too late to change course."

    —John T. Harvey, professor of economics, Texas Christian University

"Kelton's mission in this powerful book is to free us from defunct orthodox thinking about fiscal deficits rooted in the bygone era of the gold standard. Her theoretical canvas is modern monetary theory. At its core MMT offers a simple proposition: In a fiat currency world, the finances of we the people ain't the same as a summing up of our individual budget constraints, because we the people can't go broke, only deficit-spend our collective self into inflationary excesses. In the prevailing era of too-low inflation, the macro policy implication should be obvious: We the people presently have far more fiscal space than the deficit scold, pay-for crowd preaches. Kelton is a gifted writer and teacher and I confidently predict that *The Deficit Myth*, brilliantly written and argued, will become the defining book on what MMT is—and what it is not."

    —Paul Allen McCulley, retired managing director and chief economist, PIMCO, and senior fellow, Cornell University Law School

"Clear! Compelling! Eye-opening and persuasive, *The Deficit Myth* is an adventure in the world of budgets, jobs, trade, banking, and—above all—money. With the great force of common sense, Stephanie Kelton and the MMT team have broken through the closed circles of so-called sound finance, a stale orthodoxy that has weakened and impoverished us all. This book shows how they did it, and it blazes a path forward, toward a better world built on better ideas."

    —James K. Galbraith, The University of Texas at Austin

"A robust, well-reasoned, and highly readable walk through many common misunderstandings. A 'must-read' for anyone who wants to understand how government financing really works, and how it interplays with economic policy."

    —Frank Newman, former deputy secretary of the Treasury

the

DEFICIT

MYTH

Modern Monetary Theory

and the Birth of the People's Economy

STEPHANIE KELTON

PUBLICAFFAIRS

NEW YORK

PublicAffairs
Hachette Book Group
1290 Avenue of the Americas, New York, NY 10104
www.publicaffairsbooks.com
@Public_Affairs

Printed in the United States of America

First Edition: June 2020

Published by PublicAffairs, an imprint of Perseus Books, LLC, a subsidiary of Hachette Book Group, Inc. The PublicAffairs name and logo is a trademark of the Hachette Book Group.

The Hachette Speakers Bureau provides a wide range of authors for speaking events. To find out more, go to www.hachettespeakersbureau.com or call (866) 376-6591.

The publisher is not responsible for websites (or their content) that are not owned by the publisher.

Library of Congress Cataloging-in-Publication Data

Names: Kelton, Stephanie, 1969– author.
Title: The deficit myth : modern monetary theory and the birth of the people's economy / Stephanie Kelton.
Description: First edition. | New York : PublicAffairs, [2020] | Includes bibliographical references and index.
Identifiers: LCCN 2019059417 | ISBN 9781541736184 (hardcover) | ISBN 9781541736207 (ebook) | ISBN 9781541757110 (international)
Subjects: LCSH: Debts, Public—United States. | Budget deficits—United States. | Government spending policy—United States. | Fiscal policy—United States.
Classification: LCC HJ8119 .K46 2020 | DDC 339.5/30973—dc23
LC record available at https://lccn.loc.gov/2019059417

ISBN: 978-1-5417-3618-4 (hardcover); 978-1-5417-3620-7 (ebook); 978-1-5417-5711-0 (international)

LSC-C

10 9 8 7 6 5 4 3 2 1

For Bradley and Katherine

Contents

Introduction

Bumper Sticker Shock

It ain't what you know that gets you into trouble. It's what you
know for sure that just ain't so.

—MARK TWAIN

I remember when I saw a bumper sticker on the back of a Mercedes
SUV in 2008 while I made my one-hour commute from Lawrence,
Kansas, to my job teaching economics at the University of Missouri
in Kansas City. It featured a man, standing slightly hunched, with his
pants pockets turned inside out. His face bore a hardened, serious
look. He wore red-and-white striped pants, a dark-blue jacket, and
a top hat adorned with stars. It was Uncle Sam. Like the driver with
this bumper sticker, many people have come to believe that our government is flat broke and that its budget is unable to tackle the most
important issues of our time.

Whether the policy debate is health care, infrastructure, education,
or climate change, the same question inevitably arises: But how are
you going to pay for it? This bumper sticker captured a real frustration
and anxiety that exists over our nation's fiscal affairs, particularly with
the size of the federal deficit. Based on how politicians across parties

have railed against the deficit, it's understandable why anyone would get enraged when thinking about our government behaving imprudently. After all, if we as individuals behaved the way the government behaves, we'd soon be bankrupted just like the image of a destitute Uncle Sam.

But what if the federal budget is fundamentally different than your household budget? What if I showed you that the deficit bogeyman isn't real? What if I could convince you that we can have an economy that puts people and planet first? That finding the money to do this is not the problem?

Copernicus and the scientists who followed him changed our understanding of the cosmos, showing that the earth revolves around the sun and not the other way around. A similar breakthrough is needed for how we understand the deficit and its relationship to the economy. When it comes to increasing our public well-being, we have far more options than we realize, but we desperately need to see through the myths that have been holding us back.

This book uses the lens of Modern Monetary Theory (MMT), of which I have been a leading proponent, to explain this Copernican shift. The main arguments that I present apply to any monetary sovereign—countries like the US, the UK, Japan, Australia, Canada, and others—where the government is the monopoly issuer of a fiat currency.[1] MMT changes how we view our politics and economics by showing that in almost all instances federal deficits are good for the economy. They are necessary. And the way we have thought about them and treated them is often incomplete or inaccurate. Rather than chasing after the misguided goal of a balanced budget we should be pursuing the promise of harnessing what MMT calls our public money, or sovereign currency, to balance the economy so that prosperity is broadly shared and not concentrated in fewer and fewer hands.

The taxpayer, according to the conventional view, is at the center of the monetary universe because of the belief that the government has no money of its own. Therefore, the only money available to fund the government must ultimately come from people like us. MMT radically changes our understanding by recognizing that it is the currency issuer—the federal government itself—not the taxpayer, that finances all government expenditures. Taxes are important for other reasons that I will explain in this book. But the idea that taxes pay for what the government spends is pure fantasy.

I was skeptical when I first encountered these ideas. In fact, I resisted them. During my early training as a professional economist, I sought to refute MMT's claims through intense research about our government's fiscal and monetary operations. By the time I developed this into my first, published, peer-reviewed academic paper, I realized that my prior understanding had been wrong. The core idea behind MMT may have initially appeared outlandish, but it proved to be descriptively accurate. In one sense, MMT is a nonpartisan lens that describes how our monetary system actually works. Its explanatory power doesn't depend on ideology or political party. Rather, MMT clarifies what is economically possible and thus shifts the terrain of policy debates that get hamstrung over questions of financial feasibility. MMT focuses on the broader economic and social impacts of a proposed policy change rather than its narrow budgetary impact. John Maynard Keynes's contemporary, Abba P. Lerner, was a champion of this approach, which he dubbed *functional finance*. The idea was to judge policy by the way it worked or functioned. Does it control inflation, sustain full employment, and bring about a more equitable distribution of income and wealth? The particular number that falls out of the budget box each year was (and is) quite beside the point.

Do I believe the solution to all our problems is to simply spend more money? No, of course not. Just because there are no *financial* constraints on the federal budget doesn't mean there aren't *real* limits to what the government can (and should) do. Every economy has its own internal speed limit, regulated by the availability of our *real productive resources*—the state of technology and the quantity and quality of its land, workers, factories, machines, and other materials. If the government tries to spend too much into an economy that's already running at full speed, inflation will accelerate. There are limits. However, the limits are not in our government's ability to spend money, or in the deficit, but in inflationary pressures and resources within the real economy. MMT distinguishes the real limits from delusional and unnecessary self-imposed constraints.

You've probably already seen MMT's central insights in action. I saw them up close when I worked in the US Senate. Whenever the topic of Social Security comes up, or when someone in Congress wants to put more money into education or health care, there's a lot of talk about how everything must be "paid for" to avoid adding to the federal deficit. But have you noticed this never seems to be a problem when it comes to expanding the defense budget, bailing out banks, or giving huge tax breaks to the wealthiest Americans, even when these measures significantly raise the deficit? As long as the votes are there, the federal government can always fund its priorities. That's how it works. Deficits didn't stop Franklin Delano Roosevelt from implementing the New Deal in the 1930s. They didn't dissuade John F. Kennedy from landing a man on the moon. And they never once stopped Congress from going to war.

That's because Congress has the power of the purse. If it really wants to accomplish something, the money can always be made available. If lawmakers wanted to, they could advance legislation—today— aimed at raising living standards and delivering the public investments in education, technology, and resilient infrastructure that are critical for our long-term prosperity. Spending or not spending is a political decision. Obviously, the economic ramifications of any bill should be thoroughly considered. But spending should never be constrained by arbitrary budget targets or a blind allegiance to so-called sound finance.

I DON'T THINK it's a coincidence that I ended up seeing the Uncle Sam bumper sticker when I did in November of 2008. The outmoded beliefs about the government running out of money gained traction during the financial crisis that same year. Our nation was in the midst of the worst economic downturn since the Great Depression. It did feel as though we, as a country, were going broke, along with a good chunk of the rest of the world. What started as a disruption in the sub-prime mortgage market had spilled over into global financial markets and morphed into a full-blown economic meltdown that cost millions of Americans their jobs, their homes, and their businesses.[2] Eight hundred thousand Americans lost their jobs that November alone. Millions applied for unemployment insurance, food stamps, Medicaid, and other forms of public assistance. With the economy sliding deeply into recession, tax receipts fell off a cliff and spending to support the unemployed rose sharply, pushing the deficit to a record $779 billion. There was panic all around.

Proponents of MMT, myself included, saw this as an opportunity to offer bold policy ideas to the incoming Obama administration. We urged Congress to enact a robust stimulus, calling for a payroll tax holiday, additional aid for state and local governments, and a federal job guarantee.

By January 16, 2009, America's four largest financial institutions had lost half their value, and the labor market was hemorrhaging hundreds of thousands of jobs a month. Just like FDR, President Obama took the oath of office on January 20 at a time of historic urgency. Within thirty days, he had signed a $787 billion economic stimulus package into law. Some of his close advisers had pushed for substantially more, insisting that a minimum of $1.3 trillion would be needed to avoid a protracted recession. Others balked at anything ending in "trillion." In the end, Obama lost his nerve.

Why? Because he was basically a conservative when it came to fiscal policy. He was surrounded by people giving him different numbers, and he decided to err on the side of caution, picking a number toward the lower end of what was presented to him. Christina Romer, his chair of the Council of Economic Advisers, understood that a crisis of this magnitude could not be handled with the more modest $787 billion intervention. She made the case for an ambitious trillion-plus stimulus, saying, "Well, Mr. President, this is your 'holy-shit moment.' It's worse than we thought."[3] She had run the numbers, and she concluded that a package as large as $1.8 trillion might be required to combat the worsening recession. But that option was nixed by Lawrence Summers, the Harvard economist and former treasury secretary who became Obama's chief economic adviser. Summers might have preferred a bigger stimulus, but he worried that asking Congress for anything close to $1 trillion would provoke ridicule, saying that "the public wouldn't stand for it, and it would never get through Congress."[4] David Axelrod, who would go on to become senior adviser to the president, agreed, worrying that anything over a trillion would create "sticker shock" in Congress and with the American people.

The $787 billion that Congress ultimately authorized included money to help state and local governments cope with the downturn, funding for infrastructure and green investment projects, and substantial tax breaks to encourage private sector consumption and investment. It all helped, but not nearly enough. The economy shrank, and as the deficit climbed to more than $1.4 trillion, President Obama faced questions about the rising tide of red ink. On May 23, 2009, he appeared in an interview on C-SPAN. The show's host, Steve Scully, asked, "At what point do we run out of money?"[5] The president responded, "Well, we are out of money now." And there it was. The president had just reinforced what the driver with the Uncle Sam bumper sticker suspected all along. The United States was broke.

The Great Recession, which lasted from December 2007 to June 2009, left permanent scars on communities and families across the United States and beyond. It took more than six years for the US labor market to recover all 8.7 million jobs that were lost between December 2007 and early 2010.[6] Millions struggled for a year or longer before finding employment. Many never did. And some who were fortunate enough to find work often had to settle for part-time employment or take jobs that paid substantially less than they had been earning. Meanwhile, the foreclosure crisis swallowed $8 trillion in housing wealth, and an estimated 6.3 million people—including 2.1 million children—were pushed into poverty between 2007 and 2009.[7]

Congress could and should have done more, but the deficit myth had taken hold. By January 2010, with the unemployment rate at a staggering 9.8 percent, President Obama was already moving in the opposite direction. That month, in his State of the Union address, he committed to a reversal of fiscal stimulus, telling the nation, "Families across the country are tightening their belts and making tough decisions. The federal government should do the same." What followed was a sustained period of self-inflicted harm.

The Federal Reserve Bank of San Francisco (FRBSF) estimates that the financial crisis and the lackluster recovery robbed the US economy of up to 7 percent of its output potential from 2008 to 2018. Think of this as a measure of all of the goods and services (and income) we could have produced over that decade but didn't because we failed to do enough to support our economy by protecting jobs and keeping people in their homes. By not getting the policy response right, we set the stage for a slow and weak recovery that harmed our communities and translated into trillions of dollars in foregone prosperity for our economy. According to the FRBSF, the decade of subpar economic growth cost every man, woman, and child in America the equivalent of $70,000.

Why didn't we make better policy? You might think the answer is that our two-party system has become so divided that Congress was just incapable of doing the right thing, even when confronted with a national calamity that threatened the security of average Americans and big corporations alike. And there is certainly some truth to that. In 2010, Senate majority leader Mitch McConnell boasted openly that "the single most important thing we want to achieve is for President

Obama to be a one-term president." But party politics weren't the only obstacle. The politics of deficit hysteria, embraced by both sides for decades, served as an even bigger impediment.

Bigger deficits would have enabled a faster and stronger recovery, protecting millions of families and avoiding trillions in economic losses. But no one with any real power fought for bigger deficits. Not President Obama, not most of his senior advisers, not even the most progressive members of the House and Senate. Why? Did everyone really believe that the government had run out of money? Or were they just afraid of offending the sensibilities of voters like the one who placed that bumper sticker on her Mercedes?

We can't use deficits to solve problems if we continue to think of the deficit itself as a problem. Right now, about half of Americans (48 percent) say that reducing federal budget deficits should be a top priority for the president and Congress. This book aims to drive the number of people who believe the deficit is a problem closer to zero. It won't be easy. To get there, we're going to have to carefully unravel the myths and misunderstandings that have shaped our public discourse.

———

THE FIRST SIX chapters of the book dispel the deficit myths that have hobbled us as a country. To begin, I tackle the idea that the federal government should budget like a household. Perhaps no myth is more pernicious. The truth is, the federal government is nothing like a household or a private business. That's because Uncle Sam has something the rest of us don't—the power to issue the US dollar. Uncle Sam doesn't need to come up with dollars before he can spend. The rest of us do. Uncle Sam can't face mounting bills he can't afford to pay. The rest of us might. Uncle Sam will never go broke. The rest of us could. When governments try to manage their budgets like households, they miss out on the opportunity to harness the power of their sovereign currencies to substantially improve life for their people. We will show how MMT demonstrates that the federal government is not dependent on revenue from taxes or borrowing to finance its spending and that the most important constraint on government spending is inflation.

The second myth is that deficits are evidence of overspending. It's an easy conclusion to reach because we've all heard politicians lament deficits as proof that the government is "living beyond its means." That's a mistake. It is true that a deficit is recorded on the government's books whenever it spends more than it taxes. But that's only half the story. MMT paints the rest of the picture using some simple accounting logic. Suppose the government spends $100 into the economy but collects just $90 in taxes. The difference is known as the *government deficit*. But there's another way to look at that difference. Uncle Sam's deficit creates a *surplus* for someone else. That's because the government's minus $10 is always matched by a plus $10 in some other part of the economy. The problem is that policy makers are looking at the picture with one eye shut. They see the budget deficit, but they're missing the matching surplus on the other side. And since many Americans are missing it, too, they end up applauding efforts to balance the budget, even though it could mean taking money out of their pockets. It is possible for the government to spend too much. Deficits can be too big. But evidence of overspending is inflation, and most of the time deficits are too small, not too big.

The third myth is that deficits will burden the next generation. Politicians love to trot out this myth, proclaiming that by running deficits we are ruining the lives of our children and grandchildren, saddling them with crippling debt that they will eventually have to repay. One of the most influential perpetrators of this myth was Ronald Reagan. But even Senator Bernie Sanders has echoed Reagan, saying, "I am concerned about the debt. It's not something we should be leaving to our kids and our grandchildren."[8]

While this rhetoric is powerful, its economic logic is not. History bears this out. As a share of gross domestic product (GDP), the national

debt was at its highest—120 percent—in the period immediately following the Second World War. Yet, this was the same period during
which the middle class was built, real median family income soared,
and the next generation enjoyed a higher standard of living without
the added burden of higher tax rates. The reality is that government
deficits don't force financial burdens forward onto future populations.
Increasing the deficit doesn't make future generations poorer, and reducing deficits won't make them any richer.

The fourth myth we'll tackle is the notion that deficits are harmful
because they crowd out private investment and undermine long-term
growth. This myth is mostly circulated by mainstream economists and
policy wonks who should know better. It relies on the faulty assumption that in order to finance its deficits the government must compete with other borrowers for access to a limited supply of savings.
Here, the idea is that government deficits eat up some of the dollars
that would otherwise have been invested in private sector endeavors
that promote long-term prosperity. We will see why the reverse is
true—fiscal deficits actually increase private savings—and can easily
crowd-in private investment.

The fifth myth is that deficits make the United States dependent on
foreigners. This myth would have us believe that countries like China
and Japan have enormous leverage over us because they hold large
quantities of US debt. We will see this is a fiction that politicians wittingly or unwittingly propagate, often as an excuse to ignore social
programs in desperate need of funding. Sometimes this myth has used
the metaphor of irresponsibly taking out a foreign credit card. This
misses the fact that the dollars aren't originating from China. They're
coming from the US. We're not really borrowing from China so
much as we're supplying China with dollars and then allowing them
to trade those dollars in for a safe, interest-bearing asset called a US
Treasury. There is absolutely nothing risky or pernicious about this.
If we wanted to, we could pay off the debt immediately with a simple

keystroke. Mortgaging our future is yet one more instance of not understanding—or willfully misconstruing for political purposes—how sovereign currencies actually work.

The sixth myth we'll consider is that entitlements are propelling us toward a long-term fiscal crisis. Social Security, Medicare, and Medicaid are the supposed culprits. I will show you why this way of thinking is wrong. There is absolutely no good reason for Social Security benefits, for example, to ever face cuts. Our government will always be able to meet future obligations because it can never run out of money. Instead of arguing over the monetary cost of these programs, lawmakers should be fighting about whose policies stand the best chance of meeting the needs of our entire population. The money can always be there. The question is, What will that money buy? Changing demographics and the impacts of climate change are real challenges that could put stress on available resources. We need to make sure that we're doing everything we can to manage our real resources and develop more sustainable methods of production as the baby boom generation ages out of the workforce. But when it comes to paying out benefits, we can always afford to keep our promises to current retirees and to the generations that will follow them.

After we fully examine the faulty thinking underlying these six myths and counter them with solid evidence, we will consider the deficits that do matter. The real crises that we're facing have nothing to do with the federal deficit or entitlements. The fact that 21 percent of all children in the United States live in poverty—that's a crisis. The fact that our infrastructure is graded at a D+ is a crisis. The fact that inequality today stands at levels last seen during America's Gilded Age is a crisis. The fact that the typical American worker has seen virtually no real wage growth since the 1970s is a crisis. The fact that forty-four million Americans are saddled with $1.7 trillion in student loan debt is a crisis. And the fact that we ultimately won't be able to "afford" anything at all if we end up exacerbating climate change and destroying the life on this planet is perhaps the biggest crisis of them all.

These are real crises. The national deficit is not a crisis.

———————

THE CRIME OF the tax bill signed by President Trump in 2017 is not that it added to the deficit but that it used the deficit to provide help to those who needed it least. It has widened inequality, putting more political and economic power into the hands of the few. MMT understands that building a better economy isn't contingent on raising enough revenue to pay for the things we want. We can, and must, tax the rich. But not because we can't afford to do anything without them. We should tax billionaires to rebalance the distribution of wealth and income and to protect the health of our democracy. But we don't need to crack open their piggy banks to eradicate poverty or to have the federal job guarantee with a living wage that Coretta Scott King fought for. We already have the tools we need. Feigning dependence on those with incredible wealth sends the wrong message, making them appear more vital to our cause than they actually are. That's not to suggest that deficits don't matter, so we can throw caution to the wind and simply spend, spend, spend. The economic framework that I'm advocating for is asking for *more fiscal responsibility* from the federal government, not less. We just need to redefine what it means to budget our resources responsibly. Our misconceptions about the deficit leave us with so much waste and untapped potential within our current economy.

MMT gives us the power to imagine a new politics and a new economy. It challenges the status quo *across the political spectrum* with sound economics, and that is why it is generating so much interest around the world from policy makers, academics, central bankers, finance ministers, activists, and ordinary people. MMT's lens enables us to see that another kind of society is possible, one in which we can afford to invest in health care, education, and resilient infrastructure. In contrast to narratives of scarcity, MMT promotes a narrative of opportunity. Once we overcome the myths and accept that federal deficits are actually good for the economy, we can pursue fiscal policies that prioritize human need and public interest. We have nothing to lose but our self-imposed constraints.

The United States is the wealthiest country in the history of the world. But even when Americans were at their poorest during the Great Depression, we managed to establish Social Security and the minimum wage, electrify rural communities, provide federal housing loans, and fund a massive jobs program. Like Dorothy and her companions in *The Wizard of Oz*, we need to see through the myths and remember once again that we've had the power all along.

As this book was going to press, the COVID-19 virus hit with full force, giving us a vivid, real-world demonstration of the power of the MMT way of thinking. Entire industries are shutting down. Job losses are mounting, and there is the potential for an economic collapse that could put unemployment on par with the percentages last seen during the Great Depression. Congress has already committed more than $1 trillion to fight the health pandemic and the unfolding economic crisis. Much more will be needed.

The federal deficit, which was expected to top $1 trillion before the virus became a threat, will likely skyrocket beyond $3 trillion in the months ahead. If history is any lesson, anxiety over rising budget deficits will lead to pressure to reduce fiscal support in order to wrestle deficits lower. That would be an unmitigated disaster. Right now, and in the months ahead, the most fiscally responsible way to manage the crisis is with higher deficit spending.

The next year will be incredibly difficult for all of us. We will live with a heightened state of anxiety until the virus is contained and a vaccine is widely available. Many of us will experience social and economic hardship. There is enough to worry about without piling on additional concerns over our nation's fiscal situation. This is as good a moment as any to learn some important lessons about where money comes from and why the federal government—and only the federal government—can step up and save the economy.

1

Don't Think of a Household

Families across the country are tightening their belts and making tough decisions. The federal government should do the same.

—PRESIDENT OBAMA,
STATE OF THE UNION ADDRESS, 2010

MYTH #1: The federal government should budget like a household.

REALITY: Unlike a household, the federal government issues the currency it spends.

L ike many of you, I grew up watching the television show *Sesame Street*. One of the skills it helped young kids develop was the ability to sort objects according to their similarities and differences. "One of these things is not like the other one," the song began as this segment of the show started. Four images appeared in a matrix on the screen: a banana, an orange, a pineapple, and a sandwich. "The sandwich! The sandwich!" my sister and I would holler back at the TV set. I'm no longer a kid, but I still find myself hollering back at the TV whenever I hear someone talk about the federal government's budget as if it were no different from a household budget.

If you've heard someone complain that Washington needs to get its fiscal house in order, you've heard a version of the household myth. It derives from the flawed idea that we should look at Uncle Sam's budget through the same lens we use to manage our own family budgets. Of all the myths we're going to explore in the pages ahead, this is undoubtedly the most pernicious.

It's a favorite among politicians, who tend to look for the simplest possible rhetoric to connect with their constituents. And what could be easier than describing the government's finances in terms the rest of us already understand—our own. We all know it's important to keep our personal spending in line with our overall income. So, when we hear someone come along and talk about government finances in ways that remind us of our own, it hits home. It's got a folksy, kitchen-table feel to it.

We've all seen it done. In campaign ads and town halls across America, politicians point to the small businessman or the hardworking waitress, holding them up as shining examples of what responsible budgeting looks like. They empathize with the struggles of everyday Americans, reminding us that we all know what it's like to sit around the kitchen table and balance the family checkbook. Then, in the hope of drawing outrage from the crowd, they shift the conversation to the federal government, telling us that Uncle Sam's books almost never balance because irresponsible spending has become a way of life in Washington, DC.

Stories like these resonate with us because the language is so familiar. We know that we're supposed to live within our means and arrange our finances so that we aren't spending more than we bring in. We know we need to set aside some savings for the future and that we should be extra careful when it comes to borrowing money. Taking on too much debt can lead to bankruptcy, foreclosure, and even incarceration.

We know people can go broke, and we've seen iconic companies like RadioShack and Toys "R" Us get driven into bankruptcy when they could no longer afford to pay the bills. Even cities (Detroit) and states (Kansas) can run into big trouble when they're not bringing in enough money to cover their expenses. Every family sitting around the kitchen table understands these realities. What they don't understand is why the federal government (Uncle Sam) is different.

To understand why, we go right to the heart of MMT.

Issuers Versus Users of Currency

MMT takes as its starting point a simple and incontrovertible fact: our national currency, the US dollar, comes from the US government, and it can't come from anywhere else—at least not legally. Both the US Treasury and its fiscal agent, the Federal Reserve, have the authority to issue the US dollar. This might involve minting the coins in your pocket, printing up the bills in your wallet, or creating digital dollars known as reserves that exist only as electronic entries on bank balance sheets. The Treasury manufactures the coins, and the Federal Reserve creates the rest. Once you appreciate the significance of this reality, you will be able to unravel many of the deficit myths on your own.

Even though you may not have given it much thought before, something inside you probably already understands this basic truth. I mean, think about it. Can *you* create US dollars? Sure, you can *earn* them, but can you manufacture them? Maybe with high-tech engraving equipment you could set up shop in your basement and produce something that looks very much like the US dollar. Or maybe you could hack into the computer at the Federal Reserve and type up some digital dollars. But we both know you'll end up in an orange jumpsuit if you get caught trying to counterfeit the currency. That's because the US Constitution grants the federal government the *exclusive* right to issue the currency.[1] As the Federal Reserve Bank of St. Louis put it, the US government is "the sole manufacturer of dollars."[2]

The term *monopoly* refers, of course, to a market in which there is only one supplier of some product. Since the federal government is the *sole* manufacturer of US dollars, we can think of it as having a monopoly over the dollar itself. It's kind of like a being given a super copyright (one that never expires) over the ability to make additional copies of the dollar. It's an exclusive power, articulated by our founders. It's not something households, businesses, or state and local governments can do. Only the federal government can *issue* our currency. Everyone else is merely a currency *user*. It's a special power that must be exercised with great care.

Going back to *Sesame Street*, we can easily identify which of the things in Exhibit 1 is not like the others.

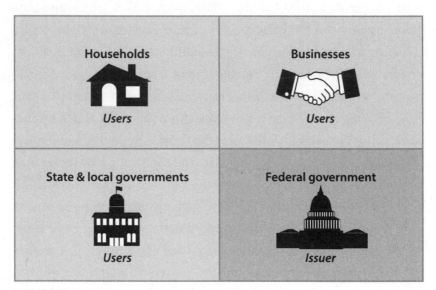

EXHIBIT 1. Currency Users Versus Issuers

The distinction between currency *users* and the currency *issuer* lies at the heart of MMT. And as we will see in the pages ahead, it has profound implications for some of the most important policy debates of our time, such as health care, climate change, Social Security, international trade, and inequality.

To take full advantage of the special powers that accrue to the currency issuer, countries need to do more than just grant themselves the exclusive right to issue the currency. It's also important that they don't promise to convert their currency into something they could run out of (e.g., gold or some other country's currency). And they need to refrain from borrowing (i.e., taking on debt) in a currency that isn't their own.[3] When a country issues its own nonconvertible (fiat) currency and only borrows in its own currency, that country has attained monetary sovereignty.[4] Countries with monetary sovereignty, then, don't have to manage their budgets as a household would. They can use their currency-issuing capacity to pursue policies aimed at maintaining a full employment economy.

Sometimes, people ask me whether MMT applies to countries outside the United States. It does! Even though the US dollar is considered special because of its status as the global reserve currency, lots of other countries have the power to make their monetary systems work for their people. So, if you're reading this book outside the USA, don't assume there are no important lessons here for you and your country. On the contrary, MMT can be used to describe and improve the policy choices available to *any* country with a high degree of monetary sovereignty—the US, Japan, the UK, Australia, Canada, and many more. And, as we'll see in Chapter 5, MMT also offers insights for countries with little or no monetary sovereignty—nations like Panama, Tunisia, Greece, Venezuela, and many more.

MMT helps us to see why countries that fix their exchange rates, like Argentina did until 2001, or that take on debt denominated in a foreign currency, like Venezuela has done, undermine their monetary sovereignty and subject themselves to the kinds of constraints faced by other currency users, such as Italy, Greece, and other eurozone countries. When countries with little or no monetary sovereignty fail to prioritize budget discipline, they can face unsustainable debts just like a household. In contrast, the United States never has to worry about running out of money. It can always pay the bills, even the big ones. The US can't end up like Greece, which gave up its monetary sovereignty when it stopped issuing the drachma in order to use the euro. America is not dependent on China (or anyone else) for financing.

Most importantly, having monetary sovereignty means that a country can prioritize the security and well-being of its people without needing to worry about how to pay for it.

Thatcher's Backward Dictum: (TAB)S

In a now-famous speech from 1983, British prime minister Margaret Thatcher declared that "the state has no source of money, other than the money people earn themselves. If the state wishes to spend more it can only do so by borrowing your savings or by taxing you more."[5] This was Thatcher's way of saying that the government's finances were constrained in the same way our personal finances are constrained. In order to spend more, the government would need to raise the money. "We know that there is no such thing as public money," she added. "There is only taxpayer money." If the British people wanted more from their government, they would have to foot the bill.

Was it an innocent mistake or a carefully crafted statement designed to discourage the British people from demanding more from their government? I'm not sure. Regardless of her motives, Thatcher's remarks concealed the currency-issuing power of the state. More than three decades later, political leaders in currency-issuing nations like the UK and the US still talk as though we, the taxpayers, are the ultimate source of the government's money. As former British prime minister Theresa May put it more recently, the government doesn't have a "magic money tree."[6] Unless they take more of *our* money, we're told, the government can't afford to top up spending on existing programs much less fund ambitious new projects.

To most of us, the idea that the government must tax more to spend more probably sounds reasonable. And our politicians know it. They also know that most of us don't want to see our taxes go up, so they twist themselves into knots, trying to figure out how to win votes by vowing to do big things without asking the majority of us to pay more. For example, Donald Trump promised the American people that Mexico would pay for his border wall, while Democrats have insisted that billionaires and Wall Street banks can foot the bill for many of their ambitious programs. The money has to come from *somewhere*, right? Actually, we've got it backward. But before we get to that, let's walk through the conventional understanding so it will be easier to contrast this backward thinking with the way things actually work.

Recall that the finances we understand best are our own, and we know that we need to come up with money before we can spend. So, the idea that the federal government must collect funds in order to spend seems intuitively correct. Extrapolating from our own experiences, we know that we can't walk out of the department store with a new pair of shoes or drive away from the car dealership in a sporty new vehicle unless we come up with the financing first. According to conventional thinking, the government relies on two sources of funding: it can raise your taxes, or it can borrow your savings. Taxes allow the government to collect money from people who have it, which means taxes are looked upon as a way to transfer money to the federal government. If the government wants to spend more than it collects by taxing, it can raise additional funds by borrowing from savers. In either case, the idea is that the government must come up with the money *before* it can spend. That's how most of us have been taught to understand the government's fiscal operations. Taxing and borrowing come first. Spending comes last. A handy mnemonic for the conventional way of thinking is (TAB)S: taxing and borrowing precede spending.

Because we've been trained to believe that, like each of us, the government must "find the money" before it can spend, everyone becomes obsessed with the question: How are you going to pay for it? We've been conditioned to expect our elected officials to offer a blueprint that maps out the source of every new dollar they wish to spend. Even the most progressive candidates fear that they'll be eaten alive if their proposals add to the deficit, so borrowing is almost never an option. To show that their policies won't add to the deficit, they hunt for ways to squeeze more tax revenue out of the economy, usually targeting those who can most easily afford to pay more. For example, Senator Bernie Sanders insists that a financial transactions tax will cover the cost of making public colleges and universities tuition-free, and Senator Elizabeth Warren claims that a 2 percent tax on fortunes above $50 million would raise enough revenue to wipe out student debt for 95 percent of students and also pay for universal childcare and free college. In both cases, the goal is to demonstrate that everything can be paid for by taxing the richest people in America. As we'll see in the pages ahead, there's often room to fund new programs without the need for higher taxes. Adding to the deficit shouldn't be looked upon as a taboo. Taxes are critically important, but there's no reason to assume the government must raise taxes whenever it wants to invest in our economy.

In practice, the federal government almost never collects enough taxes to offset all of its spending. Deficit spending is the norm, and everyone in Washington, DC, knows it. And so do voters. That's why so many politicians complain that Congress needs to get its fiscal house in order before it's too late. To demonstrate their commitment to good, old-fashioned household budgeting, the Democrats, led by Speaker Nancy Pelosi (D-CA) reinstated a budget rule known as pay as you go (PAYGO) in 2018. With PAYGO in place, borrowing to finance new expenditures is technically off limits. That reduces (TAB)S to just tax and spend (T)S, so lawmakers face intense pressure to cover any proposed new spending with revenue from new taxes.[7]

Is this a good political strategy? Is it good economics? It certainly *sounds* like a wholesome approach to budgeting. But it's rooted in a flawed understanding of how the federal government actually spends. In fact, it gets everything backward.

How the Currency Issuer Spends: S(TAB)

Because it's the dominant way of thinking, most of us probably carry a version of the (TAB)S model in our minds. Even if we have never spent a moment of our time thinking about the inner workings of the federal budget, we probably believe that the government needs *our* money to help pay the bills. We might even feel a bit patriotic about the check we send off to the Internal Revenue Service (IRS) every April, proud to have done our small part in building low-income housing, paying our men and women in uniform, and supporting our farmers with generous subsidies. I hate to be the bearer of uncomfortable news, but that's not what's actually happening. If you're not already doing so, you should probably sit down. Are you ready? Your taxes don't actually pay for anything, at least not at the federal level. The government doesn't need *our* money. We need *their* money. We've got the whole thing backward!

When I first encountered this way of understanding how taxing and spending work in actual practice, I recoiled. It was 1997, and I was midway through a PhD program in economics when someone shared a little book called *Soft Currency Economics* with me.[8] The book's author, Warren Mosler, was a successful Wall Street investor, not an economist, and his book was about how the economics profession was getting almost everything wrong. I read it, and I wasn't convinced.

According to Mosler, the government spends first and then taxes or borrows. That sequencing turns Thatcher's dictum completely around, reordering the mnemonic to give us S(TAB): spending before taxing and borrowing. By Mosler's reasoning, the government doesn't go around looking for someone else to pick up the TAB, it just spends its currency into existence. Warren saw things that most economists were missing. To many of us, his ideas initially sounded completely original, but most weren't. They were only new to us. It turns out they could be found (and we found them) in canonical texts, like Adam Smith's *Wealth of Nations* or in John Maynard Keynes's two-volume classic, *A Treatise on Money*. Anthropologists, sociologists, philosophers, and others had long ago arrived at similar conclusions about the nature of money and the role of taxes, but the economics profession had largely lagged behind.

Mosler is considered the father of MMT because he brought these ideas to a handful of us in the 1990s. He says he doesn't know how he came up with this way of understanding taxing and government spending but that it just struck him after his years of experience working in financial markets. He was used to thinking in terms of debits and credits because he had been trading financial instruments and watching funds transfer between bank accounts. One day, he started to think about where all those dollars must have originally come from. It occurred to him that before the government could subtract (debit) any dollars away from us, it must first add (credit) them. He reasoned that spending must have come first, otherwise where would anyone have gotten the dollars they needed to pay the tax? Although the logic seemed infallible, I felt certain his story couldn't be right. How could it? It turned everything I thought I understood about money, taxes, and government spending on its head. I had studied economics with world-renowned economists at Cambridge University, and none of my professors had ever said anything like this. In fact, all of the models they taught me were compatible with Thatcher's dictum that governments must tax or borrow before they can spend.[9] Was it really possible that nearly everyone had it wrong? I had to find out.

In 1998, I visited Mosler at his home in West Palm Beach, Florida, where I spent hours listening to him explain his thinking. He began by referring to the US dollar as "a simple public monopoly." Since the US government is the sole source of dollars, it was silly to think of Uncle Sam as needing to get dollars from the rest of us. Obviously, the issuer of the dollar can have all the dollars it could possibly want. "The government doesn't want dollars," Mosler explained. "It wants something else."

"What does it want?" I asked.

"It wants to *provision* itself," he replied. "The tax isn't there to raise money. It's there to get people working and producing things for the government."

"What kinds of things?" I asked.

"A military, a court system, public parks, hospitals, roads, bridges. That kind of stuff."

To get the population to do all that work, the government imposes taxes, fees, fines, or other obligations. The tax is there to create a demand for the government's currency. Before anyone can pay the tax, someone has to do the work to earn the currency.

My head spun. Then he told me a story.

Mosler had a beautiful beachfront property with a swimming pool and all the luxuries of life anyone could hope to enjoy. He also had a family that included two young kids. To illustrate his point, he told me a story about the time he sat his kids down and told them he wanted them to do their part to help keep the place clean and habitable. He wanted the yard mowed, beds made, dishes done, cars washed, and so on. To compensate them for their time, he offered to pay them for their labor. Three of his business cards if they made their beds. Five for doing the dishes. Ten for washing a car and twenty-five for tending to the yard work. Days turned into weeks, and the house became increasingly uninhabitable. The grass grew knee high. Dishes piled up in the sink, and the cars were covered in sand and salt from the ocean breeze. "Why aren't you doing any work?" Mosler asked the kids. "I told you I would pay you some of my business cards to pitch in around here." "D-a-a-a-a-ad," the kids intoned. "Why would we work for your business cards? They're not worth anything!"

That's when Mosler had his epiphany. The kids hadn't done any chores because they didn't *need* his cards. So, he told the kids he wasn't requiring them to do any work at all. All he wanted was a payment of thirty of his business cards, each month. Failure to pay would result in a loss of privileges. No more TV, use of the swimming pool, or trips to the mall. It was a stroke of genius. Mosler had imposed a "tax" that could only be paid using his own monogrammed paper. Now the cards were worth something.

Within hours, the kids were scurrying around, tidying up their bedrooms, the kitchen, and the yard. What was once considered a worthless rectangular calling card was suddenly perceived as a valuable token. But why? How did Mosler get the kids to do all that work without forcing them to do any chores? Simple. He put them in a situation where they needed to earn his "currency" to stay out of trouble. Each time the kids did some work, they got a receipt (some business cards) for the task they had performed. At the end of the month, the kids returned the cards to their father. As Mosler explained, he didn't actually need to collect his own cards back from the kids. "What would I want with my own tokens?" he asked. He had already gotten what he really wanted out of the deal—a tidy house! So why did he bother taxing the cards away from the kids? Why didn't he let them hold on to them as souvenirs? The reason was simple: Mosler collected the cards so the kids would need to earn them again next month. He had invented a virtuous provisioning system! *Virtuous* in this case means that it keeps repeating.

Mosler used this story to illustrate some basic principles about the way sovereign currency issuers actually fund themselves. Taxes are there to create a demand for government currency. The government can define the currency in terms of its own unique unit of account—a dollar, a yen, a pound, a peso—and then give value to its own otherwise worthless paper by requiring it in payment of taxes or other obligations. As Mosler jokes, "Taxes turn litter into currency." At the end of the day, a currency-issuing government wants something real, not something monetary. It's not our tax money the government wants. It's our time. To get us to produce things for the state, the government invents taxes or other kinds of payment obligations. This isn't the explanation you'll find in most economics textbooks, where a superficial story about money being invented to overcome the inefficiencies associated with bartering—trading goods without the use of money—is preferred. In that story, money is just a convenient device that sprang up organically as a way to make trade more efficient. Although students are taught that barter was once omnipresent, a sort of natural state of being, scholars of the ancient world have found little evidence that societies were ever organized around barter exchange.[10]

MMT rejects the ahistorical barter narrative, drawing instead on an extensive body of scholarship known as chartalism, which shows that taxes were the vehicle that allowed ancient rulers and early nation-states to introduce their own currencies, which only later circulated as a medium of exchange among private individuals. From inception, the tax liability creates people looking for paid work (aka unemployment) in the government's currency. The government (or other authority) then spends its currency into existence, giving people access to the tokens they need to settle their obligations to the state. Obviously, no one can pay the tax until the government first supplies its tokens. As a simple point of logic, Mosler explained that most of us had the sequencing wrong. Taxpayers weren't funding the government; the government was funding the taxpayers.[11]

It started to make sense to me, at least in theory. I began to think of the government as the currency monopolist. Mosler's argument brought back childhood memories, in this case playing the board game Monopoly with my family when I was just a kid. As I thought about the rules of the game, I began to see the parallels even more clearly. For one thing, the game can't begin until someone is put in control of the currency. The players don't pony up the money to get the game underway. They can't, because they don't have it yet. The currency has to be issued before anyone can get it. After the initial dispensation, the players move around the board, buying property, paying rent, landing in jail, or drawing a card that instructs them to pay $50 to the IRS. Each time a player rounds the board, they receive a $200 payment from the person who controls the currency. Because the players are merely *users* of the currency, they can and do go broke. The *issuer*, however, can never run out of money. In fact, the official rules[12] of the game literally read: "The Bank *never 'goes broke.'* If the Bank runs out of money, the Banker may issue *as much more money as may be needed* by writing on any ordinary paper" (emphasis mine).

I thought about this idea of writing on paper to make money when I took my own kids on a tour of the US Bureau of Engraving and Printing in Washington, DC. If you haven't done it, I highly recommend it. It's eye opening. You can schedule a tour on the government's own website: www.moneyfactory.gov. It's a far more sophisticated operation than making Monopoly money by "writing on any ordinary paper," but it amounts to much the same thing. It's one of the places where the issuer of our currency manufactures it.[13] One of the first things I noticed was an enormous neon sign, suspended high above the engraving equipment. The sign read: "We Make Money the Old-Fashioned Way. We Print It." Everyone wanted to take a picture of it, but photos aren't permitted on the tour. The crowd marveled at the sight as reams of uncut $10s, $20s and $100s spun from the machines. Then someone said what we were all thinking. "I wish I could do that!" Alas, to avoid the orange jumpsuits we need to leave the manufacturing to the US Bureau of Engraving and Printing.

Those notes make up part of the supply of US currency. As those old mason jars full of pennies, nickels, and dimes on your grandmother's shelf attest, the government also issues US currency in the form of coins. Just as the Federal Reserve describes itself as "the issuing authority for all Federal Reserve notes," the US Mint describes itself as "the nation's sole manufacturer of legal tender coinage." Finally, the Federal Reserve issues digital dollars, known as bank reserves.[14] These are created exclusively via keystrokes on a computer controlled by the government's fiscal agent, the Federal Reserve. When the Wall Street banks needed trillions of dollars to survive the 2008 financial crisis, the Fed effortlessly conjured them into existence using nothing more than a keyboard at the New York Federal Reserve Bank.

To the average person, it might seem as though the government literally takes the bills rolling off its printing press or coins tumbling from its minting machines to pay its bills. Cable news shows certainly love the imagery of the mass production of money. They'll often air a story about government spending while running a video of newly manufactured dollars spewing from the printing press. But Federal Reserve notes and coins are mostly there for our convenience. It would be way too clunky for the federal government to pay Boeing for a fleet of new fighter jets with an enormous stockpile of physical currency. That's just not how it works.

Instead of handing over fistfuls of cash, as in Monopoly, the federal government makes most of its payments the way a scorekeeper assigns points in a game of bridge. Except, instead of writing the points on a scorecard, payments simply get typed into a keyboard by someone at the Federal Reserve. Let me explain.

Take military spending. In 2019, the House and Senate passed legislation that increased the military budget, approving $716 billion, nearly $80 billion more than Congress had authorized in fiscal year 2018.[15] There was no debate about how to pay for the spending. No one asked, Where will we get the extra $80 billion? Lawmakers didn't raise taxes or go out and borrow an extra $80 billion from savers so that the government could afford to make the additional payments. Instead, Congress committed to spending money it did not have. It can do that because of its special power over the US dollar. Once Congress authorizes the spending, agencies like the Department of Defense are given permission to enter into contracts with companies like Boeing, Lockheed Martin, and so on. To provision itself with F-35 fighters, the US Treasury instructs its bank, the Federal Reserve, to carry out the payment on its behalf. The Fed does this by marking up the numbers in Lockheed's bank account. Congress doesn't need to "find the money" to spend it. It needs to find the votes! Once it has the votes, it can authorize the spending. The rest is just accounting. As the checks go out, the Federal Reserve clears the payments by crediting the sellers' account with the appropriate number of digital dollars, known as bank reserves.[16] That's why MMT sometimes describes the Fed as the scorekeeper for the dollar. The scorekeeper can't run out of points.

Think about where the points come from when you play a card game or go to a basketball game. They don't come from anywhere! They're just conjured into existence by the person doing the record-keeping. When a basketball player drains a shot from behind the three-point line, three points are added to the team's total. Does the scorekeeper reach into a bucket to get those three points? Of course not! The scorekeeper doesn't actually *have* any points. To record the three-point shot, the scorekeeper simply changes the number up, and the bigger number lights up on the scoreboard. Now, suppose the play gets reviewed and the referees determine that the shot clock had run out. The points are taken away. But note that the arena doesn't actually *collect* anything back. It's just adding and subtracting points, the same way the federal government adds and subtracts dollars from the economy when it spends and taxes. Uncle Sam doesn't *lose* any dollars when he spends, and he doesn't *get* any dollars when he taxes. That's why former Fed chairman Ben Bernanke refuted the claim that tax-payer dollars were being used to rescue banks after the financial crisis. "The banks have accounts with the Fed," he explained. "We just use the computer to mark up the size of the accounts." Taxpayers didn't bail out Wall Street. The scorekeeper did.

Bernanke's comments might remind some of you of the popular television show *Whose Line Is It Anyway?* The host, Drew Carey, in-troduced every episode by saying, "A show where everything's made up and the points don't matter." It was improv comedy, so everything really was made up. Throughout the show, Carey awarded imaginary points, based on how thoroughly he and the audience were amused by the other comedians. No one could do anything with the points, so they really didn't matter. The government's points, however, *do* matter.

For one thing, you and I need dollars to pay our taxes. And because taxes (and death) are an inescapable fact of life, the government's currency occupies a central place in our economic lives. Once a tax-backed currency like the US dollar is introduced, it usually becomes the standard unit in which everything else is priced. Walk into any restaurant or shopping mall in the United States, and you'll find a seller who is trying to earn dollars. Enter a courthouse and you'll find a judge awarding damages in US dollars. Log on to your computer to order a pizza, and you'll be expected to pay in dollars. We need the dollars, and we get them from the only place they can come from, the currency issuer. The pizza parlor and the department store need them, too, because, ultimately, they'll have to pay taxes as well. Even state and local governments rely on them because they have to pay the teachers, judges, firefighters, and police officers, all of whom expect to be paid in dollars. Only the scorekeeper is different. Uncle Sam doesn't need dollars. When he collects taxes from us, he's just subtracting away some of our dollars. He doesn't actually get any dollars.

It's jarring, I know. This is our first Copernican moment. It's why one journalist at the *Financial Times* described MMT as an autostereo-gram.[17] You know, one of those two-dimensional images that doesn't look like much until you focus your gaze a certain way and then the image behind the image comes into view, revealing an intricate 3-D visual of a painted desert or a great white shark. Once you're able to see that the government's ability to spend doesn't revolve around the taxpayer dollar, the whole fiscal paradigm shifts. Or as that journalist put it, "Once you get it, you never see things quite the same way again."

Why Bother Taxing and Borrowing?

If the federal government really can just manufacture all of the dollars it could possibly desire, then why bother taxing or borrowing at all? Why not eliminate taxes altogether? The people would rejoice! And why borrow a dollar if you don't need to? We could eliminate the national debt if we stopped borrowing. So why not skip the (TAB) altogether and just spend the money to solve our problems? These are important questions that often come up when someone realizes that currency-issuing governments don't need to rely on taxes or borrowing to spend.

In 2018, a thirteen-year-old named Amy from Bristol, England, called the hosts of a popular podcast known as *Planet Money* with this suggestion:

> AMY: I had this idea that because they print money, instead of giving it to the bank and making inflation go up, they could use it just for the public services. And it would be much easier. And it would be, in general, really good because there's lots of problems with, like, there's not enough tax to go around all of the schools and hospitals. So I thought maybe this might help. So thank you for listening. Yeah, thanks. Bye.

Out of the mouths of babes, as they say. Amy sees problems that need solving. Underfunded schools and a National Health Service that desperately needs more public investment. She also witnessed the Bank of England cranking up its digital printing press to manufacture £435 billion out of thin air, as part of its quantitative easing program following the financial crisis. To Amy, the solution seems obvious—forget about taxes and just run the printing press for the people!

The hosts of the podcast were intrigued, and they reached out to me with the following question: The government can create money. So, what's the point of taxes? Why does the government need to take my money in taxes?[18]

I told the folks at *Planet Money* that MMT recognizes at least four important reasons for taxation.[19] We've already touched on the first. Taxes enable governments to provision themselves without the use of explicit force. If the British government stopped requiring its people to settle their tax obligations using British pounds, it would rather quickly undermine its provisioning powers. Fewer people would need to earn pounds, and the government would have a harder time finding teachers, nurses, and so on who were willing to work and produce things in exchange for its currency.

Amy touches on the second important reason for taxation—inflation. If the government did as Amy suggested, merely spending loads of new money without taxing any of it away from people, it would cause an inflation problem. As we'll see in the next chapter, it's not the *printing* of money, per se, but the *spending* of money that matters. If the government wants to boost spending on health care and education, it *may* need to remove some spending power from the rest of us to prevent its own more generous outlays from pushing up prices. One way to do this is by coordinating higher government spending with higher taxes so that the rest of us are forced to cut back a little to create room for additional government spending.[20] That can help manage inflationary pressures, by balancing the strain on our economy's real productive capacity. More than any other economic school of thought, MMT emphasizes the importance of deciding *when* tax increases should accompany new spending and *which* taxes will be most effective at restraining inflationary pressures. Raising taxes when it's not necessary can undermine fiscal stimulus, and raising the wrong kind of taxes can leave a nation vulnerable to accelerating inflation. We'll see why in the next chapter.

Third, taxes are a powerful way for governments to alter the distribution of wealth and income. Tax cuts, like those passed by the Republicans in December 2017, can be structured to widen the gap between the rich and the poor, delivering windfall gains to large corporations and the wealthiest people in our societies. Today, there is more income and wealth inequality than at almost any time in US history. About half of all new income goes to the top 1 percent, and just three families own more wealth than the bottom half of America. Such extreme concentrations of wealth and income create both social and economic problems. For one thing, it's hard to keep the economy strong when most of the income goes to the thinnest slice of people at the top, who save (rather than spend) much of their income. Capitalism runs on sales. You need a reasonable distribution of income so that businesses have enough customers to stay profitable enough to provide enough employment to keep the economy running well. Extreme concentrations of wealth also have a corrosive effect on our political process and our democracy. Just as tax cuts can be used to exacerbate inequities, governments can exercise their taxing authority to reverse these dangerous trends. Stepping up enforcement, closing loopholes, raising rates, and establishing new forms of taxation are all important levers to enable the government to achieve a more sustainable distribution of income and wealth. So, MMT sees taxes as an important means to help redress decades of stagnation and rising inequality.

Finally, governments can use taxes to encourage or discourage certain behaviors. To improve public health, battle climate change, or deter risky speculation in financial markets, governments might levy a cigarette tax, a carbon tax, or a financial transactions tax. Economists often refer to these as sin taxes because they're used to deter people from engaging in harmful activities. MMT recognizes that in each case, the purpose of a sin tax is to discourage undesirable behaviors— smoking, polluting, or excessive speculation—not to raise money for the sovereign currency issuer. Indeed, the more effective the tax at discouraging these behaviors, the *less* the government will end up collecting, since the tax is only paid if the behavior continues. If a carbon tax succeeds in stamping out all $CO2$ emissions, it will yield no revenue, but the tax will have served its true purpose. Conversely, taxes can be used to incentivize behaviors. For example, the government might offer tax rebates to encourage people to buy energy-efficient appliances or electric vehicles.

For all of these reasons, taxes are an indispensable policy tool that cannot be abandoned simply because the government can manufacture its own currency. Amy was definitely on to something, though. Most governments, including hers, routinely spend more than they tax. And they do it, year after year, without creating an inflation problem. In fact, many of the world's largest economies have been actively trying to get their inflation rates to move *higher*. So, why not just spend more without worrying about raising taxes? And what's the point of borrowing your own currency if you can manufacture it yourself? We turn to these questions below.

The Role of Borrowing in MMT

Until I switched my own thinking from the household model (TAB)S to the currency-issuer model S(TAB), I wasn't able to see clearly what taxes and borrowing were really about. Flipping that mental switch wasn't easy, and I initially resisted Mosler's sequencing. It didn't *feel* right. But something about it gnawed at my brain. I was training to become a professional economist, and it seemed more important for me to try to get it right than to cling to the conventional way of thinking simply because the textbooks had decided that the taxpayer was at the center of the monetary universe. So, I went in search of answers.

I spent months researching the intricacies of government finance. I poured over official documents from the Federal Reserve and the US Treasury, read countless books and articles about monetary operations, and talked with numerous government insiders. Then I began writing. I organized my thoughts around a single question: *Do taxes and bonds finance government spending?* Everything I had been taught suggested this was a pointless exercise. Everyone "knew" the purpose of taxing and borrowing was to finance government spending. I thought of that Mark Twain quote—"It ain't what you know that gets you into trouble. It's what you know for sure that just ain't so"—and decided to keep an open mind. As I began to write, I honestly had no idea where I would arrive. I was committed to letting the research be my guide. In 1998, I published an early draft of the paper, and two years later a more polished version became my first peer-reviewed, academic publication.[21] The answer to the question I had posed was *no*.

It's not easy to see how it all works. In fact, it's impossible to disentangle the government's monetary operations in discrete time. On any

given day, there are, literally, millions of moving parts. Throughout
the year, the Federal Reserve handles trillions of dollars in US Treasury
payments. Each month, millions of households and businesses write
checks to Uncle Sam, and those payments clear between commercial
banks and the Federal Reserve.[22] The Treasury, the Federal Reserve,
and the primary dealers coordinate about when to auction Treasuries,
what mix of maturities to offer, and how many total securities to offer
at each auction. The whole thing is like a perfectly choreographed water ballet. A perpetual motion machine, clearing tax payments, federal
spending, and borrowing in perfect unison.

To the naked eye, it can appear that the government is collecting
dollars from taxpayers and bond buyers because it needs those dollars
to pay its bills. Viewed this way, the purpose of taxes and bonds is
to finance government spending. That's how Thatcher wanted us to
see it, through the lens of a household. MMT looks at what's happening through the lens of the currency issuer. The government doesn't
need our money. Just as the reason for taxation is not to provide the
government with its own currency, the purpose of auctioning US
Treasuries—that is, borrowing—isn't to raise dollars for Uncle Sam.

Then why does the government need to borrow? The answer is,
it doesn't. It *chooses* to offer people a different kind of government
money, one that pays a bit of interest. In other words, US Treasuries
are just interest-bearing dollars. To buy some of those interest-bearing
dollars from the government, you first need the government's currency. We might call the former "yellow dollars" and the latter "green
dollars." When the government spends more than it taxes away from
us, we say that the government has run a fiscal deficit. That deficit
increases the supply of green dollars. For more than a hundred years,
the government has chosen to sell US Treasuries in an amount equal
to its deficit spending. So, if the government spends $5 trillion but
only taxes $4 trillion away, it will sell $1 trillion worth of US Treasuries. What we call government borrowing is nothing more than Uncle

Sam allowing people to transform green dollars into interest-bearing yellow dollars.

MMT shows why it is a mistake to look at government borrowing through the household lens. If you and I borrow to purchase a home or an automobile, we don't walk into a bank, hand over a stack of cash to the loan officer, and then ask to borrow that money to buy a house or a car. The reason we borrow the money is because we don't have it. Unlike a household, the government spends first, supplying the dollars that can then be used to buy government bonds. As we will see in Chapter 3, it does this to support interest rates, not to fund expenditures.

Staying Within the Limits

Once you internalize the difference between the currency issuer and a currency user, you can begin to see, through a new lens, why so much of our political discourse is broken. Free of the constraints that bound us in a gold-standard world, the US now enjoys the flexibility to operate its budget, not like a household, but in the true service of its people.

To get there, we must break free of Thatcher's dictum. That means shedding the myth that the government has no money of its own, that it must ultimately get the money it needs from us, the taxpayer. MMT shows that this is exactly backward. In purely financial terms, our government can afford to purchase whatever is for sale in its own currency. It can never "run out of money," as President Obama once claimed.

Does that mean there are no limits? Can we just print our way to prosperity? Absolutely not! MMT is not a free lunch. There are very real limits, and failing to identify—and respect—those limits could bring great harm. MMT is about distinguishing the real limits from the self-imposed constraints that we have the power to change.

It may seem like Congress is already spending without limit. The US is projected to run trillion-dollar deficits, and the publicly held debt is on track to rise from $16 trillion in 2019 to $28 trillion by 2029. In many ways, it looks like there's nothing holding Congress back. Technically, there is.

Congress has adopted a number of technical procedures and budgetary conventions that are meant to slow or impede new federal spending. Let's look at just a handful of them. First, as noted earlier, is PAYGO, a rule that currently operates in the House of Representatives. PAYGO is a self-imposed rule that makes it harder for lawmakers to approve new spending. If you want to put more federal dollars into, say, education, you don't just have to win enough votes to fund that priority, you also have to win support for the tax increase or spending cut you're attaching to the legislation to "pay for" it. Adding to the deficit is not an option under PAYGO. The rule is there to force Congress to budget like a household. Another self-imposed constraint, known as the Byrd rule, exists on the Senate side. Under the Byrd rule, deficits can increase, but they can't continue to rise beyond the ten-year budget window. Third, both the House and Senate are required to seek a budget score from agencies like the Congressional Budget Office or the Joint Committee on Taxation before lawmakers can even vote on major legislation. A poor score from one of these agencies can literally stop a bill in its tracks. Finally, Congress faces a debt ceiling limit, which places a legal limit on the total amount of federal debt the government can accrue.

Because all of these constraints were imposed by Congress, they can all be waived or suspended by Congress.[23] In other words, they are binding only if Congress wants them to bind. Congress can, and frequently does, rewrite the playbook. For example, House Republicans quickly suspended the PAYGO rule to pass their Tax Cuts and Jobs Act in 2017. To pass their version of the bill, Senate Republicans had to deal with the Byrd rule. They did this by assuming wildly optimistic

economic growth[24] and scheduling personal income tax cuts to ex-
pire after 2025. Together, these maneuvers allowed Republicans to
gimmick their way around the Byrd rule, producing "evidence" that
the tax cuts wouldn't increase the deficit outside the ten-year budget
window. And, of course, we have all borne witness to the recurring
dramas over the debt ceiling limit. In theory, this limit, first enacted
in 1917, is there to do just that—*limit* the size of the national debt. In
practice, lawmakers have increasingly viewed any approaching debt
ceiling limit as a political opportunity to grandstand or extract legisla-
tive concessions. But, at the end of the day, Congress always musters
the will to avert default by raising the limit. It has done so some one
hundred times since the limit was enacted.

If Congress frequently unshackles itself, then what's the point of
all these nonbinding constraints? Why not eliminate PAYGO, the
Byrd rule, the debt limit statute, and other self-imposed checks on
government spending? Why not stop pretending that Congress needs
to budget like a household? The truth is, many lawmakers find the
self-imposed constraints *politically* useful.

For one thing, members of Congress routinely face pressure from
voters seeking more generous funding for health care, education, and
so on. The budget rules give them political cover. Instead of explaining
that they're philosophically opposed to boosting Pell Grant funding to
help low-income students attend college, lawmakers can feign empa-
thy with their constituents while claiming their hands are tied because
of the deficit. If they couldn't hide behind *the deficit myth*, what excuse would they use to justify withholding support? It helps to have a
bad cop.

Others in Congress look for ways to turn self-imposed constraints
into political opportunities. Lemons into lemonade, so to speak. Instead of fighting to overturn the constraints, they find ways to pair
their spending objectives with other policy goals. For example, a progressive Democrat might embrace PAYGO by calling for an array of

new taxes on the rich to "pay for" new programs aimed at helping poor and middle-income families. Robin Hood was beloved by the people, after all.

Our Real Limits

Viewed through the lens of MMT, we see that the US government is nothing like a household or a private business. The key difference is simple and inescapable. The government *issues* the currency (the US dollar), and everyone else—households, private business, state and local governments, and foreigners—merely *uses* it. This gives Uncle Sam an incredible advantage over the rest of us. Uncle Sam doesn't need to come up with dollars before he can spend. The rest of us do. Uncle Sam can't face mounting bills that he can't afford to pay. The rest of us can. Uncle Sam will never go broke. The rest of us could.

So why not tell Congress to just keep spending until all our problems are solved? Ah, if only it were that easy. Inflation, the subject of our next chapter, is a real danger. To be clear, MMT is not about removing all limits. It's not a free lunch. It's about replacing our current approach, one obsessed with budget outcomes, with one that prioritizes human outcomes while at the same time recognizing and respecting our economy's real resource constraints. In other words, MMT redefines what it means to engage in fiscally responsible budgeting. To paraphrase Democratic political strategist James Carville (who during Bill Clinton's 1992 presidential campaign famously coined the phrase "It's the economy, stupid"), MMT points out, "It's the economy's real resources, stupid!" We are a nation rich with real resources—advanced technologies, an educated workforce, factories, machines, fertile soil, and an abundance of natural resources. We are blessed to have enough of what matters. We can build an economy that provides a good life for all. We just need to budget our real resources.

2

Think of Inflation

MYTH #2: Deficits are evidence of overspending.

REALITY: For evidence of overspending, look to inflation.

I n 2015, I took a leave of absence from my job teaching economics at the University of Missouri–Kansas City and moved to Washington, DC, to serve as the chief economist for the Democrats on the US Senate Budget Committee. I thought it would be interesting to step outside the academic world, where anything is theoretically possible, and into the sausage factory, where budgets are formulated and spending decisions impact the lives of real people. I'm not sure exactly what I expected to find, but what I discovered was incredibly disheartening. None of the senators who sit on the powerful Budget Committee seemed to realize that the federal budget didn't work like a household budget.

The top Republican on the committee was its chairman, Senator Mike Enzi from Wyoming. Enzi had a background in accounting and had run a shoe-sale business before getting involved in politics. He spent a decade as a state legislator, serving in Wyoming's house of

representatives as well as its state senate. In all of these jobs, he operated under a constrained budget. As a businessman, he had to control
costs, meet payroll, and turn a profit to remain viable. As a member
of the Wyoming legislature, he operated in an environment where
the governor is constitutionally required to submit a balanced budget
each year. Before coming to Washington, he had only seen the world
through the lens of a currency user.

The committee held regular hearings on budget-related matters,
and I typically sat close behind Senator Enzi and the ranking Democratic member of the committee, Senator Bernie Sanders, who had
hired me for the job. At the start of each hearing, the chairman would
read aloud several minutes of prepared remarks. Senator Enzi's comments never changed much. He looked at the federal budget as if it was
an income statement for his shoe-sale business. To him, the problem
was obvious. Uncle Sam was operating at a loss. Deficits and debt had
become a way of life, and the whole thing was just plain irresponsible.
You didn't need an accounting degree (like Senator Enzi) to see the
problem. Time and again he would simplify the situation by declaring,
"Deficits are evidence of overspending!"

The economist in me wanted to leap from my chair. The chief economist in me was forced to sit quietly and hope that one of the other
twenty-one senators on the committee had a background in economics. As we teach our first-year students, excessive spending manifests
as inflation. A deficit is only evidence of overspending if it sparks inflation. Since prices weren't accelerating, the deficit couldn't possibly
be too big.

To my great disappointment, none of the other senators challenged
Enzi's claim. They were all using the same flawed lens and comment-
ing on the need to match spending with receipts. Republicans saw
too much on the expenditure side of the ledger—a spending problem.
Democrats saw too little on the income side—a revenue problem.
Everyone was convinced the deficit was too big. The argument was

about whether to cut spending to match revenue or increase revenue to match spending. Kitchen-table budgeting.

What were they missing?

Three big things.

First, as we learned in the previous chapter, the currency monopolist doesn't face the same constraints as currency users (households, businesses, or state and local governments). August 15, 1971, marked a major turning point in monetary history. President Nixon's decision to suspend dollar convertibility increased monetary sovereignty to the United States, forever changing the nature of the relevant constraint on federal spending. Under the Bretton Woods system, the federal budget had to be fairly tightly controlled to protect the nation's gold reserves. Today, we have a purely fiat currency. That means the government no longer promises to convert dollars into gold, which means it can issue more dollars without worrying that it could run out of the gold that once backed up the dollar. With a fiat currency, it's impossible for Uncle Sam to run out of money. Yet these senators were talking as if overspending could lead to bankruptcy. They needed to update their monetary lens.

Second, the government's budget isn't supposed to balance. Our economy is. The budget is just a tool that can be used to add or subtract dollars from the rest of us. A fiscal deficit adds more dollars than it subtracts, while a fiscal surplus subtracts more dollars than it adds. MMT provides the evidence that neither outcome is inherently good or bad. It's a balancing act, and the goal is to allow the government's budget to move in ways that deliver a broadly balanced economy for the people it is meant to serve.

Finally, the federal government has historically almost always kept its deficit too small. Yes, too small! Evidence of a deficit that is too small is unemployment. Of course, MMT recognizes that deficits can also be too big. But Senator Enzi had it all wrong. A fiscal deficit isn't evidence of overspending. For evidence of overspending, we must think of inflation.

Inflation: Common Ways of Thinking

No one wants to live in a country where inflation gets out of hand. Inflation means a continuous rise in the price level. A bit of inflation is considered harmless and even something economists like to see in a healthy, growing economy. But if prices start rising faster than most people's incomes, it means a widespread loss of purchasing power. Left unchecked, this would mean a decline in society's real standard of living. In extreme cases, prices can even spiral out of control, gripping a country in hyperinflation.

There isn't just one way to think about inflation. There's not even just one way to measure it. In the United States, the Bureau of Labor Statistics produces consumer price indices (CPI-U and CPI-W), a producer price index (PPI), and chained–consumer price indices (C-CPI-U), among others. The Bureau of Economic Analysis generates a GDP price deflator, an index known as a personal consumption expenditure (PCE), and many more. The Federal Reserve prefers a measure known as core PCE, and well, you get the picture. Lots of statisticians are employed to produce a wide range of estimates to help policy makers, investors, businesses, unions, and others get a sense of what's happening to prices in our economy.

We can only get a general sense of what's happening to prices because it's literally impossible to track what's happening to the price of every item that's for sale in our economy. You might find yourself paying more for your morning coffee, a gallon of gas, or your monthly cable, but that doesn't mean that the overall price level is accelerating. To understand what's happening at the macro level, we have to rely on price indices like those above. An index like the Consumer Price Index tells us whether the price of a standard basket of consumer goods and services is becoming more expensive over time. The basket includes everything from housing and health care to food, transportation, entertainment, clothing, and more. Obviously, not all households consume identical baskets of goods, so indices like the CPI are constructed to reflect the spending habits of a typical household. Expenses that eat up a bigger share of the typical household budget—for example, housing—count more (i.e., are weighted more heavily) than items that are less important to the average family. Because housing is weighted more heavily than, say, entertainment, a 5 percent spike in the cost of housing will have a bigger impact on the CPI than an equivalent 5 percent rise in the cost of entertainment. In the real world, some categories of goods and services have gotten more expensive (housing, education, and health care) while others have become cheaper over time. What matters is how the overall price of the basket changes from month to month and year to year, and whether average earnings are rising fast enough to keep up with rising prices.

People worry about inflation because it can eat away at their real standard of living. You might have no trouble affording the typical basket of goods today, but if the price of that fixed basket starts rising, you may discover that you can no longer afford to buy it. It depends what's happening to your income. If the price of the basket keeps going up by 5 percent each year while your annual earnings rise by just 2 percent, then in real (inflation-adjusted) terms you'll be 3 percent worse off each year. That means a real loss in terms of the actual amount of stuff—real goods and services—you can afford to buy.

So what causes prices to rise, and what can we do to prevent inflation from eroding our standard of living over time?

Before we turn to these questions, it's worth noting that many of the world's major countries have been desperately trying to solve the opposite problem—underinflation—for a decade or more. Too little, not too much, inflation has plagued the US, Japan, and Europe. In each of these regions, 2 percent is officially considered the "right" amount of inflation, so that's the rate the Federal Reserve, the Bank of Japan, and the European Central Bank have been trying to achieve. But none of them has been successful in bringing inflation up to a steady 2 percent. Japan has had a particularly rough time, fighting not just low inflation but periodic bouts of outright deflation—a drop in the overall

price level—a rare phenomenon that gripped the US during the Great
Depression of the 1930s. You might wonder why anyone would worry
about inflation getting too low. It sounds great! Yet economists worry
because when there's little or no inflation, it's usually considered a re-
flection of weakness in the broader economy.

The long battle against low inflation is considered a puzzle by most
economists. Some argue that a combination of factors is probably responsible for low inflation across much of the world. Many believe
rapid improvements in technology, demographics, and globalization
probably explain the phenomenon. Others believe central banks simply haven't used their tool kits aggressively enough. They think inflation has been stubbornly low because people at the European Central
Bank, the Bank of Japan, and the Federal Reserve haven't done enough
to create a different psychology, so people continue to expect inflation to remain low. For this group, raising actual inflation is simply
a matter of getting people to raise their inflation expectations. If central banks can convince people that inflation will move higher, people
will begin spending more money today (why wait to buy something
if prices are heading up?), and the added demand will actually move
prices higher. Still others see inequality and wage stagnation as key
drivers of slow growth and *de minimis* pressure on wages and prices.
Some say wage growth and a more equitable distribution of income
would help bolster demand among lower- and middle-income households, thereby helping to create some inflationary pressure.

No one knows how long the current bout of low inflation will
last or what will eventually give rise to higher prices.[1] Economists typically distinguish between *cost-push* and *demand-pull* drivers of inflationary pressures. As Texas Christian University economist John T.
Harvey puts it, cost-push inflation can happen because of "acts of
God" or "acts of power."[2] For example, a serious drought could lead
to massive crop failures and food shortages that send prices soaring
as supply collapses. Or powerful storms could wipe out oil refiner-
ies, causing the price of energy to spike. A sustained increase in food

and energy costs, which feed directly into the CPI, can therefore set off an inflationary process. Prices could also increase when workers gain enough bargaining power to bid up their wages. To prevent the increase in wages from squeezing profit margins, businesses may pass these costs on to consumers in the form of higher prices. As the battle over income shares rages back and forth, it can set off a wage-price spiral that results in accelerating inflation. Companies with enough market power can also unilaterally raise prices in a quest for greater and greater profits. For example, pharmaceutical companies that enjoy patent protections can raise the price of prescription drugs, adding to overall health care costs, which then feed into inflation.[3]

Demand-pull inflation occurs when businesses raise prices due to changes in buying habits. Most often, it happens when people are spending faster than the economy can churn out new goods and services. Think of it this way. Every economy has its own internal speed limit. It's only possible to produce so much, at any point in time, given the real resources—people, factories, machines, raw materials— available in that moment. During a recession, people lose jobs and companies turn off machines and allow them to sit idle. In that environment, spending can safely increase because workers can be rehired, and machines can be brought back online to produce more output. That's why the $787 billion fiscal stimulus passed in 2009 didn't cause an inflation problem. The Great Recession left millions unemployed and businesses operating far below their productive capacity. When there's that much slack in the economy, it's easy for businesses to increase supply in response to more spending. But as an economy moves closer to its full employment limit, real resources become increasingly scarce. Rising demand can begin to put pressure on prices, and bottlenecks can develop in industries that are experiencing the greatest strain on capacity. Inflation can heat up. Once the economy hits this full employment wall, *any* additional spending (not just government spending) will be inflationary. That's overspending, and it can even happen if the government's budget is balanced or in surplus.

Another common way to think about inflation is closely associated with the economic doctrine of monetarism.[4] The father of this
approach is Nobel Prize–winning economist Milton Friedman. Monetarism dominated economic thinking in the 1970s, and versions of
the monetarist cannon still permeate debates today. According to
Friedman, "inflation is always and everywhere a monetary phenomenon." What he meant was that too much money is the culprit in any
inflationary episode. If prices weren't stable, it was because the central
bank was trying to force the economy to create too many jobs by allowing the money supply to increase too rapidly.

Before Friedman came along, Keynesian thinking dominated
macroeconomics.[5] Keynesian economists believed that expanding
the money supply was a perfectly legitimate tool for central banks to
use in pursuit of low unemployment. More money would mean more
spending, which would mean businesses needed to hire more workers
and produce more output to satisfy higher demand. Unemployment
would fall, and the possibility of inflation would increase as more hiring led to higher wages and prices. You got more of something good—
jobs—at the cost of something bad—inflation.[6] It was up to the central
bank to decide how to exploit this trade-off over time.

Friedman challenged the Keynesian paradigm. In his view, a certain amount of unemployment is basically impossible to eliminate. He
called it the "natural rate of unemployment." The central bank could
fight against the natural rate, but it would be fighting a losing and
increasingly costly battle. Friedman's argument against the Keynesians was that workers would find themselves in a continual trap, with
excessive growth in the money supply causing inflation to rise faster
than paychecks. Workers would end up working more (i.e., the unemployment rate would fall) but for lower real pay. Eventually, they
would figure this out and demand better compensation. But the whole
thing would end in tears, as inflation would spiral higher while unemployment would return to its "natural rate," as companies chose to
shed workers rather than boost paychecks. The takeaway was simple.

Keynesians were offering a devil's bargain. Trying to hold the unemployment rate down would simply condemn you to a world of accelerating inflation.

The only solution was to tie the hands of macroeconomic policy makers.[7] Instead of giving the Federal Reserve discretion to trade lower unemployment for higher inflation, the central bank should be forced to accept the fact that a certain amount of unemployment was necessary to keep inflation stable. As we will see, MMT contests this framework.

How We Fight Inflation Today

Since 1977, the Federal Reserve has operated under what is commonly referred to as a dual-mandate from Congress. The dual-mandate directs the Fed to pursue maximum employment and stable prices. Basically, Congress put the Fed in charge of jobs and inflation. Congress doesn't tell the Federal Reserve how many jobs it's expected to support or how much inflation is considered too much. The central bank is treated as independent in the sense that it gets to pick its own inflation target and decide for itself what maximum employment means.[8] Like most central banks, the Federal Reserve has chosen a 2 percent inflation target.[9] To keep from overshooting that rate, the Fed aims to keep just the "right" amount of unemployment in the system, much like Friedman prescribed a half century ago.

The Federal Reserve can't spend money directly into the economy, and it can't tax money out of the economy either. Those powers are reserved for the fiscal authority—Congress. So how is the Fed supposed to deliver on its dual-mandate?

There was a time, in the late 1970s and early 1980s, when many central banks, including the Federal Reserve, claimed that by directly controlling the growth of the money supply, they could control inflation.[10] Today, virtually all central banks have adopted a different approach, targeting a key interest rate that is supposed to help them indirectly manage inflationary pressures.[11] The idea is that by influencing the price of credit—that is, how much it costs to borrow money—the central bank can regulate how much money consumers and businesses borrow and spend into our economy.

When it lowers its policy rate, the central bank is said to be easing credit conditions. They do this when they think the jobless rate is *above* the so-called natural rate of unemployment. The goal is to bring the unemployment rate down. If everything works as intended, lots of people take out loans to purchase things like homes and automobiles, and businesses borrow to invest in new machines and build new factories. As all of this borrowed money gets spent, the economy picks up, and more people find jobs. With fewer people out of work, the labor market is said to tighten, causing wages to rise, and with them, the risk of wage-price inflation.

And there's the rub. The Fed subscribes to the idea that if it induces too much spending, the labor market will get too hot, and unemployment will dip below its "natural" rate, causing inflation to accelerate. This is exactly what conservative economist Marvin Goodfriend had in mind when he warned in 2012 that if the Fed allowed the unemployment rate to dip below 7 percent, it would "give rise to a rising inflation rate in the next few years, which would just be disastrous for the economy." But Goodfriend was wrong. Three years after his warning, unemployment had dropped to 5 percent, yet inflation was *lower* than it was when he made his initial prediction.

Why did he (and others) get it so wrong? One problem is that the natural rate of unemployment—if it exists at all—isn't something the Fed (or anyone else) can observe or even calculate. Instead, it's more like a description of an economy in its ideal state. The natural rate can change over time, but there's only one unique natural rate at any particular moment. And no one can tell you what it is. You discover it by trial and error. You've found it when any further decline in unemployment causes inflation to accelerate.

In other words, whether or not an economy is at its natural rate of unemployment is a *conclusion* drawn after the fact. In that respect, reaching the natural rate for economists is sort of like falling in love for the rest of us: you rarely see it coming but know it when it happens.[12] Economists have a name for it. They call it the NAIRU (nī-rū), the non-accelerating inflationary rate of unemployment. Sexy, isn't it? To understand how it works, think of the classic children's story, "Goldilocks and the Three Bears." Just replace porridge with unemployment, and you basically have it. Whenever the unemployment rate is too cold, the Fed lowers the interest rate, hoping to warm things up by inducing more borrowing and spending. When it gets too hot, the Fed raises the interest rate, hoping to cool things off by discouraging further borrowing and spending. Hence, the solution is to keep adjusting monetary policy back and forth so that the unemployment rate stays just right.

But there's a wrinkle here. The Fed doesn't like to wait until inflation becomes a problem before acting. Instead, it prefers to fight the inflation monster preemptively before it rears its ugly head. As New York Federal Reserve Bank president William C. Dudley explains: "we do not know with much precision how low the unemployment rate can go without prompting a significant rise in inflation. We do not directly observe the non-accelerating inflation rate of unemployment, or NAIRU. Rather, we only infer it from the response of wage compensation and price inflation as the labor market tightens."[13]

In other words, the Fed watches the labor market for evidence that wages might be accelerating and interprets rising pay as a prelude to higher inflation. The idea is not to wait to see the whites of the inflation monster's eyes. Shoot now and ask questions later. This kind of preemptive bias often leads the Fed to err on the side of overtightening, raising the interest rate even when it may be premature or a false alarm. Errors like these carry real consequences in the form of millions of people unnecessarily locked out of employment.

The dual-mandate framework is predicated on the belief that there's a delicate balance between too much employment and too little. It also assumes that the Federal Reserve has the ability to move the economy to its sweet spot, where just the "right" number of people are kept on the sidelines, wanting to work but trapped in unemployment for the sake of keeping prices in check. To put it crudely, the Fed uses unemployed human beings as its primary weapon against inflation.

In theory, this is all pretty easy to do. In practice, well, that's another story.

In theory, the Fed can use a mathematical model to determine exactly where to set the interest rate to keep the inflation rate stable. After the 2008 financial crisis, the Fed lowered the interest rate all the way to zero and left it there. The unemployment rate fell from a peak of 10 percent in October of 2009 to 5 percent by the end of 2015. More people were finding jobs, including many low-skilled and minority workers who often have the hardest time securing employment. In December of 2015, the Fed raised its interest rate target from 0 percent to 0.25 percent, even though the inflation rate remained below its 2 percent target. Over the next three years, the Fed raised its policy rate another eight times, despite persistently undershooting its inflation target. Some people criticized them for raising rates when inflation was clearly not expected to accelerate. But the Fed believed the rate hikes were justified to bring the unemployment rate back to its NAIRU estimates and preemptively keep inflation at bay. Although the Fed was trying to cool things off, unemployment continued to decline further below their estimates, and inflation didn't accelerate. According to the NAIRU framework, that wasn't supposed to happen.

Despite the apparent breakdown in any relationship between low unemployment and inflation, the Fed remains committed to the NAIRU concept. Indeed, Federal Reserve chairman Jerome Powell testified in July 2019 at a hearing before the House Committee on Financial Services that "we need the concept of a natural rate of unemployment." He continued, "We need to have some sense of whether unemployment is high, low or just right."

Regardless of whether Chairman Powell is right or wrong, it is indisputable that the Fed's recent estimates of the NAIRU—the level of unemployment that can be achieved without causing inflation to accelerate—have been consistently wrong. This failure was put on full display in another exchange from the same July 2019 committee hearing, when newly elected Congresswoman Alexandria Ocasio-Cortez posed the following question to Chairman Powell:

> **AOC:** The unemployment rate has fallen three full points since 2014, but inflation is no higher today than it was five years ago. Given these facts, do you agree that the Fed's estimate of the lowest sustainable unemployment rate has been too high?
> **POWELL:** Absolutely.

It's unusual to see a Fed chairman so frankly admit error. But notice that Powell didn't question the legitimacy of the NAIRU as an essential policy guide. Instead, he blamed himself for having misjudged precisely where the NAIRU lies. It's this underlying faith in the idea that there's some inescapable constraint on the economy's employment potential that caused the Fed to systematically underestimate the extent to which the unemployment rate could safely fall. This misreading drove the Fed to raise interest rates in the hope of choking off a further drop in unemployment, essentially aiming to deny millions of underemployed and unemployed people access to jobs on the belief that the NAIRU limit had already been reached. You're considered unemployed if you are actively seeking paid employment but not currently working. Some people are underemployed. They're currently working part-time, but what they really want is a full-time job. Because they're employed, they're not counted in the official measure of unemployment known as U-3. Instead, they're included in a broader measure of unemployment known as U-6, which also includes people who want to work but have basically given up hope of finding a job. And the problems don't end there. As former Fed governor Daniel Tarullo confessed, the Fed has no reliable theory of inflation guiding its day-to-day decision-making. It has various conjectures, assumptions, and models, but many of these are unproven or indeed unprovable.[14] It's all something of a guessing game, where people's lives are on the line.

Far from being an exact science, the core guiding principle of the Fed's approach is best described as faith. Faith that their understanding of inflation is more accurate than not. Faith that their tools are powerful enough to manage inflation. And faith that, whatever other uncertainties may exist, excessive inflation is always and everywhere a greater threat to our collective well-being than excessive unemployment.[15]

Faith Contested

Even as scientists and engineers constantly innovate, creating new medicines, technologies, and techniques to eradicate diseases and solve human problems, the majority of economists remain wedded to a fifty-year-old doctrine that relies on human suffering to fight inflation. In recent years, a few senior insiders have voiced concerns about the Fed's framework and indicated an openness to rethinking their approach. But most mainstream economists remain wedded to the idea that there is some lower boundary below which unemployment cannot safely be permitted to decline. Some slack must be maintained in the form of a human sacrifice—forced idleness—lest we condemn ourselves to the ravages of accelerating inflation. Because they accept the concept of an inherent trade-off between inflation and unemployment, the Fed is forced to think in terms of how much unemployment to keep in the system as a sort of insurance policy against inflation. They simply see no other way to achieve low and stable inflation.

Why not just strive for a better mix of fiscal and monetary policy to keep the economy operating at its full employment potential? Couldn't we achieve true full employment by asking the Fed to improve the way it runs monetary policy? Or maybe Congress could help fine-tune the economy with better real-time adjustments in government spending and taxation?

Recall that the Fed chooses its own definition of full employment. For them, maximum employment is defined as the level of unemployment it believes is necessary to hit its inflation target. In other words, although it's legally responsible for full employment and price stability, one goal takes clear priority over the other. If it takes eight or ten million unemployed people to stabilize prices, then that is how the Fed defines full employment. It's counterintuitive to define full employment as *a certain level of unemployment*. But politically speaking, it is useful for the Fed as it means they get to claim success by defining away the very problem they were tasked to solve. No matter how many people remain jobless, the Fed can claim it's done its best, and there's simply no way to reduce unemployment further without causing inflation. For those who are still without jobs, tough luck. Thanks for your service in the inflation war. There's nothing more the Fed can do to help you.

It's sometimes argued that there are actually plenty of jobs for the unemployed but that there are structural problems in matching the people who want to work with the jobs that are currently available. Maybe workers are just too picky, refusing to take entry-level jobs because they have too much education to justify accepting low-paid work. Or maybe it's the opposite problem: those without work lack the education and skills that are required to fill the high-tech jobs of the future. Either way, the problem is matching people to chairs, not a lack of chairs. If only they had gotten the right education, or the right skills, or had the right motivation and personal discipline, they could find jobs.

It's a convenient argument for those who are content to leave millions behind, but it's not reality. In reality, no matter how smart or hardworking the population may be, the Fed sees too much risk in allowing everyone who wants to work to do so. Some people view this as rigging the game in a way that chronically leaves too many people without jobs. If the Fed believes the NAIRU is 5 percent, then it's only safe to allow ninety-five musical chairs for every one hundred people in the game.

Others take the opposite approach, pointing to recent evidence that lower unemployment hasn't come at the cost of rising inflation. This is interpreted as evidence that the Fed could do more to increase the availability of chairs. Critics from both the left, organizations like the activist group FedUp, and the right, such as conservative economics writer Stephen Moore, have complained that the Fed has unnecessarily stomped on the brake pedal. In their view, the problem is not with the Fed's tools but with the way it wields them. In particular, they believe the Fed is too quick to raise interest rates, thereby snatching away jobs that would have materialized if the Fed had let things run their course. In other words, they believe the Fed could help the unemployed by cutting rates or at least waiting more patiently for additional chairs to materialize.

But even a more patient Fed can never guarantee that everyone who wants to work can find a job. Outside of World War II, the US has never sustained anything approximating true full employment. The reason was spelled out in 1936 by John Maynard Keynes in his most famous book, *The General Theory of Employment, Interest, and Money*. Capitalist economies chronically operate with insufficient aggregate demand. That means there is never enough combined spending (public and private) to induce companies to offer employment for every person who wants to work. You can come close, and you might even get there for brief periods in wartime, but peacetime economies don't operate at full capacity. There is always slack in the form of unemployed resources, including labor.[16]

Most economists are content to allow the market to figure out how many jobs to provide. Congress, if it is to play any role at all, might dedicate some resources to helping the jobless acquire more skills to make them more attractive to potential employers. More education, better workforce training, subsidized private sector employment, and the like are seen as pathways out of poverty for the unemployed. MMT sees these proposals as half measures that do little to address the problem of chronic underemployment and unemployment. When there is a chronic lack of jobs, the best these solutions can offer is a sort of shuffling around of joblessness or taking turns experiencing bouts of unemployment. As Nobel Prize–winning economist William Vickrey put it, when the number of jobs is insufficient, "attempts to push [the unemployed] into jobs is simply a game of musical chairs in which local agencies instruct their clients in the art of rapid sitting."[17]

The truth is, we have placed far too much responsibility on central banks, not just in the US but around the world. They cannot alter taxes or spend money directly into the economy, so the best they can do to promote employment is to try to establish financial conditions that will give rise to more borrowing and spending. Lower interest rates *might* work to induce enough new borrowing to substantially lower unemployment. But they might not. As Keynes famously observed, "You can't push on a string." What he meant was that the Fed can make it cheaper to borrow, but it cannot force anyone to take out a loan. Borrowing money puts companies and individuals on the hook for the debts they incur. Loans must be repaid out of future income, and there are good reasons why the private sector might be reluctant to increase its indebtedness at various stages of the business cycle. Remember, households and businesses are currency users, not currency issuers, so they do need to worry about how they're going to make their payments.

In the wake of the Great Recession, which was itself precipitated by a massive buildup in private (subprime mortgage) debt, it became clear that the Fed was struggling to fix the economy on its own. It had already cut the interest rate to zero, and it had embarked on a new strategy known as quantitative easing.[18] It was doing everything in its power to hold things together. So, it was a frustrating moment for Fed chairman Ben Bernanke when he appeared before Congress and was grilled about why the Fed's extreme measures didn't seem to be doing much to help the economy recover. Pressed by Congressman Jeb Hensarling of Texas, Bernanke responded, "Let me just agree with you on the following. Monetary policy is not a panacea. It is not the ideal tool."[19]

Not the ideal tool? Monetary policy is *the* tool. By statute, Congress put the Fed in charge of running the economy—in good times and bad. The Fed is supposed to do it all. And that's the problem. Monetary policy has limited potency. It works mainly by driving consumers and businesses into debt. And debt for the private sector is not the same as debt for the public sector. When the bottom fell out of the housing market, most Americans wanted to borrow less, not more. Millions of homeowners were underwater on their mortgages; they owed more than their homes were worth. After a long period of borrowing to finance spending in excess of its income, the private sector wanted relief from debt, not more debt. Without actually using the F-word (fiscal), Bernanke delivered the message. The Fed's policy lever wasn't powerful enough on its own. It was time for the other policy tool—fiscal policy—to get back in the game.

The problem is that the recession pushed the budget deep into deficit, and Congress had already passed a $787 billion stimulus package to fight the effects of the Great Recession. When Bernanke made his not-so-subtle plea for additional help in 2011, it fell on deaf ears. Congress had become preoccupied with the state of its own balance sheet. When the Fed realized it was essentially on its own, Bernanke pushed in all the chips with an open-ended round of quantitative easing that some experts believe contributed to widening inequality and risky speculation in financial markets. Over time, the unemployment rate fell from 9 percent to less than 4 percent.

It took seven years, but eventually the labor market clawed back all of the jobs that were lost in the aftermath of the financial crisis. For some, this is a testament to the capacity of monetary policy to rebalance the economy after a recession. To the economists behind MMT, it reveals the shortcomings in the dominant approach to macroeconomic stabilization. A recession that could have been quickly reversed with the right fiscal prescription instead became the longest and most protracted downturn in the post–World War II era. To make sure that never happens again, MMT recommends a shift away from the current reliance on central banks to deliver on the twin goals of full employment and price stability.

Inflation and Unemployment: The MMT Approach

The economists behind MMT recognize that there are real limits to spending, and that attempting to push beyond those limits can manifest in excessive inflation. However, we believe there are better ways to manage those kinds of inflationary pressures and that it can be done without trapping millions of people in perpetual unemployment. In fact, we argue that it is possible to use *true* full employment to help stabilize prices.

Instead of relying on the concept of a NAIRU to try to figure out when the economy is approaching its productive limit, MMT urges us to think about slack more broadly. Currently, policy makers look at the official unemployment rate, a measurement known as U-3, and then try to divine how close that number is to the invisible NAIRU rate. As the Fed admits, they often underestimate the degree of slack in the labor market, thereby trying to slow the economy even before it has maxed out its productive capacity. That's like leaving money on the table in the sense that every person who could have been employed, performing useful tasks for society, is forever lost to us. A sort of free lunch not eaten.

When we run our economy below its productive capacity, it means that we are living below our collective means. The federal budget might be in deficit, but we are *underspending* whenever there is unused capacity. It's like building a high-performance automobile and then driving it like it's a golf cart. It's inefficient. When we tolerate mass unemployment, we're sacrificing whatever might have been produced if we had harnessed the time and energy of those who wanted to work but were denied access to jobs. Eliminating this kind of involuntary unemployment has been a concern of Keynesian economists for decades.

In the 1940s, an economist with a flair for advancing new ways of thinking suggested a way to permanently close the output gap—the difference between what the economy is capable of producing and what it actually produces at any point in time. His name was Abba P. Lerner, and his idea was to allow the private sector to come as close as possible to achieving full employment on its own and then to rely primarily on fiscal policy to make up any shortfall in total spending. With enough *aggregate* spending, he reasoned, policy makers could maintain prosperity by holding the economy at full potential through a permanent application of fiscal policy. Monetary policy could help, but Lerner wanted fiscal policy—adjustments in taxes and government spending—in charge of the economic steering wheel.[20] He argued, even more strongly than Keynes before him, that the federal government should adjust its own budget to offset any and all departures from full employment. The budget outcome was irrelevant. Only real economic outcomes mattered.

He labeled his approach functional finance because he wanted Congress to make decisions based on the way its policies would work or function in the real economy rather than worrying about how they would impact the budget. The goal was to produce a balanced economy—one in which jobs were sufficiently plentiful and inflation was low. Achieving those goals might require fiscal deficits, a balanced budget, or a fiscal surplus. Any one of those outcomes was deemed acceptable, as long as the overall economy remained in balance.

Functional finance turned conventional wisdom on its head. Instead of trying to force the economy to generate enough taxes to match federal spending, Lerner urged policy makers to think in reverse. Taxes and spending should be manipulated to bring the overall economy into balance. That might require the government to add in (spend) more dollars than it subtracts (taxes) away. It might even need to do this on an ongoing basis, meaning sustained fiscal deficits over many years or even decades. Lerner saw this as a perfectly responsible way to manage the government budget. As long as any resulting deficits didn't push inflation higher, the deficit shouldn't be labeled overspending.

This fundamentally changes the way we conceive of what it means to deploy the federal budget in a fiscally responsible way. Instead of blaming Congress for failing to bring spending in line with taxes, we should accept *any* budget outcome that delivers broadly balanced conditions in our economy. Thus, if the budget outcome depicted in Exhibit 2 on the left gives rise to the balanced economic conditions pictured on the right, then fiscal policy requires no further adjustment and we should consider the budget in balance.

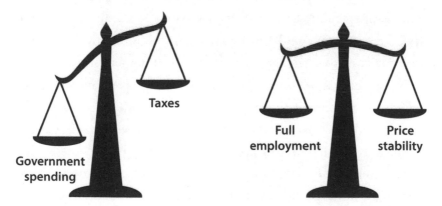

EXHIBIT 2. Redefining a Balanced Budget

To maintain full employment and keep inflation low, Lerner wanted the government to keep constant watch on the economy. If something happened to move the economy out of balance, Lerner wanted to the government to respond with a fiscal adjustment, either changing taxes or altering government spending. Tax cuts could work to fight against unemployment if they could be enacted quickly and were well targeted, meaning they had to benefit those who would most likely spend that money right back into the economy. To work well, tax cuts need to benefit those with a high propensity to spend out of new income. The reason Trump's personal income tax cuts did little to boost the overall economy is because they were heavily skewed in favor of those at the very top of the income distribution. More than 80 percent of the benefits went to those in the top 1 percent. Compared with lower- and middle-income earners, who would spend a high percentage of any new dollar you give them, the rich just don't spend all that much more when you shovel more money into their pockets. Well-targeted tax cuts can work, but a more direct way to maintain spending would be for the government to simply spend more on its own. Just as well-targeted tax cuts will work better than poorly targeted cuts, well-targeted government spending works better than poorly targeted spending. Economists usually prefer spending projects that have a high fiscal multiplier because it means that the initial round of government spending will multiply into many more rounds of spending as dollars change hands again and again, each time creating some additional demand in the economy. To ensure that government spending provided the maximum boost to the economy, Lerner was adamant that any increase in spending take place *without* an accompanying tax increase to "pay for it." Instead of following a PAYGO-like rule, he wanted the government to refrain from raising taxes until it became necessary to fight inflationary pressures.[21] If inflation began to creep up, Lerner believed that Congress could respond by raising taxes or cutting back its own expenditures. And if unemployment suddenly shot higher, he thought lawmakers should cut taxes or find a way to spend more money and fast.

Lerner's insights are important to MMT, but they don't go far enough. We agree that we should rely on adjustments in taxes and spending (fiscal policy) rather than interest rates (monetary policy) to balance our economy. We also agree that fiscal deficits, in and of themselves, are neither good nor bad. What matters is not whether the government's budget is in surplus or deficit but whether the government is using its budget to achieve good outcomes for the rest of the economy. We agree that taxes are an important way to reduce spending power and that taxes should never be increased simply to appear fiscally responsible. But we think Lerner's prescriptions will still leave too many people without jobs.

Even if all 535 members of Congress woke up tomorrow and agreed to conduct fiscal policy the way Lerner recommended, involuntary unemployment would remain a permanent feature of our economy. There's just no way for Congress to react to changing economic conditions by turning the steering wheel quickly enough to ensure that everyone who is looking for work can always find a job. At best, we might arrive at a closer approximation to full employment, but there would always be a significant cohort that remains locked out of employment. It's also not enough to rely exclusively on Congress to adjust government spending and taxation to fight off inflation once it begins to accelerate. To supplement discretionary fiscal policy (the steering wheel), MMT recommends a federal job guarantee, which creates a nondiscretionary automatic stabilizer that promotes both full employment and price stability.

Think of a poorly maintained roadway. You get a smooth ride until you encounter a pothole or a bump in the road. You can try to steer clear of hazards, but at some point, you're destined to hit one. At that point, you could be in for a rough ride. If you've got a vehicle with good shock absorbers, they'll buffer the impact, and you won't get jostled around too much. But if the shock absorbers are weak, you'd better hang on! MMT enhances Lerner's steering wheel with a powerful new shock absorber in the form of a federal job guarantee.

Here's how it would work.

The federal government announces a wage (and benefit) package for anyone who is looking for work but unable to find suitable employment in the economy. Several MMT economists have recommended that the jobs be oriented around building a care economy.[22] Very generally, that means the federal government would commit to funding jobs that are aimed at caring for our people, our communities, and our planet. This effectively establishes a public option in the labor market, with the government fixing an hourly wage and allowing the quantity of workers hired into the program to float.[23] Since the market price of an unemployed worker is zero—that is, no one is currently bidding on them—the government can create a market for these workers by setting the price it is willing to pay to hire them. Once it does, involuntary unemployment disappears. Anyone seeking paid employment has guaranteed access to a job at a rate of remuneration established by the federal government.

The job guarantee has its origins in the tradition of Franklin Delano Roosevelt, who wanted the government to guarantee employment as an economic right of all people. It was also an integral part of the civil rights movement led by Dr. Martin Luther King Jr., his wife, Coretta Scott King, and the reverend A. Philip Randolph. The influential economist Hyman Minsky advocated such a program as a key pillar in his antipoverty work. It's important to note that the job guarantee doesn't require policy makers to try to divine the amount of slack in the labor market using something like a NAIRU. Instead, the government simply announces a wage and then hires everyone who turns up looking for a job. If no one shows up, it means the economy is already operating at full employment. But if fifteen million people show up, it reveals substantial slack. In a real sense, it's the only way to know for sure how substantially the economy is underutilizing available resources.

Why does the financing have to come from Uncle Sam? Simple. He can't run out of money. It would be nearly impossible for a currency user, such as a state or local government, to commit to hiring anyone and everyone who showed up asking for a job. Imagine what would happen if the mayor of Detroit announced that the city was prepared to offer a job to anyone who wanted to work but couldn't find employment anywhere in the region. It would be swamped with applicants. Even in a relatively good economy, tens or hundreds of thousands of people would show up, placing an enormous strain on the local government budget. Now think about what would happen if the economy went into recession and the number of applicants doubled at the same time Detroit's tax revenues were falling off a cliff. Remember, state and local governments really do depend on tax revenue to pay the bills. They can't simply commit to spending more when their revenues dry up in a recession. But that's precisely when the program is under the greatest strain (and when it's most critical).

Recall from the previous chapter that Mosler got his kids to do chores around the house by imposing a tax payable only in his business cards. In this sense, the tax (at least from inception) is the thing that causes people to seek employment. MMT reckons that since the government imposes the tax that causes people to look for ways to earn the currency, the government should make sure that there is always a way to earn the currency.

With a job guarantee in place, the economy can pass through a rough patch without throwing millions of people into unemployment. The rough patches are inevitable. There isn't a capitalist economy on earth that has found a way to eradicate the business cycle. Economies grow and create jobs and then, eventually, something happens to throw them into recession. We can and should use discretionary policy to try to tame the business cycle. Smoother rides are preferable to bumpy ones. But no country has figured out how to steer clear of every possible hazard. Over the past sixty years, the US has been hit with recessions in 1960–1961, 1969–1970, 1973–1975, 1980, 1981–1982,

1990–1991, 2001, and 2007–2009. Good times are followed by bad times, which eventually set the stage for the next round of good times.

A major benefit of the job guarantee is that it helps to insulate the economy as it passes through the inevitable boom-bust cycle. Instead of throwing millions of people out of work when the economy softens, the job guarantee allows people to transition from one form of paid employment into another. You might lose a job sorting boxes for a private retailer, but you could immediately secure employment performing a useful job in public service. Because the job guarantee allows workers to transition into alternative *employment* rather than joining the ranks of the unemployed, the program helps to cushion the overall economy by supporting wages and preserving (or enhancing) skills until the economy recovers and workers begin to transition back into private sector jobs. And because spending to hire workers into the program becomes automatic once the job guarantee is in place, we don't have to rely on discretionary spending to smooth the ride.[24]

The federal government guarantees the financing, establishes the broad parameters that define the types of jobs the program aims to support, and provides oversight to ensure compliance and accountability. Virtually everything else is handled in a decentralized way, bringing decision-making as close as possible to the people and communities who will benefit most directly from the tasks that will be performed. The key feature of the program is that it will act as a powerful new automatic stabilizer for the economy as a whole.

MMT fights involuntary unemployment by eliminating it. In our view, the most effective full employment policy is one that targets the unemployed directly. Instead of aiming spending at infrastructure and hoping jobs will trickle down to the unemployed, MMT proposes what Bard College economist Pavlina Tcherneva describes as a bottom-up approach.[25] It takes workers as they are, and where they are, and it fits the job to their individual capabilities and the needs of the community. We're not talking about creating just any old job. This isn't a make-work scheme, aimed simply at giving the unemployed a shovel in order to justify paying them a wage. It's a way to enhance the public good while strengthening our communities through a system of shared governance. As Vickrey put it, these public service jobs would enable us to "convert unemployed labor into improved public amenities and facilities of various types."[26] The idea is to task people with useful work that is valued by the community and to provide compensation for that work in the form of a decent wage and benefit package.

If the economy were to crash the way it did in 2008, the federal job guarantee would catch hundreds of thousands of people instead of allowing them to fall into unemployment.[27] The private sector would shed jobs, but new jobs would immediately spring forth in public service. Since the federal government has committed to providing the funding for these new jobs, the downturn is cushioned by an expansion of the fiscal deficit. It happens automatically, without any need to wait for Congress to deliberate and haggle over whether to rescue the economy with fiscal stimulus. Because the program supports incomes, the economy stabilizes more quickly than it would in the absence of the job guarantee. The downturn is less severe, and the recovery arrives sooner. And because it's a permanent program, it's there to buttress the economy in good times and in bad.

Since it's always in effect, the job guarantee provides for a smoother overall economic ride, which helps to stabilize inflation. Without it, incomes would fall more sharply when businesses lay off workers as customers disappear, causing inventories to pile up and businesses to look for ways to quickly mark down prices to liquidate unsold items. When the recovery eventually arrives, companies can raise prices to reestablish customary profit margins. The more the economy swings around, the more prices may move in response. By stabilizing consumer income, the job guarantee helps to avoid wider adjustments in consumer spending that may result in more price variation.

The job guarantee also helps to stabilize inflation by anchoring a key price in the economy—the price paid to workers in the job guarantee program. By establishing a wage floor, the government sets the minimum compensation, say $15 per hour. This becomes the rate of remuneration against which all other employment can be priced. Right now, the minimum wage is zero. Yes, the federal minimum wage is $7.25 per hour, but as the economist Hyman Minsky often observed, the minimum wage available to the unemployed is $0. You have to be employed to earn at least the federal minimum wage, and millions of unemployed Americans don't have access to that wage. To establish a universal minimum, there must be a standing offer to bid for labor at some positive price. The job guarantee establishes that minimum bid, making the job guarantee wage the de facto minimum wage through-out the economy. Once established, any other form of employment would be expected to offer a premium over the base wage.[28] We al-ready do this with interest rates, where the Federal Reserve sets the overnight rate, which becomes the base rate against which mortgages, credit cards, auto loans, and so on are priced. When the Fed raises the short-term rate, other rates usually move higher.[29] By anchoring the price of labor, the job guarantee imparts greater stability across a spectrum of wages and prices in the economy.

Finally, the job guarantee helps to fight inflationary pressure by maintaining a ready pool of *employed* people from which businesses can easily hire when they're looking to expand production. We know from surveys of employers that the least appealing job applicant is the one who has suffered a long bout of unemployment. Employers just don't want to take a chance on hiring someone who has no re-cent employment record.[30] To the extent possible, they want to know what they're getting. Hiring the unemployed involves substantial risk. There's no way to find out whether the long-term unemployed have retained good work habits, if they can be expected to interact well with others, and so on. An efficient typist or a skilled craftsman may have seen their skills deteriorate from lack of use. You're rolling the dice when you hire someone who's been out of work for a relatively long period of time. To avoid the uncertainty, companies often try to lure workers away from their current positions by bidding up wages to the level necessary to entice them to switch jobs. If every employer follows suit, then we're in a game of musical chairs, where those with chairs are constantly moving to better-paying chairs and those without chairs stay locked out of the game. Bidding up wages in this way introduces an inflationary bias that is mitigated when businesses have the option to hire from a pool of employed public service workers instead. With the job guarantee in place, employers have an expanded pool of potential workers from which to hire. It benefits not only employers and those who would otherwise languish in unemployment but the rest of us as well.

Because it's an automatic stabilizer, the job guarantee moves the federal budget up and down—more money is spent when the economy is weak and less is spent when it grows stronger—ensuring that deficits move countercyclically to avoid overspending in this area of the budget. Of course, Congress would still retain *discretionary* control over other parts of the budget. As the currency issuer, Uncle Sam wields the power of the purse, and he can always decide to spend more on things like infrastructure, education, or defense. If there are goods and services for sale and Uncle Sam wants them, he has the power to outbid the rest of us. He's not financially constrained. As the currency issuer, he has the power to commit to spending money he doesn't have, and he can't go broke as a result. That's the reality that MMT exposes.

———

AS STAN LEE, the creator of the Spider-Man comic books, taught us, "With great power there must also come—great responsibility." Senator Enzi was right to express concerns about overspending. But he failed to identify the real danger. The threat to our common well-being isn't the budget deficit. It's excessive inflation.

So how do we take advantage of the potential benefits that a sovereign currency affords the people of our nation while at the same time guarding against the risk of overspending? You might be tempted to argue that we already have safeguards in place. The debt ceiling limit, the Byrd rule, and PAYGO might look like effective checks on over-spending. They aren't. And it's not because it's easy for Congress to get around the rules. It's because under current budgeting procedures, Congress doesn't have to consider inflation risk when it wants to spend more. Remember, it put the Federal Reserve in charge of price stability. So, members of Congress only ask whether new spending will increase the deficit, not inflation. That's the wrong question.

In fact, as MMT shows, it sidesteps the great responsibility that should be demanded of any government that wields the power of the fiscal purse. To see why, let's consider an example. Suppose the econ-omy is close to its maximum speed limit, with most workers and busi-nesses already churning out as many goods and services as it's possible to produce. Now suppose Congress wants to spend $2 trillion mod-ernizing and upgrading America's crumbling infrastructure (airports, hospitals, highways, bridges, water treatment facilities, etc.).[31] Because no one in Congress thinks like a currency issuer, they all believe the important thing to worry about is whether the spending will increase the deficit. To avoid adding to the deficit, suppose they pair the spend-ing with a proposal to raise $2 trillion by leveling a small tax on a handful of Americans whose net worth exceeds $50 million. Today, that bill would go to the Congressional Budget Office (CBO), where it would likely receive a good score on the grounds that it doesn't add to the deficit over time. With a green light from the CBO, members of Congress would be free to move forward with a vote to authorize the spending. What happens next could be a disaster.

As the Department of Transportation tries to contract out the work, it quickly discovers that there aren't enough unemployed resources available for the government to hire. That's because the tax fell on a small number of people (about seventy-five thousand) who weren't go-ing to spend much (if any) of that money in the first place. This should *not* be construed as an argument against taxing the rich. It is an argu-ment against arbitrary decision-making when it comes to tax policy.

There is a strong case to be made for taxing the rich, and we need to do it. But we need to do it strategically, recognizing that the purpose of the tax is not to pay for government expenditures but to help us rebalance the distribution of wealth and income because the extreme concentrations that exist today are a threat to both our democracy and to the functioning of our economy. Think about it. Jeff Bezos, the richest man in America, has an estimated net worth of $110 billion. How many fewer cars, swimming pools, tennis courts, or luxury vacations will Bezos purchase after 2 percent of his wealth is taxed away? The answer is not many. A small, annual tax on a fraction of his net worth isn't going to crowd out much of his spending. When it comes down to it, he's more of a saver than a spender. Billionaires save their wealth in the form of financial assets, real estate, fine art, and rare coins. A wealth tax might make the infrastructure bill *appear* fiscally responsible, but it makes a lousy offset if the government wants to increase spending in an economy that doesn't have much available slack.

In a deeply depressed economy, this wouldn't matter. There would be plenty of "fiscal space" because business would be operating with lots of spare capacity and there would be loads of unemployed workers available for hire. But as we get close to full employment, these real resources become increasingly scarce. Once the economy exhausts its real productive capacity, the only way for the government to get the construction workers, architects and engineers, steel, concrete, paving trucks, cranes, and so on that it needs is to bid them away from their current use. That bidding process pushes prices higher, giving rise to inflationary pressures. To mitigate that risk, the tax needs to offset enough current spending to free up the real resources the government is trying to hire. The problem is that because this particular tax is levied on a tiny cadre of uber-rich people, it won't open up much (if any) fiscal space.

That doesn't make it a bad idea on other grounds! It just means it's not an effective way to mitigate inflation risk, and that's especially important when the economy is running close to its maximum speed limit.

That's why MMT recommends a different approach to the federal budgeting process, one that integrates inflation risk into the decision-making process so that lawmakers are forced to stop and think about whether they have taken the necessary steps to guard against inflation risk *before* approving any new spending. MMT would make us *safer* in this respect because it recognizes that the best defense against inflation is a good offense. We don't want to allow excessive spending to cause inflation and then fight inflation after it happens.[32] We want agencies like the CBO helping to evaluate new legislation for potential inflation risk *before* Congress commits to funding new programs so that the risks can be mitigated preemptively. At its core, MMT is about replacing an artificial (revenue) constraint with a real (inflation) constraint.[33]

The reality is that Uncle Sam faces no binding revenue constraint. He spends first and removes dollars by taxing later. Instead of starting with the premise that every dollar of new spending should be paired with a dollar of new revenue, MMT urges us to begin by asking, How many dollars should be subtracted away? This turns PAYGO on its head. Instead of accepting the presumption that we should always avoid adding to the deficit, MMT tells us to start by asking whether any of the proposed spending needs to be offset to mitigate inflation risk.

Sticking with the $2 trillion infrastructure proposal, MMT would have us begin by asking if it would be safe for Congress to authorize $2 trillion in new spending *without* offsets. A careful analysis of the economy's existing (and anticipated) slack would guide lawmakers in making that determination. If the CBO and other independent analysts concluded it would risk pushing inflation above some desired inflation rate, then lawmakers could begin to assemble a menu of options to identify the most *effective* ways to mitigate that risk. Perhaps one-third, one-half, or three-fourths of the spending would need to be offset. It's also possible that none would require offsets. Or perhaps the economy is so close to its full employment potential that PAYGO is the right policy. The point is, Congress should work *backward* to arrive at the answer rather than beginning with the presumption that every new dollar of spending needs to be fully offset. That helps to protect us from unwarranted tax increases and undesired inflation. It also ensures that there is always a check on any new spending. The best way to fight inflation is before it happens.

In one sense, we have gotten lucky. Congress routinely makes large fiscal commitments without pausing to evaluate inflation risks. It can add hundreds of billions of dollars to the defense budget or pass tax cuts that add trillions to the fiscal deficit over time, and for the most part, we come out unscathed—at least in terms of inflation. That's because there's normally enough slack to absorb bigger deficits. Although excess capacity has served as a sort of insurance policy against a Congress that ignores inflation risk, maintaining idle resources comes at a price. It depresses our collective well-being by depriving us of the array of things we could have enjoyed if we had put our resources to good use. MMT aims to change that.

MMT is about harnessing the power of the public purse to build an economy that lives up to its full potential while maintaining appropriate checks on that power. No one would think of Spider-Man as a superhero if he refused to use his powers to protect and serve. With great power comes great responsibility. The power of the purse belongs to all of us. It is wielded by democratically elected members of Congress, but we should think of it as a power that exists to serve us all. Overspending is an abuse of power, but so is refusing to act when more can be done to elevate the human condition without risking inflation.

3

The National Debt (That Isn't)

MYTH #3: One way or another, we're all on the hook.

REALITY: The national debt poses no financial burden whatsoever.

When I arrived in Washington, DC, in January 2015, I was the only staffer on the US Senate Budget Committee who looked at the world through the lens of a currency issuer. I knew the federal government wasn't like a household or a private business. I knew Uncle Sam could never run out of money. I knew that inflation, rather than insolvency, was the relevant punishment for overspending. I also knew I was alone in this thinking.

Everyone else fell into one of two camps: deficit hawks and deficit doves. The hawks were the hard-liners. Mainly, but not exclusively, Republicans, who looked at fiscal deficits as evidence of an epic mismanagement of our nation's finances. Budgets should balance. Period. Any imbalance between spending and taxation ruffled their feathers. They warned of a looming debt crisis and called for swift action to rein in fiscal deficits. The label was meant to symbolize their hawkish determination—at least rhetorically—to balance the budget and zero out the national debt. The hawks taunted their opponents, the deficit doves, accusing them of being too sanguine (dovish) about the threat posed by the nation's mounting debt. The hawks mostly blamed entitlement programs—Social Security, Medicare, and Medicaid—while the doves pointed to tax cuts for the rich and trillion-dollar wars as the main drivers of government debt.

While beltway pundits and Washington insiders depicted them as polar opposites, I saw them as birds of a feather. Both considered the long-term fiscal outlook a problem that needed to be fixed. The main differences came down to disagreements about who (and what) had gotten us into this mess and how quickly we should act to repair the damage. Most Republicans wanted to slash entitlements, while most Democrats wanted to raise taxes. Different paths to the same destination.

By the time I joined the Budget Committee, I had established myself as a contrarian in this arena. As word spread that I would be heading to the nation's capital to advise the Democrats, journalists fired off articles with headlines like "Sanders Hires Deficit Owl." I had coined the term in 2010, as a way to distinguish the views held by MMT economists from those of the more deficit-anxious birds. I decided the owl would make a good mascot for MMT because people associate owls with wisdom and also because owls' ability to rotate their heads nearly 360 degrees would allow them to look at deficits from a different perspective.

Most of the senators on the committee had never heard of MMT. Even the senator who hired me, Bernie Sanders, was initially surprised by the media attention surrounding his pick. When I met with the members of the committee for the first time, Virginia senator Tim Kaine told me that he had read about my appointment in the *Kansas City Star*. No one was rude, but I could sense that there was reticence about expanding the deficit aviary.

It wasn't easy being the new bird in town. I knew that my views differed sharply from theirs. The Democrats I was there to serve included a number of senators who had earned reputations as fiscal conservatives. Three of them had even been anointed "Fiscal Heroes" by the notorious debt-shaming front group Fix the Debt.[1]

The job was frustrating in a lot of ways. On fiscal matters, I didn't share the views of the members I was there to serve. I looked for ways to help the committee without reinforcing myths and misunderstandings about our nation's finances. I wrote carefully scripted talking points and drafted prepared remarks to be read aloud by the committee's ranking member. Sometimes, what you don't say is as important as what you do. So, I sought ways to reshape thinking in subtle ways, sometimes by pressing fellow staffers to strike a sentence or two from a press release or an op-ed. I was still an educator at heart, so I couldn't totally suppress the urge to introduce new ways of thinking. Besides, bad reasoning leads to bad policy. And bad policy affects all of us.

One of the most eye-opening things I learned came from a game I would play with members of the committee (or their staffers). I did this dozens of times, and I always got the same incredible reaction. I'd start by asking them to imagine that they had discovered a magic wand with the power to eliminate the entire national debt with one flick of the wrist. Then I'd ask, "Would you wave the wand?" Without hesitation, they all wanted the debt gone. After establishing an unflinching desire to wipe the slate clean, I'd ask a *seemingly* different question: "Suppose that wand had the power to rid the world of US Treasuries. Would you wave it?" The question drew puzzled looks, furrowed brows, and pensive expressions. Eventually, everyone would decide against waving the wand.

I found it fascinating! These people served on a committee that was literally created to deal with issues related to the federal budget, and not one of them seemed to catch on to the trick. They all had a love-hate relationship with the national debt. They loved US Treasuries, as long as they thought of them as financial *assets* held by the private sector. But they hated the very same securities when they considered them *obligations* of the federal government. Unfortunately, you can't wave away the national debt without also eliminating the instrument that composes the national debt—US Treasuries. They are one in the same.

Eventually, I'd point out that I had asked two versions of the same question. It was like asking folks if they preferred the weather when its 77 degrees F or 25 degrees C. That was sometimes awkward. Some of them told me they understood that waving the wand entailed eliminating the entire US Treasury market, but they wanted the debt wiped out anyway, because it scares voters.

It's $0,000,000,000,000 Big

Of course voters are terrified! How could they not be? Unless you manage to steer clear of all political discourse, it's virtually impossible to get through the workweek without encountering some form of hysteria over fiscal deficits and the national debt. Newspaper headlines scream of record indebtedness and looming disaster. A debt clock towers over pedestrians on West 43rd Street in New York City, delivering the daunting numbers in real time. Political cartoonists depict the federal debt as a hungry T-Rex eating its way through city streets or as an ever-expanding balloon on the verge of exploding. Bookstores are replete with bombastic titles featuring anxiety-inspiring words like *Endgame, Red Ink,* and *Fiscal Therapy*. Social media circulates breaking news alerts to report the latest dire projections from the Congressional Budget Office. Talk radio plays alarming audio of former secretary of state Hillary Clinton warning that "our rising debt levels pose a national security threat." Even ordinary citizens, like the one who put the sticker of a broke Uncle Sam on the bumper of her SUV, have become messengers of doom.

It's a wonder we're not all holed up in a bunker, bracing for Armageddon. The end is always near.

The truth is, we're fine. The debt clock on West 43rd Street simply displays a historical record of how many dollars the federal government has added to people's pockets without subtracting (taxing) them away. Those dollars are being saved in the form of US Treasuries. If you're lucky enough to own some, congratulations! They're part of your wealth. While others may refer to it as a *debt clock*, it's really a US dollar *savings clock*. But you won't hear that from anyone in Congress. You can imagine why. Think about what would happen if a member of Congress returned to his or her district and tried to convince a roomful of panicked constituents that everything they deeply fear about our ballooning national debt is really a big nothing burger. With every other voice of authority delivering exactly the opposite message, the words of the soothsayer would go over like a lead balloon. Sometimes, as Mark Twain put it, "it's easier to fool people than to convince them that they have been fooled."

Even if their own thinking wasn't so broken, there are reasons why members of Congress might not want the rest of us to see the so-called debt for what it really is—nothing more than those yellow interest-bearing dollars called US Treasuries that we talked about in Chapter 1. For some politicians, attaching the word *debt* to a really *big* number creates the perfect foil. Meganumaphobia—the fear of large numbers—might not be a medically recognized anxiety disorder, but plenty of politicians seem to think it's real enough.

I remember being struck by this during a meeting with members of the US Senate Budget Committee. The Congressional Budget Office (CBO) had just released its 2015–2025 budget outlook, and the senators were pouring over the report's findings.[2] The CBO had projected that the fiscal deficit would stand at $1.1 trillion and the gross federal debt would reach $27.3 trillion in 2025. The committee's chairman, Mike Enzi, found the numbers startling. But not startling enough. He was worried that by using decimal points instead of commas, the report would fail to stoke the right emotional response from our citizenry. To dramatize the numbers, he suggested that the CBO be required to write the numbers out in long form: $1,100,000,000,000 and $27,300,000,000,000.

Recall that Senator Enzi ran a shoe-sale business before getting involved in politics. As a businessman, he must have understood the importance of a good marketing campaign. A more comfortable fit, a wider selection, a more fashionable design. Finding the right message to appeal to shoppers is critical for sustaining your customer base. Tap into the right emotions, and a good marketing campaign will bring people in off the streets. If you think about it, Enzi was basically looking for a way to market information about the government's finances in a way that would elicit a certain emotional reaction from voters. Once politicians like Senator Enzi succeed in making us anxious about the sheer size of this thing we label debt, they can weaponize that fear in a number of ways.

By persuading voters that something must be done about these big scary numbers, politicians can push for cuts to popular programs, like Social Security and Medicare.[3] Winning support for an agenda that calls for painful cuts requires sustaining public outrage over our national finances. These are programs that benefit enormous constituencies. People will fight tooth and nail to protect them. Unless, of course, they can be convinced that there is no alternative. That we must act to "fix the debt" before it's too late.

MMT shows that we don't need to fix the debt. We need to fix our thinking. Not just to prevent senseless cuts to programs that support tens of millions of Americans but also to have a more enlightened debate about the full range of things we could accomplish if we weren't so afraid. The debt isn't the reason we can't have nice things. Our broken thinking is. To fix our broken thinking, we need to overcome more than just an aversion to big numbers with the word *debt* attached. We need to beat back every destructive myth that hobbles our thinking.

China, Greece, and Bernie Madoff

I doubt the woman who placed that bumper sticker on her SUV was simply nervous about the size of the US Treasury market—that is, the national debt. Chances are, she had other concerns. Maybe she'd heard presidential candidate Barack Obama complain that the US was borrowing from China and "driving up our national debt, that we are going to have to pay off." The debt clock on West 43rd Street doesn't just provide a real-time record of the outstanding total. It also divides that total by the size of the US population, calculating "your share" of the national debt. Maybe she was a mother, who carried around a sense of guilt because she heard Wisconsin congressman Paul Ryan say that we need to deal with the debt to "protect our children and grandchildren from a crushing burden of debt and taxes." Or perhaps she was thinking about our nation going broke. We all know what happened to Greece. Maybe she feared for our great nation. After all, Obama had described the national debt as "irresponsible" and "unpatriotic."

I'm a mother and a patriot, and none of these things worry me. That's because I'm also an MMT economist, who looks at all of this through a fundamentally different lens. I can read the latest CBO report and not panic over the projected increase in the national debt. I don't agonize over "my share" of the national debt, and I never worry about the US ending up like Greece. I don't fret over the possibility that China might one day shut off the spigot and starve the US of the dollars we need to pay our bills. Heck, I don't even think we should be referring to the sale of US Treasuries as borrowing or labeling the securities themselves as the national debt. It just confuses the issue and causes people unnecessary grief. Even worse, misguided fears stand in the way of better public policy. And that hurts all of us. So, let's try to fix our thinking.

It was at a campaign stop in Fargo, North Dakota, where Obama told a small crowd that America was relying on "a credit card from the Bank of China." His choice of words was important because it taps into two of our basic anxieties. For one thing, there's the fear of relying on borrowed money to pay the bills. We know from personal experience that taking on too much debt can cause financial distress. Borrowing to buy a home, a car, or even groceries puts you on the hook for future

payments. Before long, the house payment, car loan, or credit card bill
will arrive, and you'll need to come up with the money to pay back
the loan. Hearing that our country is running up trillions of dollars
in credit card debt is enough to make anyone worry. Learning that we
owe that money to a foreign nation—an adversary even—only height-
ens the anxiety.

It's not that we don't have anything to worry about when it comes
to our international trading partners. As we'll discover later in Chapter 5 ("Winning at Trade"), there are legitimate reasons for concern.
But relying on China to pay our bills isn't one of them. To see why,
let's take a step back and think about how China (and other foreign
countries) ended up holding US government bonds in the first place.[4]
Where did China get the $1.11 trillion in US Treasuries it held as of
May 2019? Did Uncle Sam travel to Beijing, star-spangled hat in hand,
to ask the Chinese government for a loan? Not at all.

What happens, first, is that China decides it wants to sell some of
what it produces to buyers outside China, including the United States.
The US does that, too, but America exports less than it imports from
other countries. In 2018, the US exported $120 billion in US manufac-
tured goods to China, while China shipped $540 billion of its prod-
ucts to the US. The difference gave China a $420 billion trade surplus
(the US carried the opposite, a $420 billion trade deficit with China).
Americans paid for those goods with US dollars, and those payments
were credited to China's bank account at the Federal Reserve. Like any
other holder of US dollars, China has the option to sit on those dollars
or use them to buy something else. Uncle Sam doesn't pay interest on
the dollars China keeps in its checking account at the Fed, so China
usually prefers to move them into what is effectively a savings account
at the Fed. It does this by purchasing US Treasuries. "Borrowing
from China" involves nothing more than an accounting adjustment,
whereby the Federal Reserve subtracts numbers from China's reserve
account (checking) and adds numbers to its securities account (savings). It's still just sitting on its US dollars, but now China is holding

yellow dollars instead of green dollars. To pay back China, the Fed simply reverses the accounting entries, marking down the number in its securities account and marking up the number in its reserve account. It's all accomplished using nothing more than a keyboard at the New York Federal Reserve Bank.

What Obama was missing is the fact that the dollars don't originate from China. They're coming from the United States. We're not really borrowing from China so much as we're supplying China with dollars and then allowing those dollars to be transformed into a US Treasury security. The problem, really, is with the words we use to describe what's actually happening. There is no national credit card. And terms like *borrowing* are misleading. So is labeling those securities the national debt. There is no *real* debt obligation. As Warren Mosler likes to put it, "The only thing we owe China is a bank statement." You could argue that this is actually a bad deal for China (and other countries that run trade surpluses against the United States). After all, it means their workers are using their time and energy to produce real goods and services that China doesn't hold on to for its own people. By running trade surpluses, China is essentially allowing the US to take its stuff in exchange for an accounting entry that says we're keeping track of how much of its output we took. But as we'll see in Chapter 5, China benefits from trade with the US in a number of ways.

Although China is the largest foreign holder of US Treasuries, it owned less than 7 percent of the publicly held total at the time of this writing. Still, some people worry that this gives China enormous leverage over the US because China could decide to sell off its holdings, driving the price of US government bonds down and the yield on those bonds (i.e., the interest rate) up. The worry is that Uncle Sam could lose access to affordable financing if China refuses to keep buying Treasuries. There are a number of problems with this thinking. For one thing, China can't avoid holding dollar assets without wiping out its trade surplus with the United States. That's not something China wants to do, since shrinking its exports to the US would tend to slow its economic growth. Assuming it wants to keep its trade surplus intact, it's going to end up holding dollar assets. As financial commentator and former investment banker Edward Harrison put it, "the only question for China is which dollar assets [green dollars or yellow dollars] it will buy, not whether it will go on a US dollar strike."[5] And even if it does decide to hold fewer US Treasuries (yellow dollars) in its portfolio, this situation won't leave Uncle Sam strapped for cash. Remember, the US is a currency issuer, which means it can never run out of dollars. Moreover, as Marc Chandler, popular television commentator and author of the book *Making Sense of the Dollar*, observed, China reduced its holdings of US Treasuries by 15 percent from June 2016 through November 2016, and the ten-year Treasury yield "was virtually unchanged."[6]

Even though it can't happen to the United States, it is possible for a country to lose access to affordable financing. That's what happened to Greece in 2010. But that's because Greece undermined its monetary sovereignty by abandoning the drachma in favor of the euro in 2001. Adopting the euro changed everything. All of the Greek government's existing debt was redenominated into euro, a currency that the Greek government could not issue. From that point on, anyone who bought bonds from the Greek government was taking on a new kind of risk—default risk. Lending to Greece was now a lot like lending to an individual US state, say Georgia or Illinois. As we learned in Chapter 1, individual states are currency users, not currency issuers. They really *are* dependent on tax revenue and borrowing to pay the bills. Sure, they can sell bonds to raise money, but financial markets normally demand a premium for the added risk of lending to someone who might not be able to repay. It's a lesson Greece learned the hard way (along with Ireland, Portugal, Italy, and Spain).

As the 2008 financial crisis spread through Europe, the Greek economy suffered a severe economic downturn. Jobs began disappearing at breakneck speed, and tax revenues fell off a cliff. At the same time, the Greek government was making larger payments to support the ailing economy. That combination of forces—collapsing tax revenue and rising spending—pushed Greece's budget deficit to more than 15 percent of its GDP in 2009. Under the rules that established the euro, member governments were supposed to prevent budget deficits from rising in excess of 3 percent of their country's gross domestic product (GDP). But the downturn was so severe that it pushed the Greek budget deficit well above the 3 percent limit. To cover those deficits, Greece had to borrow. The problem is that under the euro, the Greek government no longer had a national central bank that could act on its behalf by clearing all of its payments. To finance its spending, the government really did need to "find the money" ahead of time. The (TAB)S model doesn't apply to a currency-issuing government like the United States, but it does apply to a country like Greece, which turned itself into a currency user when it severed the link between the Greek central bank and the Greek parliament. The problem, as Greece quickly discovered, was that lenders weren't willing to buy Greek government bonds unless they got a substantial premium for the obvious risk they were taking in lending billions of euros to a currency user who might have trouble paying it back. From 2009 to 2012, the interest rate on ten-year Greek government bonds rose from less than 6 percent to more than 35 percent.

Compare that with what happened in currency-issuing countries like the US or the UK, where fiscal deficits more than tripled from 2007 to 2009. By 2009, both countries saw deficits rocket from less than 3 percent to around 10 percent of GDP. And yet, over the same period, the average interest rate on ten-year government bonds *fell* from 3.3 percent to 1.8 percent in the United States and from 5 percent to 3.6 percent in the United Kingdom. That's because both countries have a central bank that acts on behalf of the government as a monopoly supplier of the currency. That backstop reassures investors, who understand that the central bank has ironclad control over its short-term interest rate, along with substantial influence over rates on longer-dated securities.[7] Greece gave up that backstop when it adopted the euro. It could literally run out of money, and everyone knew it. That's why it couldn't keep the bond vigilantes at bay. The term *bond vigilantes* refers to the power of financial markets (or, more accurately, investors in financial markets) to force sharp movements in the price of a financial asset like government bonds so that the interest rate swings unexpectedly. Ultimately, the European Central Bank *did* keep the vigilantes at bay, but not without helping to impose painful austerity on the Greek people.[8]

By 2010, many European countries, including Greece, were ensnared in a full-blown debt crisis. Credit-rating agencies like Fitch Group, Moody's, and Standard & Poor's downgraded Greek government bonds, and borrowing costs spiraled out of control. As the crisis deepened the Greek government came close to defaulting on its debt. American politicians saw the crisis engulfing parts of the eurozone and began urging Congress to act to reduce deficits here at home, warning that a Greek-style debt crisis could soon visit America.[9] Savvy investors, like Warren Buffett, billionaire investor and CEO of Berkshire Hathaway, knew better. As Buffett explained, the US cannot "have a debt crisis of any kind as long as we keep issuing our notes in our own currency."[10] Buffett also understood that the Greek debt crisis happened because "Greece lost the power to print their money. If they could print drachmas, they would have other problems, but they would not have a debt problem."[11]

Still, isn't there some limit? As Isaac Newton taught us, "what goes up must come down." Surely the debt can't go on rising forever. If the government never pays it down, then it has to keep finding new buyers for its bonds.[12] It seems risky. As Margaret Thatcher famously quipped, the problem is that "eventually you run out of other people's money." To some people, finding new investors to purchase a never-ending mountain of government debt can start to look like a fraudulent pyramid scheme.[13] The kind run by the notorious huckster Bernie Madoff. It isn't.

Madoff was defrauding investors. The United States Treasury is not. As Alan Greenspan explained in an appearance on NBC's *Meet the Press*, investors face "zero probability of default" when it comes to US Treasuries.[14] And here we should distinguish between voluntary and involuntary default. Greenspan's statement referred to the latter. His point was that the US could not end up like Greece, desiring to make scheduled payments to bondholders but lacking the authority to instruct its central bank to clear the payments. Congress could do something stupid, like refusing to raise the debt ceiling limit, which might trigger a *voluntary* default. But there is zero risk of the US being forced into default by its creditors. That's because the federal government can always meet its obligation to turn those yellow dollars back into green dollars. All it has to do is change the relevant numbers on the Federal Reserve's balance sheet. There's also no risk of running out of "other people's money." Remember, Thatcher had it backward. Her model treated the British government like a household that had no alternative but to collect taxes or borrow other people's money to pay the bills.

MMT flips this around, showing that the more appropriate, real-world sequencing is S(TAB). The government spends first, making dollars available to pay taxes or purchase government bonds. Take an example. Suppose S (spending) equals $100, meaning that the government spends $100 into the economy. Now suppose that the government taxes $90 away from us, meaning the government's deficit has left us with $10 to hold on to. Currently, the government coordinates any deficit spending by selling an equivalent amount of securities— that is, "borrowing." The important point is that the $10 that is needed to buy the bonds has been supplied by the government's own deficit spending. In that sense, the currency issuer's spending is *self-financing*. It's not selling bonds because it needs the dollars. Bond sales just allow holders of reserve balances (green dollars) to trade them in for US Treasuries (yellow dollars). It's done to support interest rates, not to fund the government.

Since our lawmakers have not yet had the benefit of seeing MMT's insights, they view debt service as a growing financial burden on the federal government. That's a mistake. In truth, paying interest on government bonds is no more difficult than processing any other payment. To pay the interest, the Federal Reserve simply credits the appropriate bank account. Right now, Congress looks at the federal budget as a zero-sum game. Lawmakers look at rising interest expenditure the way we might look at a rising cable bill—it means less money to spend on everything else. So, when the CBO says that the federal government is on track to "spend more on interest payments than the entire discretionary budget, which includes defense and all domestic programs, by 2046," many lawmakers begin to panic.[15] They think it shrinks the amount of money that's left over, forcing them to spend less on other priorities. That's just not true. The congressional budget is limited only by Congress. To avoid cutting back on programs people value, Congress can simply authorize a *larger budget* to fund its other priorities. There's no fixed pot of money. There is, however, only so much room in the economy to safely absorb higher spending. That's the constraint Congress needs to worry about.

The limit, as we saw in Chapter 2, is our economy's capacity to absorb that additional spending without pushing inflation higher. Every dollar that is paid in the form of interest becomes *income* to bondholders. If those interest payments become too large, the risk is that total spending could push the economy above its speed limit. MMT has emphasized that rising interest income can serve as a potential form of fiscal stimulus. The federal government is a net payer of interest, and all of the interest it pays out is received by holders of government securities. At least *some* of that interest income goes to people who turn around and spend it back into the economy, buying newly produced goods and services. If a high percentage of interest income was spent back into the economy, it could potentially push aggregate spending above potential, fueling some inflationary pressure. Though, as Vice President Joe Biden's former chief economist, Jared Bernstein, notes, it seems unlikely that the government's interest payments will fuel overheating anytime soon, in part because "about 40 percent of our public debt [is] now held by foreigners," which means "an increasing share of interest payments now leak out of the country."[16] Even if bondholders aren't spending enough of their interest income to fuel *ordinary price inflation* (like the CPI), they might still fuel *asset price inflation* by using their interest income to bid up the prices of commodities, real estate, stocks, and so on.

There is the potential for inflation, and there are *distributional* implications involved, but paying interest on government securities poses no financial challenge for the federal government. Some people complain that the government shouldn't be paying interest at all. They see Treasuries as a kind of luxury good, something that is only available to people who already have a lot of money. By turning their green dollars into yellow dollars, the government ends up adding to their riches over time, potentially widening the gap between those at the bottom and those at the top of the income distribution. That's one way to look at it. Of course, Treasuries are also safe assets that help diversify risk, so they provide a layer of protection to many working-class people who have pensions or other kinds of retirement plans that invest some of their money into government bonds. Distributional issues aside, Uncle Sam can always handle the interest payments.

We Could Pay It Off Tomorrow

In April 2016, *Time* magazine devoted its cover to the US national debt. It began, "Dear Reader, You owe $42,998.12. That's," the cover continued, "what every American man, woman and child would need to pay to erase the $13.9 trillion US debt."[17] I don't know about you, but I don't have $43,000 lying around. I'm also not squirreling away money in anticipation of one day being asked to write Uncle Sam a big fat check for "my share" of the national debt. It's never going to happen. The idea that the rest of us are personally liable for some portion of the national debt is preposterous. It's an extension of the household budgeting philosophy that wrongly assumes that the government must ultimately depend on us—the taxpayer—to pay its bills. I hope it's clear by now why that logic makes no sense when it's applied to a currency-issuing government. Because the truth is, the entire national debt could be paid off tomorrow, and none of us would have to chip in a dime.

That's not how most economists see it. Some will argue that faster growth would help us deal with our "debt problem" because it's the ratio of debt relative to the size or our economy (debt versus GDP) that really matters. The numerator (the debt) is rising, but the ratio will fall if the denominator (economy) grows faster than the debt. For many economists, that's the right way to look at the problem. The trick, then, is to keep the debt ratio from heading northward in perpetuity. At some point, it must come down, or the debt path is considered mathematically unsustainable. For decades, conventional thinking held that the US debt was on an unsustainable path because the formal models used to evaluate the debt trajectory all showed the ratio rising steadily higher into the indefinite future.[18]

Today, some of the most influential economists in the world are telling us the debt might be sustainable after all, at least for now. These mainstream economists don't arrive at the paradigm-shifting conclusions of an MMT economist, but some of them have softened their rhetoric in ways that have tempered anxieties about a looming debt crisis. For example, in January 2019, Olivier Blanchard, world-renowned economist and former head of the International Monetary Fund, made this the focus of his presidential address at the annual meeting of the American Economic Association.[19] In that speech, Blanchard explained that the debt trajectories for many countries, including the United States, appear to be on a sustainable path, at least in the near term. That's because Blanchard expects the future to look a lot like the recent past, which is to say he expects interest on the debt (r) to remain below the economy's growth rate (g), a condition (r < g) that ensures that the debt ratio will not head off to infinity. If he's right, then his model predicts that the US will not experience a debt crisis anytime soon. But Blanchard does not dismiss the possibility of a future crisis. For him, we're safe until one day in the future, when financial markets push the interest rate above our economy's growth rate (r > g). When that day arrives, we're right back on an unsustainable debt trajectory unless the budget has moved into surplus in the interim. Until then, we can relax and perhaps even safely increase the size of the fiscal deficit. Because Blanchard's findings ran so counter to the dominant (media and political) narrative about public debt, his findings received significant media attention. Within days of his speech, MarketWatch ran an article featuring the headline, "Leading Economist Says High Public Debt 'Might Not Be So Bad.'"[20] Shortly thereafter, the Wall Street Journal asked, "Worry About Debt? Not So Fast, Some Economists Say."[21] These were important findings, but it should be pointed out that MMT economist Scott Fullwiler made a similar observation thirteen years earlier.[22]

The difference between Fullwiler's early work and Blanchard's more recent study is that Fullwiler looks at the question of debt sustainability through the MMT lens.[23] Unlike Blanchard, he recognizes that a government that borrows in its own sovereign currency can always maintain the critical condition for sustainability (r < g). It never has to accept a market rate of interest. For Fullwiler, Blanchard's "concept of fiscal sustainability is flawed due to its assumption that a key variable—the interest rate paid on the national debt—is set in private financial markets."[24] In other words, Blanchard's more cautious take on sustainability rests on the possibility that interest rates could eventually jump higher, leading to the kind of debt crisis that unfolded in Greece or Argentina. But the US is not like Greece (which borrows in euros) or Argentina (which defaulted on US dollar–denominated debt). It can't lose control of its interest rate. As Fullwiler observed, interest on the national debt is "a matter of political economy," meaning that policy makers can always overrule market sentiment.[25] Or, as

James Galbraith humorously put it, "It's the interest rate, stupid!" To prevent interest on the debt from rising above the economy's growth rate, Galbraith simply advised the central bank to "keep the projected interest rate down."[26] It's a critically important insight that distinguishes the MMT perspective on debt sustainability from more conventional thinking. Under MMT, it is inflation—not the relationship between interest rates and growth rates—that matters. Still, it's easy enough for the US (and other monetary sovereigns) to satisfy the conventional criteria for sustainability.

Just look at Japan. At 240 percent, Japan's debt-to-GDP ratio is the highest in the developed world. At the end of September 2019, Japan's national debt hit a record ¥1,335,500 billion.[27] That's more than a million billion. Imagine the horror Senator Enzi would experience at the thought of more than a *quadrillion* in debt. That's a lot of zeroes! If it was featured in *Time* magazine, the cover would read, "You Owe ¥10.5 million" (about $96,000 per person in US dollar terms). But Japan, like the US, is fine, at least when it comes to debt sustainability, because it's a currency-issuing government with a central bank that can clear every payment obligation that comes due. Financial markets can't push Japan into crisis because the Bank of Japan (BOJ) can override any unwanted move in interest rates. It could also, essentially, retire the entire debt using nothing more than a computer keyboard at the Japanese central bank.

Most of the world's leading central banks focus on setting just one interest rate—a very short term interest rate known as the overnight rate. They rigidly fix this rate and then allow longer-term rates to reflect market sentiment about the expected future path of the short-term policy rate. That means that the interest rate that's paid on longer-term government bonds is related to the overnight rate that its own central bank is setting. As Fullwiler put it, "This means that longer-term rates are based upon current and expected actions of the [central bank]."[28] That leaves investors with *some* influence over the interest rate that the US government pays on Treasuries or the British government pays on gilts. (In the UK, government securities are known as gilt-edged bonds or gilts for short.) But—and this is really important—the government can always strip markets of any influence over the interest rate on government bonds. Indeed, that's exactly what the Federal Reserve did during and immediately after World War II, and it's what the Bank of Japan is doing today.[29]

To keep a lid on interest rates during World War II, the Federal Reserve "formally committed to maintaining a low-interest-rate peg of 3/8 percent on short-term Treasury bills" and "also implicitly capped the rate on long-term Treasury bonds at 2.5 percent."[30] Even as deficits exploded and the national debt climbed from $79 billion in 1942 to $260 billion by the time the war ended in 1945, the federal government paid just 2.5 percent interest on long-term bonds. To hold rates at 2.5 percent, the Fed simply had to buy large quantities of US Treasuries. It required an open-ended commitment on the part of the Fed, but it was an easy commitment to fulfill since the Fed purchases bonds (yellow dollars) simply by crediting the seller's account with reserves (green dollars). Even after the war ended, the Fed continued to anchor the long-term interest rate on behalf of the government. Coordination with fiscal policy officially ended in 1951, with an agreement known as the Treasury–Federal Reserve Accord, which freed the Fed to pursue independent monetary policy.[31]

Elsewhere, central banks are returning to explicit coordination of fiscal and monetary policy.[32] For more than three years, the BOJ has been engaged in a policy known as yield curve control. In addition to anchoring the short-term interest rate, the BOJ committed to pinning rates on ten-year government bonds (known as Japanese Government Bonds or JGBs) near zero. In carrying out that policy, the BOJ has purchased massive amounts of government debt, buying up ¥6.9 trillion in June 2019 alone.[33] As a result of its aggressive bond-buying program, the BOJ now holds roughly 50 percent of all Japanese government bonds. So, while Japan is often described as the most indebted developed country in the world, half of its debt has already been essentially retired (i.e., paid off) by its central bank. And it could easily go all the way to 100 percent. If it did, Japan would become the least indebted developed country in the world. Overnight.

MMT economists understand this. But not many others seem to realize how easy it would be for a country like Japan (or other currency-issuing sovereigns) to pay off the entire public debt. It could be done tomorrow, without collecting a penny from taxpayers.

One of the few people who appears to understand this is economist Eric Lonergan. In 2012, he published a thought experiment asking, "What if Japan monetized 100% of outstanding JGBs?"[34] It was a fancy way of asking what would happen if the central bank retired the entire national debt. How? The same way the BOJ got the bonds it already holds, namely by crediting the sellers' bank accounts. It's a thought experiment, so Lonergan imagines the BOJ doing this with a one-time flick of the wand. "Let's assume the BOJ comes out tomorrow and purchases the entire stock of JGBs by creating bank reserves (money) and cancels the debt." Poof! The debt is gone. Lonergan then asks, "What would happen to inflation, growth and the currency?" In his view, "nothing would change if you had 100% monetization of the stock of JGBs!"

To some, this might seem preposterous.[35] How can the BOJ manufacture ¥500 trillion out of thin air without devastating inflationary consequences? Most economists are trained to accept some version of the quantity theory of money (QTM). Strict adherents to the theory, such as followers of Milton Friedman, will likely scream, "Zimbabwe!" "Weimar!" or "Venezuela!"[36] That's because the QTM teaches that "inflation is always and everywhere a monetary phenomenon."[37] The idea of conjuring up ¥500 trillion of new cash to buy up government debt causes them to immediately anticipate hyperinflation. Lonergan, who works in financial markets, knows better. He correctly observes that swapping JGBs for cash has no effect on the private sector's net wealth. Instead of holding government bonds, investors now "hold the same value in cash." While *net wealth* is unaffected, buying up JGBs does have an effect on *income*. That's because the bonds are interest-bearing instruments, and the cash is not. When the BOJ replaces bonds with cash, the private sector loses out on any interest that would have been paid. So, retiring the debt siphons interest income out of the private sector. With this in mind, Lonergan asks, "Why on earth would the Japanese household sector rush out and buy things when their interest income has fallen, their wealth is unchanged, and they are used to falling prices?" The short answer is, they wouldn't. If anything, transferring all of the outstanding government debt onto the central bank's balance sheet would tend to push prices lower, not higher. I would think twice about stripping the private sector of all of its interest-bearing government bonds at once, but the Japanese government could certainly pull it off. The US could do it too.[38]

A Life Without Debt?

Just think of it. No more government shutdowns as lawmakers engage in theatrical uprisings over raising the debt ceiling limit. No one comparing Uncle Sam to a spendthrift who's running up the credit card and borrowing from China. No fear of losing access to the bond market and being forced into default like Greece. No economists arguing about whether interest rates will be low enough to keep the debt on a sustainable path. And best of all, no more stress about how to cover "your share" of the national debt. We could rip the bumper sticker right off.

We actually did it once.[39] It was 1835—Andrew Jackson was president—and it was the only time in US history when the public debt was paid all the way down. That was long before the Federal Reserve was created, so the debt wasn't gobbled out of existence by the central bank.[40] Instead, it was eliminated the old-fashioned way—that is, by reversing fiscal deficits and paying off bondholders. It didn't end so well.

It took more than a decade to retire the entire debt. It happened because the government ran fiscal surpluses from 1823 to 1836. Since it was taxing away more money than it was spending in each of those years, it didn't issue new debt. Instead, as bonds matured, the government simply paid them off.[41] By 1835, the US was debt free. It was also headed for one of the worst economic downturns the country has ever experienced. In hindsight, it seems obvious why things unfolded the way they did.

Fiscal surpluses suck money out of the economy. Fiscal deficits do the opposite. As long as they're not excessive, deficits can help to maintain a good economy by supporting incomes, sales, and profits.[42] They're not imperative, but if they disappear for too long, eventually the economy hits a wall.[43] As Frederick Thayer, the prolific writer and professor of public and international affairs at the University of Pittsburgh, wrote in 1996, "the US has experienced six significant economic depressions," and "each was preceded by a sustained period of budget balancing."[44] Table 1 details his findings.

TABLE 1. US History of Budget Surpluses and Debt Reduction

Years when debt is paid down	Percent decline in debt	Year depression began
1817–1821	29%	1819
1823–1836	100%*	1837
1852–1857	59%	1857
1867–1873	27%	1873
1880–1893	57%	1893
1920–1930	36%	1929

The historical record is clear. Each and every time the government substantially reduced the national debt, the economy fell into depression. Could it have been a remarkable coincidence? Thayer didn't think so. He blamed the "economic myths" that drove politicians to wrestle their budgets into surplus on the flawed belief that paying down debt was both morally and fiscally responsible.[45] As we see from the insights of MMT, government surpluses *shift deficits* onto the nongovernment sector.[46] The problem is that currency users can't sustain those deficits indefinitely. Eventually, the private sector reaches the point where it can't handle the debt it has accumulated. When that happens, spending grinds sharply lower and the economy falls into depression.

Since Thayer's work was published, the US experienced one other brief period (1998–2001) of sustained fiscal surpluses. It happened during Bill Clinton's presidency, and many Democrats still look back on it as a crowning achievement. The red ink was eliminated, and Uncle Sam was back in the black for the first time in decades. The surpluses began in 1998, and by 1999 the White House was ready to party like it was, well, 1999.[47] The following year, White House economists began working on a report titled "Life After Debt." It was supposed to deliver the celebratory news that the United States was on track to retire the entire national debt by 2012.

At first, paying off the debt seemed like the kind of accomplishment that might be worthy of a national parade. The White House was preparing to feature the news in its annual *Economic Report of the President*. But then everyone got cold feet, and that chapter of the report was hidden from public view. We only know about it because National Public Radio's *Planet Money* "obtained a secret government report outlining what once looked like a potential crisis: The possibility that the US government might pay off its entire debt."[48] Instead of shouting it from the rooftops, White House officials quietly tucked it away. The reason? They were worried about the broader implications of wiping out the entire US Treasury market. It was a return to the love-hate relationship many public officials have with the national debt. On the one hand, the White House would have loved to eliminate the national debt. On the other hand, it couldn't risk getting rid of all Treasuries.

What worried policy makers the most was the prospect of depriving the Federal Reserve of the key instrument it relied on to conduct monetary policy—government debt. At the time, the Fed was relying on government bonds to manage the short-term interest rate. When the Fed wanted to raise interest rates, it sold some of its Treasuries. Buyers paid for those bonds using a portion of their bank reserves. By removing enough reserves, the Fed could move the interest rate up.[49] To cut rates, the Fed would do the opposite, buying Treasuries and paying for them with newly created reserves. Without Treasuries, the Fed would need to find some other way to set interest rates.[50]

In the end, the problem solved itself. By 2002, the surpluses were gone, and the US was no longer on track to pay down the national debt, much less retire the full amount. The federal budget moved back into deficit after 2001, when the stock market bubble—which had been supporting consumer spending—burst. A recession began in 2001. It was a fairly mild recession, but the damage had been done.[51] As we'll see in the next chapter, the Clinton surpluses had weakened private sector balance sheets, magnifying the damage caused by the arrival of the Great Recession, which began in 2007.

The Great Recession changed the way the Federal Reserve conducts monetary policy. In November 2008, the Fed launched the first of three rounds of a massive bond-buying program called quantitative easing.[52] Among other things, the Fed hoped its program would help stimulate the US economy by lowering long-term interest rates. By the time it was over, the Fed had gobbled up some $4.5 trillion in bonds, including nearly $3 trillion in US Treasuries.[53] In addition to using quantitative easing to push *longer-term* interest rates lower, the Fed also changed the way it managed its *short-term* interest rate. Instead of buying and selling Treasuries to add and subtract reserves, the Fed switched to a "more direct and more efficient method of interest rate support."[54] It simply started paying interest on reserve balances. Today, the Fed can adjust the short-term interest rate any time it chooses, simply by announcing that it will pay a new rate.

What this means is that times have changed. The dollar is no longer tied to gold. The US issues a freely floating fiat currency so it doesn't need to tax or borrow before it can spend. Indeed, as we learned in Chapter 1, the S(TAB) model reflects the way the economy actually

works. Taxes aren't important because they help the government pay
the bills. They're important because they help to prevent government
spending from creating an inflation problem. Similarly, bond sales
aren't important because they allow the government to finance fiscal deficits. They're important because they drain off excess reserves,
which enables the Fed to hit a positive interest rate target. But today
the Fed pays interest on reserve balances, so it no longer relies on
Treasuries to hit its rate target.[55]

So why keep them around? Should we love 'em or leave 'em? Is the
national debt a "national treasure," as Alexander Hamilton believed?
Or is it "irresponsible" and "unpatriotic," as Barack Obama described
it? Should we treasure it or trash it?

One thing is for sure. We don't want to start wiping out US Treasuries the ugly way. The 1835 way. The Clinton way. By building fiscal
surpluses on the back of unsustainable private sector deficits. As we'll
see in the next chapter, that has predictably negative consequences for
our economy. If we really want to make the national debt disappear,
there are more painless ways to go about it. The most straightforward
option is to do it the way Lonergan described. Simply let the central
bank buy up government bonds in exchange for bank reserves. A pain-
free transaction that turns yellow dollars back into green dollars. It can
be carried out using nothing more than a keyboard at the Federal Reserve. Another option would be to phase out the issuance of Treasuries
over time. Instead of selling bonds to drain off the reserve balances
that result from deficit spending, we could just leave the reserves in the
system.[56] We can do it without interfering with the Federal Reserve's
ability to conduct monetary policy because the Fed doesn't need government bonds to hit its short-term interest rate target. Over time,
all of the outstanding bonds will mature, and the debt will gradually
disappear.[57]

There is another option. We could learn to live with 'em. There's
nothing inherently dangerous about offering a safe, interest-bearing
way for people to hold on to dollars.[58] If we choose to live with 'em, we

should come to grips with the fact that the thing we call the national debt is nothing more than a footprint from the past. It tells us where we've been, not where we're going. It records the history of the many deficits that have been run since the birth of our government in 1789.[59] The bloody world wars, our many recessions, and the decisions taken by the thousands of people elected to Congress over the years. What matters is not the size of the debt (or who holds it) but whether we can look back with pride, knowing that our stockpile of Treasuries exists because of the many (mostly) positive interventions that were taken on behalf of our democracy.

If we're not going to eliminate Treasuries, then we must find a way to make peace with the national debt. Perhaps we should start by giving it another name. The national debt is nothing like household debt, so using the word *debt* just leads to confusion and unnecessary angst. We could just refer to it as part of our net money supply. I doubt *yellow dollars* will catch on, but hey, it's worth a shot! In Shakespeare's *Romeo and Juliet*, Juliet famously inquires, "What's in a name?" She wasn't troubled when she learned that Romeo was a Montague. For her, "A rose by any other name would smell as sweet." Love, as they say, is blind. On the political stage, words matter. It's time to come up with a new name for these interest-bearing dollars.

4

Their Red Ink Is Our Black Ink

MYTH #4: Government deficits crowd out private investment, making us poorer.

REALITY: Fiscal deficits increase our wealth and collective savings.

M ost of the time, we're bombarded with fairly simple deficit myths. We're told to think of the federal government like a household (Chapter 1) that is recklessly overspending (Chapter 2) and running up the national credit card (Chapter 3). These myths are built for mass consumption. They make great soundbites on television and in political stump speeches because they're so easy to articulate. You don't need a background in economics (or anything else) to quickly absorb the message. Other myths are harder to package for effective messaging because they're rooted in the jargon of mainstream economics and mainly espoused by academics and so-called policy wonks. We may not encounter them as frequently, but that doesn't make them any less dangerous. The quintessential example of this kind of myth is known as crowding out.

In its most common form, the crowding-out myth says that fiscal deficits require government borrowing, which forces Uncle Sam into competition with other would-be borrowers. As everyone competes for a limited supply of available savings, borrowing costs move higher. With interest rates on the rise, certain borrowers—especially private businesses—won't be able to secure funding for their projects. This causes private investment to fall, leading to a future where there are fewer factories, machines, and so on. With a smaller stock of capital goods, society ends up with a less productive workforce, slower wage growth, and a less prosperous economy. It *does* sound ominous!

It's a complex narrative that rests on a number of theoretical propositions. If you've encountered it at all, it was probably on C-SPAN rather than Fox News or MSNBC. Even those of us who follow politics fairly closely might go a lifetime without hearing someone carefully articulate the crowding-out story. But in Washington, DC, it's everywhere.

It appears as boilerplate in the CBO's *Long-Term Budget Outlook*, one of the most widely anticipated budget reports to come out each year. Pick up virtually any edition, and you'll find a section outlining the crowding-out thesis. The 2019 report described the supposed risk of fiscal deficits this way: "The projected path of federal borrowing would reduce output in the long run. When the government borrows, it borrows from people and businesses whose savings would otherwise finance private investment in productive capital, such as factories and computers."[1]

A professional class of budget wonks, academics, and Washington insiders treat it as an article of faith. Technical jargon and a heavy smattering of charts and data give the narrative an impressive veneer of credibility that can leave readers with the impression that crowding out is something that happens in a mechanical and inevitable way, much like a mathematical series of rigorously tested *if-then* statements. *If* deficits require more borrowing, *then* the supply of savings available to finance private investment is reduced. *If* the supply of savings is reduced, *then* interest rates will rise. *If* interest rates rise, *then* private investment will decline. *If* private investment declines, *then* the economy will grow more slowly over time. Tap the first domino, and the rest obediently give way.

The whole story is rooted in a version of mainstream economics that dominates our public discourse. You hear it from liberal icons like the *New York Times*'s Paul Krugman[2] as well as conservative commentators like the *Washington Post*'s George Will.[3] And if you do happen to watch C-SPAN, you might have heard someone like Jason Furman, a Harvard-trained economist who worked in the Obama White House as chair of the Council of Economic Advisers, invoking it in testimony before Congress. For example, on January 31, 2007, he appeared before the US Senate Budget Committee, urging members of Congress to "stem the flow of red ink." He described the budget outlook as "a major fiscal challenge" that "drives down national savings." He warned that the chain reaction of events that would ultimately jeopardize our economic well-being would be "slow and gradual but relentless and inevitable."[4]

Crowding out is a story that depicts government deficits as the villains of progress. Saving is considered an act of virtue because it is believed to supply the fuel that is used to fund the kinds of private sector investments that make us a wealthier society. Deficits are said to undermine that prosperity by siphoning away some of that fuel for its own use. Fiscal deficits and private investment are therefore considered to be in tension with each other, as government borrowing necessarily leaves behind a smaller pool of savings to support the needs of private industry.[5] This is the conventional wisdom among mainstream economists. It may appear straightforward and compelling, but it is best thought of as a series of domino-linked myths.

Two Buckets

When Furman urged lawmakers in 2007 to "stem the flow of red ink," he was worried about a projected fiscal deficit of $198 billion, about 1.5 percent of GDP. He encouraged Congress to restore PAYGO to prevent deficits from climbing any further. He also complained that "the private savings rate [was] at its lowest level since 1939." In his view, the deficit was "driving down national saving." He had it completely backward.

To see why, imagine two buckets. One belongs to Uncle Sam. The other belongs to the rest of us, a sort of collective bucket in the name of everyone who is not Uncle Sam. It's a simple way to think about how dollars flow back and forth between these two parts of any economy—a government bucket on the one hand and a nongovernment bucket on the other.

I learned the value of thinking along these lines from Wynne Godley, a British economist who pioneered the sector balance framework. It was 1997, and I had just been awarded a yearlong research fellowship that took me to the Levy Economics Institute, a think tank located in New York's Hudson Valley. That's where I met Godley. I was still in graduate school, but I was given the office adjacent to his, and we would sit and talk for hours.

Godley was soft-spoken but intense. He played the oboe (often in his office) and had trained to become a professional musician. He had lived most of his life in the UK, where he had performed as the principal oboist in the BBC Welsh Orchestra before directing the Royal Opera (1976–1987). His other professional love was economics. After a long career at the British Treasury, he was persuaded to move to Cambridge University, where he became the head of the Department of Applied Economics. He was a highly regarded figure in British circles, serving as one of the chancellor of the exchequer's "seven wise men." He always seemed to be able to anticipate where the economy was headed. The *Times of London* referred to him as "the most insightful macroeconomic forecaster of his generation—though often a renegade."[6] Three years after his death, the *New York Times* payed tribute to his legacy, featuring him in an article entitled "Embracing Wynne Godley, an Economist Who Modeled the Crisis."[7]

I was fortunate to arrive at the Levy Economics Institute just two years after Godley took up residency in New York. He was a tall, slender man with wispy white hair that he would tug in frustration as he worked to find the perfect turn-of-phrase before allowing any of his work to be published. Godley was a macroeconomist, like me, but his way of thinking about the economy seemed completely original. He built macro models and used them to analyze the US economy. One morning, he invited me to sit with him while he used his model to simulate the effects of an increase in government spending. "You see," he said, "every payment has to come from somewhere and then it has to go somewhere."

Godley was obsessed with building models that didn't leave anything out. He constructed huge matrices with lots of rows and columns in order to connect up all the moving parts in the economy. He told me it was the only way he could be sure he had accounted for every financial payment as it moved through the system. Each time a payment was made by someone in the economy, it had to be received by someone else. That's what he meant when he said everything had to come from somewhere and go somewhere. He built some pretty sophisticated models, but the one he seemed to find most useful was the one he called his "one-equation model of the world." It wasn't like any of the models I had learned about in graduate school. This one didn't depend on conjecture. There were no hidden behavioral assumptions tucked inside. In fact, it wasn't really an economic model at all. It was just a simple accounting identity, true by definition under all circumstances.

We don't need a complicated matrix to understand Godley's most simple model. It has just two moving parts: the government's financial balance and ours. Since there are only two players in this game—Uncle Sam and everyone else—it stands to reason that every payment the government makes only has one place to go. By the same logic, there's only one place any payment received by the government could have come from. It's a simple but powerful way to think about the way the government's financial balance—its surplus or deficit—impacts the rest of us. And it shows why the crowding-out story gets it wrong, beginning with the first domino.

The equation looks like this:

$$\text{Government financial balance} +$$
$$\text{Nongovernment financial balance} = \text{Zero}$$

Because it's not a theory, it doesn't rest on any set of assumptions that might not hold in the real world. It's an ironclad accounting identity that will always produce an accurate statement of fact. You can think of it as a twist on Isaac Newton's third law of motion, which states that "for every action, there is an equal and opposite reaction." In the Godley model, we can see that for every deficit that exists in one part of the economy, there is an equal and opposite surplus in some other part. There's just no way around it. If one part of the economy is paying out more dollars than it's receiving, the other part must be receiving exactly that many dollars. On the other side of every minus sign (−) lies a plus sign (+) of equal size. Putting the same equation differently, Godley wrote:

$$\text{Government deficit} = \text{Nongovernment surplus}$$

It's a most powerful observation, and one that deals a fatal blow to the simple crowding-out story. To see why, let's translate Godley's model into even simpler language. We'll need just two buckets. The goal is to look at the part of the crowding-out story that claims that government deficits eat up part of our savings. First, let's look at an example of how financial payments move between the two parts of our economy. Suppose the government spends $100 on a fleet of new vehicles for the presidential motorcade. The vehicles will be produced by workers and businesses in the nongovernment part of the economy. Every dollar the government spends has to go somewhere, and there is only one place those dollars can go—into the nongovernment bucket. Let's also assume that the rest of us, collectively, pay the government $90 in the form of taxes.

Fiscal Deficit

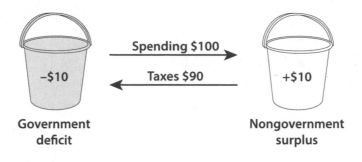

EXHIBIT 3. Government Runs a Fiscal Deficit

If these were the only payments made by and to Uncle Sam, the CBO would report that the government had run a fiscal deficit, and it would record a minus $10 in its annual budget report. But wait! That's not all that happened. The government's fiscal deficit is mirrored by an equal and opposite financial surplus in the nongovernment part of our economy. Uncle Sam's red ink is our black ink! His deficit is our financial surplus. Just follow the money: $100 goes into our bucket; $90 goes back out to pay taxes; $10 is left in our bucket. Every fiscal deficit makes a *financial contribution* to the nongovernment bucket.

Godley was a stickler for details. His models were, as he put it, stock-flow consistent. It's a fancy way of saying that all of the financial contributions that *flowed* into our bucket over time would exactly match the *stockpile* of dollar assets we must end up accumulating. In other words, every financial outflow had to become a financial inflow, and over time, those flows must accumulate into corresponding stocks of financial assets. To grasp the point, think of your bathtub. Water flows into the tub when you turn on the faucet, and water flows out of the tub when you open the drain. If the water is draining at least as fast as it's flowing in, the tub will never accumulate any standing water. But if you add water faster than you siphon it away, the water level will rise as the tub begins to fill. That's what's happening in Exhibit 3 above. The government is letting $100 dollars flow into our bucket and only siphoning $90 down the drain. The flow of red ink lamented by Jason Furman fills our bucket with dollars. Fiscal deficits don't eat up our savings; they enlarge them!

If Uncle Sam continues to deficit spend at this pace, he will drop another $10 into our bucket every year. Over time, those dollars will accumulate and build up our financial wealth. At this pace, a decade from now, we'll end up with a stockpile of $100 in our bucket. We'll get to the borrowing in just a bit. But first, let's consider what would happen if Congress had followed Furman's advice, eliminating budget deficits and running its budget on a PAYGO basis, as shown in Exhibit 4.

Balanced Budget

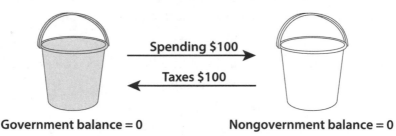

Government balance = 0   **Nongovernment balance = 0**

EXHIBIT 4. Government Balances Its Budget

By holding its spending in line with taxes, the dreaded red ink is eliminated. But what's this? The nongovernment bucket has lost its financial surplus. Now, it's possible that this is a good outcome. Remember, MMT asks us to focus on *economic* outcomes, not *budgetary* outcomes. So, if a balanced budget can deliver good overall conditions in our economy—that is, full employment and price stability—then there's no reason to complain that the government has balanced its books. Most of the time, however, our economy will need the support of fiscal deficits to keep things in balance. The trick is to prevent the deficit from getting too big or too small.

As we learned in Chapter 2, spending too much or taxing too little can lead to problems. Imagine an extreme scenario, where the government allowed us to keep every dollar it put into our bucket, never taxing anything away. That's like closing the drain in the bathtub and letting every drop of spending accumulate in our bucket. Before long, the tub would overfill, and our economy would overheat. Inflation would quickly take hold as too much money sloshed around in our bucket. The right size deficit is the one that provides just enough support to keep our economy humming along without rising inflation.

Deficits can be too big, but they can also be too small. We can use our two buckets to look, one last time, at the much-celebrated Clinton surpluses (1998–2001). Prior to 1998, the government had been running persistent deficits. Then, suddenly, the situation reversed itself. Instead of dollars flowing from Uncle Sam's bucket into ours, they started moving in the opposite direction. As Exhibit 5 shows, Uncle Sam got the (+) sign, and we got the (−) sign. We can illustrate this using simple numbers. To put Uncle Sam in surplus, the government had to tax away more dollars ($100) than it spent ($90) into our bucket in 1998. The only way for Uncle Sam to collect more dollars than he *currently* spends is to take back some of the dollars he supplied us with in *prior* years.

Fiscal Surplus

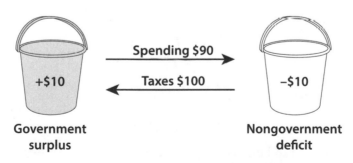

EXHIBIT 5. Government Runs a Fiscal Surplus

Once again, we've eliminated the dreaded red ink on the government's balance sheet. Indeed, Uncle Sam is now in the black. But don't break out the champagne just yet. Remember, on the other side of every financial surplus is a financial deficit of equal size. That means the government's black ink became our red ink! The Clinton surpluses forced us to sacrifice some of the dollars we had been saving in our bucket. The crowding-out story gets it completely backward. It's fiscal surpluses, not fiscal deficits, that eat up our financial savings.

Why do so few economists bother to point this out? When the CBO publishes its annual budget outlook, they're only telling half the story. They report the government's current (and projected) financial balance, but they don't bother to point out what it implies for those of us in the other bucket. They supply the data—big scary deficit numbers— that politicians and pundits use to terrorize the population, but they make no attempt to show how those deficits *necessarily* impact our financial balances. So, the public is bombarded with one-sided coverage that only looks at fiscal deficits from one vantage point. For example, in July 2019, the editorial board at the *New York Post* ran an opinion piece under the headline "Locking in a Future of Trillion-Dollar Deficits."[8] A year earlier, the *Wall Street Journal* had foreshadowed this with a similar headline: "Why Trillion-Dollar Deficits Could Be the New Normal." The problem is that no one bothers to show readers how the pieces fit together. The government's fiscal outlook is considered the whole story. It's not.

To improve the public discourse, we need to think like a deficit owl. Those hawks and doves we met in Chapter 3 spend too much time squawking about red ink and not enough time helping the public to see what that red ink means for the rest of us. To see the full picture, you have to be able to look at the flow of payments from a different angle. That's what makes the deficit owl a better budget bird. (Say that three times fast.) The owl has full range of motion: it can turn its head to see what the others are missing. A handy guy to have around if you want the entire picture.

Godley was a deficit owl. That's why he was able to see what so many others were missing as the government's budget moved into surplus beginning in 1998. While Democratic politicians and the vast majority of economists cheered the Clinton surpluses, Godley sounded the alarm.[9] Because his model didn't leave anything out, he was able to see that the government's surpluses were siphoning away a portion of our financial savings. As the president's Council of Economic Advisers was busy drafting the infamous "Life After Debt" report,[10] Godley was publishing reports that shined a spotlight on the *private sector deficits* that nearly everyone else was ignoring. He was virtually alone in predicting that the Clinton surpluses would undermine the recovery and ultimately drive the federal budget back into deficit.[11] That's because fiscal surpluses rip financial wealth away from the rest of us, leaving us with less purchasing power to support the spending that keeps our economy going.

Godley's approach shows that *in purely financial terms*, every fiscal deficit is good for someone. That's because government deficits are always matched—penny for penny—by a financial surplus in the nongovernment bucket. At the macro (big picture) level, Uncle Sam's red ink is always our black ink. When he spends more dollars into our bucket than he taxes away, we get to accumulate those dollars as part of our financial wealth. But who, exactly, is *we*?

From a thirty-thousand-foot level, all we know is that those dollars flow into a giant bucket that includes everyone not named Uncle Sam. You're in the big bucket, and so am I. Companies like Boeing and Caterpillar are in there with us. Our trading partners—China, Mexico, Japan, and so forth—are in there, too. President John F. Kennedy liked to say that "a rising tide lifts all boats." He meant that when our economy does better, all of us do better, too. Godley's model shows that fiscal deficits will *always* lift our collective, nongovernment (financial) boat. But what about all of the individual boats that are floating around inside that big bucket?

Fiscal deficits have the *potential* to lift millions of small boats, but too often the benefits of Uncle Sam's deficits aren't spread widely throughout the economy. Tax cuts that go disproportionately to the biggest corporations and the wealthiest people in society funnel riches into their buckets, while millions of families struggle to keep their boats afloat. If the goal is broadly shared prosperity, then we need fiscal deficits that channel resources more equitably. For example, investing in health care, education, and public infrastructure won't just benefit the medical professionals, teachers, and construction workers who get paid to do those jobs, it will also benefit the patients, students, and drivers who benefit from better public services.[12] And, when fiscal deficits help low- and middle-income families, those dollars aren't hoarded in off-shore bank accounts. They get spent back into the economy, helping to lift the boats that belong to families like theirs.

The point is, not every deficit serves the broader public good. Deficits can be used for good or evil. They can enrich a small segment of the population, lifting the yachts of the rich and powerful to new heights, while leaving millions behind. They can fund unjust wars that destabilize the world and cost millions their lives. Or they can be used to sustain life and build a more just economy that works for the many and not just the few. What they can't do is eat up our *collective* savings.[13]

The Interest Rate Is a Policy Variable

The crowding-out story is rooted in the (TAB)S model we introduced in Chapter 1. Remember, that model treats Uncle Sam as a currency user, who must finance his expenditures either by taxing or borrowing. If he wishes to spend (S) more than he expects to collect in taxes (T), then he must cover the shortfall (i.e., the deficit) by borrowing (B). According to conventional economists—hawks and doves alike— *if* the government borrows to cover deficits, *then* it will use up some of the savings that would otherwise have been available to private companies and other borrowers. The story continues that *if* the supply of savings is reduced *then* interest rates will rise as borrowers compete for a dwindling pool of available funding, driving borrowing costs higher.

We have already shown that deficit spending increases our collective savings. But what happens if Uncle Sam borrows when he runs a deficit? Is that what eats up savings and forces interest rates higher? The answer is no.

The financial crowding-out story asks us to imagine that there's a *fixed* supply of savings from which anyone can attempt to borrow. Picture an enormous mountain of US dollars sitting in some corner of the world. Now imagine that those dollars were put there by savers, people who have dollars but don't wish to spend everything they have. Savers make those funds available to borrowers, but only at a price. Savers earn interest on the money they lend, while borrowers pay savers for the use of those funds. It's a straightforward supply-and-demand story, where the interest rate balances the demand for funding against the available supply. In the absence of government deficits, all demand comes from private borrowers. There's still competition for these loanable funds, but companies are just competing with other private sector actors for a slice of the available supply.[14] With no competition from Uncle Sam, all savings are used to finance private investment. But, if the government's budget moves into deficit, Uncle Sam will lay claim to some of that cash. As a consequence, the supply of funds available to fund private investment is diminished, borrowing costs go up, and some companies are left without financing for their projects. It's not government deficits, per se, but deficits financed by borrowing that supposedly leads to crowding out via higher interest rates.

MMT rejects the loanable funds story, which is rooted in the idea that borrowing is limited by access to scarce financial resources. As MMT economist Scott Fullwiler put it, the conventional "analysis is simply inconsistent with how the modern financial system actually works."[15] To see why, let's take a closer look at what's actually happening when the federal government sells bonds in coordination with its deficit spending. Since MMT recognizes that the federal government doesn't operate its budget like a household, we reject the (TAB)S model and use the currency issuer's S(TAB) model instead. Remember, this model recognizes that the government is not revenue constrained (like a household) so it can spend first and then tax or borrow. Suppose Congress authorizes $100 of new spending. As the government begins making payments, those dollars flow into the nongovernment bucket. Let us again assume that $90 is used to pay taxes.

Fiscal Deficit

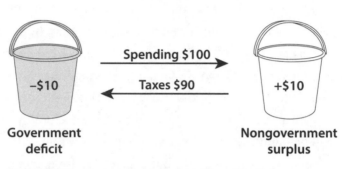

Spending $100

Taxes $90

−$10

+$10

Government
deficit

Nongovernment
surplus

EXHIBIT 6. Government Runs a Fiscal Deficit

As Exhibit 6 shows, the government's deficit deposits $10 into the nongovernment bucket. If that's all that happened, those dollars would simply sit in the form of digital or physical currency—green dollars. (Recall our use of green dollars from Chapter 1. Green dollars exist in the form of bank reserves or notes and coins.) If the government simply left us holding green dollars, it could run a fiscal deficit without selling the government bonds that end up adding to the thing we (unfortunately) call national debt. But that's not the way things currently work. Under current arrangements, the government sells US Treasuries whenever it runs a fiscal deficit. This is normally referred to as borrowing, but as we learned in Chapter 3, that is very much a misnomer. That's because *the government's own deficit supplies the dollars that are needed to purchase the bonds*. To match its $10 deficit with bond sales, the government simply pulls 10 green dollars out of our bucket and re-cycles them into 10 yellow dollars—US Treasuries. Exhibit 7 shows the government removing green dollars from the nongovernment bucket and replacing them with interest-bearing government bonds.

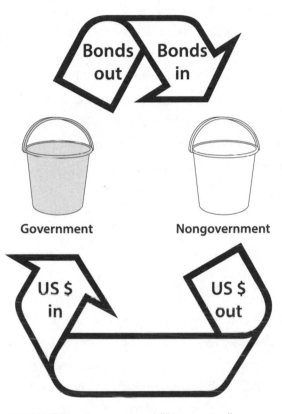

EXHIBIT 7. Government "Borrowing"

When the whole process is over, Uncle Sam will have spent (S) $100 into our bucket, taxed $90 (T) back out, and transformed the remaining $10 into yellow dollars called US Treasury bonds (B). Those bonds are now part of the wealth that is held by savers at home and around the world. As Godley's model reveals, government deficits al-ways lead to a dollar-for-dollar *increase* in the supply of net financial assets held in the nongovernment bucket.[16] That's not a theory. That's not an opinion. It's just the cold hard reality of stock-flow consistent accounting.

So fiscal deficits—even with government borrowing—can't leave behind a smaller supply of dollar savings. And if that can't happen, then a shrinking pool of dollar savings can't be responsible for driving borrowing costs higher. Clearly, this presents a problem for the conventional crowding-out theory, which claims that government spending and private investment compete for a *finite* pool of savings.

The reason the loanable funds story is not in sync with reality is that it asks us to treat the federal government like a currency *user*. When we reject this naïve lens, we see that countries like the US aren't dependent on borrowing to fund themselves, nor are they at the mercy of private investors when they do sell bonds.[17] Uncle Sam is not a beggar, who must go hat in hand, in search of funding to support his desired spending. He's a muscular currency issuer! He can choose to borrow (or not), and Congress can always decide what rate of interest it will pay on any bonds it decides to offer. That's not true of all countries, but it is true of those with monetary sovereignty.[18]

The distinction is incredibly important, for there is an element of truth in the conventional narrative that budget deficits can force interest rates higher. But we must be careful in telling that story. By focusing on the monetary arrangements and the actual mechanics of deficit financing, MMT helps us avoid an overly simplistic story about how this can happen. What matters most is the *currency regime* under which the country is operating. Unlike Greece, Venezuela, or Argentina, countries with monetary sovereignty are not at the mercy of financial markets. To see why, let's take a closer look at what happens when a monetary sovereign like the US runs a fiscal deficit.

MMT shows that the US government spends by crediting the reserve balances of private banks, which in turn credit the bank accounts of those receiving payments from the government. If you deposit $1,000 check from Uncle Sam, your bank will get a $1,000 credit to its reserve account at the Federal Reserve, and you will get a $1,000 credit to your own personal bank account. Payments made by you to the federal government have the opposite effect. For example, if you write a $500 check to pay your federal income taxes, your bank will subtract that much from your current balance, and the Fed will subtract $500 from your bank's reserve balance. When the government is spending more than it's taxing away, it leaves the banking system with a larger quantity of reserve balances. In other words, fiscal deficits increase the *aggregate* supply of reserve balances.

What happens next depends entirely on the policy response. The government might borrow, as it does today, replacing the newly created reserve balances with US Treasuries. Doing this allows the government to run fiscal deficits *without altering the quantity of reserves in the banking system.* From an MMT perspective, the purpose of selling bonds is not to "finance" government expenditures (which have already taken place) but to prevent a large infusion of reserves from pushing the overnight interest rate below the Fed's target level.[19] Selling bonds is entirely voluntary in the sense that Congress could always decide to do things differently.[20]

Because it has monetary sovereignty, the US has many options when it comes to borrowing and managing its interest rate. It could exert rigid control of the short-term interest rate but allow financial markets to have *some* influence on longer-term borrowing costs. That's how it works in the US today. Or, it could take control of longer term borrowing costs, the way it did during and immediately after World War II or the way the Bank of Japan (BOJ) does it today. It could even dispense with Treasuries altogether, which would make it all but impossible for anyone to tell a crowding-out story based on the argument that government *borrowing* is what drives interest rates higher. The point is, deficits pose no inherent crowding-out risk. The loanable funds theory is simply wrong. Fiscal deficits—with or without bond sales—do not mean an inevitable increase in interest rates.

To understand why, let's take a brief look at how it all works today. Today, the US Treasury issues what are known as risk-free securities whenever it runs a fiscal deficit. The securities are considered risk-free in the sense that a currency-issuing government can always make good on any promise to repay bondholders as long as the bonds are denominated in the government's own unit of account. Japan can always repay yen. The US can always pay US dollars. And the British government can always meet any payment obligation denominated in British pounds. In each of these countries (and others), the federal government has adopted its own procedures for placing government bonds in the hands of private buyers.

The US relies on an auction system to sell bonds into the private market. Whenever the federal government is expected to run a fiscal deficit, the Treasury Department offers a quantity of government securities that matches the anticipated deficit. Treasury officials decide how many securities to offer, and market participants—that is, investors—compete for the limited supply. The initial sale takes place in what's known as the primary market, where a certain category of buyers, called primary dealers, bid for the securities. Primary dealers are defined as trading counterparties of the New York Federal Reserve Bank. There are currently two-dozen primary dealers, including familiar names like Wells Fargo, Morgan Stanley, Bank of America, and Citigroup. After their initial purchase in the primary market, US Treasuries can change hands in the secondary market. That's where they become available to pensions, hedge funds, state and local governments, insurance companies, foreign investors, and others. The interest rate on government bonds comes out of the competitive bidding process, as primary dealers "make the market" by tendering bids for the entire supply at each auction.[21]

If the government expects to run a fiscal deficit of $200 billion, the Treasury Department will arrange an auction for that amount.[22] Before each auction, Treasury officials decide the auction date, how big the auction will be, the face value of the securities, and which maturities to offer.[23] As part of its $200 billion auction, officials might offer a block of ten-year Treasuries with face value of $1,000 each. When the auction opens, each primary dealer bids for its share of the total allot-ment. One of them might signal a willingness to buy a certain number of bonds but only if they pay out $20 per year. Another primary dealer might ask for $18 and still another might submit a bid seeking $22 per year. Each bid carries an implied rate of return. In this example, primary dealers are seeking 2 percent, 1.8 percent, and 2.2 percent, respectively. If the primary dealer seeking $20 wins a piece of the auc-tion, the Federal Reserve will charge them the appropriate number of bank reserves and credit them with Treasury bonds that will pay out 2 percent interest in each of the next ten years.[24] After ten years, each of these bonds will have paid out $200 of interest income.[25]

Primary dealers are required to bid at reasonable rates, but they don't have to submit identical bids. If they think 2 percent is too low, they can try to get a higher yield by submitting a weaker bid. How-ever, weaker bids reduce the likelihood of winning the auction. There's an old trick that will help you understand the relationship between bond yields (interest rates) and bond prices. Using your thumbs, give a thumbs-up for strong demand from investors. Strong bids mean bond prices go thumbs-up. There's an inverse relationship between bond prices and bond yields, so a thumbs-up for higher bond prices implies a thumbs-down for interest rates. It's cheaper to borrow when primary dealers indicate a willingness to buy at low interest rates. When dealers submit weaker bids, it means they're asking for higher returns. If the weakness is widespread, the Treasury Department may end up paying somewhat more than it anticipated when the auction was announced.

In practice, Treasury auctions are always oversubscribed, meaning that there are always more bids than there are securities to go around. As former deputy secretary of the US Treasury Frank Newman wrote to me: "There is always more demand for treasuries than can be allo-cated from a limited supply of new issues in each auction; the winners in the auctions get to place their funds in the safest most liquid form of instrument there is for US dollars; the losers are stuck keeping some of their funds in banks, with bank risk."[26] Since demand always tends to exceed supply, submitting a relatively weak bid means you're likely to walk away empty-handed. The most enthusiastic bidders get to swap some of their reserve balances for US Treasuries. To separate the winners from the losers, the government ranks the bids from highest to lowest. The outright strongest bid—that is, the lowest interest rate— always wins. The next allotment goes to the next highest bidder and so on down the line until the entire amount is sold.

This might sound like the loanable funds market imagined in the crowding-out story. It's not. The primary dealer market is a real-world market established by the federal government for the purpose of dealing exclusively in newly issued government securities.[27] In other words, the government created the primary dealer market for the sole purpose of placing US Treasuries in private hands as part of its fiscal operations. Uncle Sam doesn't enter the market in competition with other borrowers. On the contrary, it's the two-dozen primary dealers (lenders) who compete with one another to win a piece of the auction. Every auction involves coordination between the Treasury Department and the Federal Reserve. This means that even large, *unanticipated* fiscal deficits never pose any kind of financing problem. That's because the Fed backstops the primary dealers. Backstopping basically means that if there's ever any hiccup in the process, the Fed makes sure the primary dealers have all the funding they require to make it profitable for them to place reasonable bids for the entire allotment. With these arrangements in place, it's clear that interest rates on government bonds are a policy choice and not something imposed on the federal government by lenders.

So, what *is* the relationship between deficits and interest rates? In one respect, there's an indisputable answer. Deficits push the overnight interest rate *down*. In a world without bond sales or some other defensive action by the central bank, deficits will drive the short-term interest rate to zero. That's because deficit spending fills the banking system with excess reserves, and a huge increase in the supply of reserves will push the federal funds rate to zero.[28] If the central bank doesn't want to accept the zero rate, then it must do something to move the rate into positive territory. Historically (pre-2008), it did this by performing open-market operations, selling US Treasuries and draining reserve balances until the interest rate rose to the Fed's target. Today, the Fed hits its interest rate target by proclamation. If it wants to adjust rates, it simply announces a new target and—*voilà!*—the interest rate is now set at the new (higher or lower) level. The point is that without some explicit form of intervention, fiscal deficits would naturally drive the short-term interest rate to zero.[29]

What about other interest rates? Being a primary dealer is sort of like owning the goose that laid the golden egg. You're guaranteed a profit simply for occupying a special place in the monetary apparatus that facilitates the Treasury's fiscal operations. It's a privileged position that no primary dealer wants to jeopardize. To remain in good standing, all they have to do is present reasonable bids that win them their share of Treasuries at each auction. *Reasonable* is the key word. It means that dealers need to submit bids that come in very close to current interest rates, which are themselves largely governed by Federal Reserve policy. So, while primary dealers formally submit bids that express their desired rate of return, the interest rate they must ultimately accept is a largely beyond their control. This becomes even more obvious when you look around the world and realize that roughly one-third of the global government bond market trades at negative (nominal) rates of interest. That's because the Bank of Japan, the European Central Bank, Sweden's Riksbank, the National Bank of Denmark, and the Swiss National Bank have all set the short-term interest rate below zero.

Selling bonds to private investors gives the impression—illusion—that the government is dependent on savers for financing and that financial markets can force the government to borrow on terms set by private lenders. That's not how it works in practice. A currency-issuing government doesn't need to borrow its own currency from anyone in order to spend. And even if it does borrow, it can exert substantial influence over the interest it pays on those securities. Primary dealers can signal a *desire* for higher rates, but the Fed can always manage rates lower if it chooses to do so. There's a popular saying among savvy investors: "Don't fight the Fed." If the Fed is determined to bring rates down, it's best to prepare for falling interest rates. Investors who bet against a determined central bank are virtually guaranteed to suffer financial losses. One of the most high-profile (bad) trades was carried out by an investor named Kyle Bass. Bass felt certain that the Japanese government debt had become unsustainable, so he bet against it by shorting JGBs. When an investor shorts government bonds, they're betting that the price of the bonds is going to go down (price thumbs-down) and the yield (interest rate thumbs-up) is going to go up. Bass (and others like him) lost huge sums of money with this trading strategy. Shorting JGBs became known as the widowmaker's trade because few investors survived the resulting losses.

In spite of what most economists say, there's simply no preor-dained relationship between fiscal deficits and interest rates. If the central bank is committed to holding rates in place or managing them lower, then fiscal deficits can't force them to rise as the conventional crowding-out story imagines. A little history will prove the point.

From 1942 until 1947, the Federal Reserve—at the behest of the Treasury Department—actively managed the government's borrowing costs. Even as spending to fight World War II drove the federal deficit to more than 25 percent of GDP in 1943, interest rates trended lower. That's because the Fed pegged the T-bill rate at 0.375 percent and held the rate on twenty-five-year bonds at 2.5 percent. As MMT economist L. Randall Wray put it, "the government can 'borrow' (issue bonds to the public) at any interest rate the central bank chooses to enforce. It is relatively easy for the central bank to peg the interest rate on short-term government debt instruments by standing ready to purchase it at a fixed price in unlimited quantities. This is precisely what the Fed did in the United States until 1951—providing banks with an interest-earning alternative to excess reserves, but at a very low rate of interest."[30]

The Treasury-Fed Accord of 1951 ended the Fed's official commitment to managing rates on behalf of the Treasury, but it did not usurp its power to do so. Indeed, the Federal Reserve retains the ability to move rates lower even if deficits soar. It's a reality that should be obvious to any casual observer of Fed policy over the last decade. When the bottom fell out of the US economy in 2008, the budget deficit rocketed to more than 10 percent of GDP. As deficits climbed, the Federal Reserve cut the overnight rate to zero and held it there for seven straight years. In addition, the Fed conducted three rounds of quantitative easing, buying US Treasuries and mortgage-backed securities, which allowed the Fed to push long-term interest rates down as well. Anyone who tells you that fiscal deficits must force interest rates higher has forgotten their World War II history and ignored recent experience, and not just in the United States.

Since 2016, Japan's central bank has been explicitly targeting its yield curve.[31] That means the BOJ isn't just controlling the overnight interest rate (as the Fed does in the US) but also effectively setting long-term rates as well. The practice is known as yield curve control because it literally involves controlling the yield on ten-year government bonds. Today, the BOJ is committed to holding the ten-year rate at around zero percent. To do that, the central bank simply buys bonds in whatever quantity is necessary to prevent yields from rising above zero. It's a bit akin to quantitative easing in that lower interest rates are the objective. However, yield curve control is a stronger form of commitment since the quantity of bonds the BOJ will buy in any given time period is not determined ahead of time. Yield curve control is about committing to an interest rate (price) target rather than committing to purchase a certain amount (quantity) of bonds. The BOJ's policy clearly demonstrates that the central bank can set both short-term and long-term interest rates, *even as government borrowing rises.* By exercising its power as a sovereign currency issuer, Japan can always prevent the kind of interest rate pressure imagined in the loanable funds story.

Not every country has these powers. As Fullwiler explains, "the implications for economic policy are paradigm shifting for monetary sovereigns." To put it simply, the crowding-out story doesn't work in countries that borrow in their own sovereign currencies.[32] For the United States, Japan, the United Kingdom, and other monetary sovereigns, the interest rate on the national debt is a policy variable. As currency issuers, they don't need to borrow their own currency in order to spend. Bond sales are entirely voluntary, and the interest rate paid on any bonds the government chooses to offer is always a policy choice.[33] That's not true of countries that lack monetary sovereignty.

Countries like Greece and Italy, along with the other seventeen members of the eurozone, gave up their sovereign currencies in order to use the euro. Since they can't issue the euro, member governments must cover fiscal deficits by selling bonds. That means finding investors who are willing to give up euros in exchange for government debt. The problem is that lending to these countries became especially risky once they started promising to repay bondholders in a currency that they could no longer issue themselves. This became painfully clear in the wake of the 2008 financial crisis, as the global recession pushed the budgets of Greece and other eurozone countries deeply into deficit. To finance their deficits, each country had to seek funding in a marketplace not entirely unlike that imagined in the crowding-out story. Governments had no choice but to borrow in private financial markets, and they had to pay whatever the market demanded to secure the funding they needed. Investors were rightly worried about lending to governments that could no longer guarantee repayment. To compensate for the added risk they were taking, financial markets demanded higher and higher interest rates. Before long, a full-blown debt crisis unfolded. In Greece, the poster child for the crisis, interest rates on ten-year government bonds skyrocketed from 4.5 percent in September 2008 to nearly 30 percent by February 2012. Eventually, the currency issuer—the European Central Bank (ECB)—came to the rescue, and interest rates moved sharply lower.[34]

Borrowing in a currency they couldn't issue opened eurozone nations up to the kind of interest rate pressures predicted in the conventional crowding-out story. Something similar tends to happen when countries tether the value of their domestic currencies to gold or tie them to some other currency—that is, fix their exchange rates. Russia and Argentina, for example, once pledged to convert their domestic currencies (rubles and pesos, respectively) into US dollars at a fixed exchange rate. The problem is that in order to defend the exchange rate peg, the government has to give up control of the interest rate.

Here's what happened in Russia. You could hold the domestic currency—the ruble—or you could ask the central bank to convert your rubles into something else. You could swap your rubles for US dollars at the fixed exchange rate. Or, you could use your rubles to buy Russian government bonds (known as GKOs). As Forstater and Mosler observed, "government securities can be thought of as 'competing' with the conversion [to US dollars] option."[35] As long as most people were willing to hold rubles or GKOs, things worked pretty well. The Russian government could issue both. But all hell broke loose in 1998, when suddenly everyone wanted US dollars. As demand for GKOs evaporated, the price of Russian bonds collapsed, and yields rose sharply. Just as the Greek government was incapable of preventing a spike in borrowing costs, countries that fix their exchange rates sacrifice control of their interest rates. From an MMT perspective, "this explains the very high interest rates paid by governments with perceived default risk in fixed exchange rate regimes, in contrast to the ease a nation such as Japan has in keeping rates at 0 in a floating exchange rate regime, despite deficits that would undermine a fixed exchange rate regime."[36]

The lesson is simple. Currency regimes matter. The simple crowding-out story was built for a world that no longer exists. Yet conventional economic theory treats the sequence of falling dominoes as an inevitable consequence of deficit spending. The truth is the story has limited applicability. As Timothy Sharpe put it, "financial crowding-out theory was initially proposed and analysed in the context of a convertible currency system, that is, the gold standard and the Bretton Woods fixed exchange rate agreement (1946–1971)." Taking into account different currency regimes changes everything. That's what Sharpe discovered in a sweeping empirical investigation, where he separated countries that fit the MMT model—that is, those with monetary sovereignty—from those that fix their exchange rates or borrow in a foreign currency. Consistent with MMT, he concluded that "the empirical evidence reveals crowding-out effects in nonsovereign economies, but not within sovereign economies." In other words, it's a mistake to apply the crowding-out story to monetary sovereigns like the US, Japan, the UK, or Australia.[37]

The truth is, government deficits aren't the villains of progress. They don't make it harder for the private sector to borrow and invest. In almost all cases, they make it easier. That's because Uncle Sam's deficits feed dollars into our bucket. Whether those dollars arrive in the form of tax cuts or increased spending, they leave some of us with greater spending power. And spending is the lifeblood of capitalism. Without it, businesses would have no customers, no sales revenue, and no profits to keep them afloat. As Nobel Prize–winning economist William Vickrey put it, well-targeted deficits "will generate added disposable income, enhance the demand for the products of industry, and make private investment more profitable."[38] In other words, well-designed fiscal policies, including those that increase fiscal deficits, can catalyze private investment, sparking a virtuous cycle that leads to the crowding in of private investment, rather than crowding it out.

5

"Winning" at Trade

MYTH #5: The trade deficit means America is losing.

REALITY: America's trade deficit is its "stuff" surplus.

I remember watching Donald Trump battle his way through the Republican primary debates with my son, Bradley, who was just nine years old at the time. It was 2015, and Trump was blustering on about trade, complaining that countries like Mexico, China, and Japan were ripping us off and vowing to bring an end to the thievery if voters would put him in the White House. It became a central theme of his campaign: *We are losing the trade war against foreigners.* "We don't win anymore," Trump thundered during a 2015 primary debate in Cleveland, Ohio. "We don't beat China in trade. We don't beat Japan, with their millions and millions of cars coming into this country, in trade."[1] It's a message that resonated with millions of Americans, especially in states like Ohio, Michigan, Pennsylvania, North Carolina, and Wisconsin, where many voters traced the hollowing out of their communities and the loss of good-paying jobs to import competition and rising trade deficits.

As president, Trump remained obsessed with the gap between imports and exports, that is, America's trade deficit with the rest of the world. To him, the trade deficit is *prima facie* evidence that America is losing at trade. On the one hand, he sees the losses in monetary terms, tweeting, "The United States has been losing for many years, 600 to 800 Billion Dollars a year on Trade. With China, we lose 500 Billion Dollars. Sorry, we're not going to be doing that anymore!"[2] The problem, he seems to believe, is that foreigners are running off with our money. And when he looks at the *real terms of trade*—the actual goods that are being traded between Americans and foreigners—he again sees America getting the raw end of the trade deal. In exchange for the millions of cars Japan is sending us, Trump explained in August 2019, "We send them wheat, wheat. That's not a good deal."[3] At that point, my son, Bradley, then thirteen, turned to me with a puzzled look and said, "So, the problem is that we take their cars and they only take our wheat? That would be like me giving Ian two of my low-value trading cards and getting ten of his high-value cards in exchange. I would be very happy with that deal!"

Viewed from this perspective, you could say that a country "wins" by maximizing its benefits (imports) and minimizing its costs (exports). But that would imply, counterintuitively, that America's roughly $700 billion trade deficit is evidence that the United States is already winning at trade. Could this be right? Does Trump have it completely backward? Instead of using tariffs to wage a trade war aimed at reducing the volume of goods coming into the United States from China and elsewhere, should the US be trying to run even bigger trade deficits? Would that make us the undisputed global trade champion? As we'll see below, it's much more complicated than the simple black and white of winning and losing at trade.

So why do so many Americans feel like everyone is "killing us" when it comes to trade? In a word, jobs. As Richard Trumka, the leader of the largest federation of unions, explained to Trump, just one week before his inauguration, bad trade deals have cost millions of Americans their good-paying union jobs. "Entire communities have lost their purpose and identity," he told the president-elect, "and we have to fix that."[4] He vowed to support Trump's commitment to renegotiating the North American Free Trade Agreement (NAFTA) and other deals, saying, "Working people are looking for a new way forward on trade."

Uncle Sam by the Ankles

Just like many workers in America, millions of workers in China, Japan, and elsewhere depend on their jobs for their livelihoods. If demand for the things they help to produce suddenly dries up, their jobs could disappear. That's why we often hear politicians and unions urging consumers to buy American or pressing companies like Ford or Apple to manufacture more of their products in the United States. When Americans spend money buying things that are produced abroad, that demand supports jobs in other parts of the world instead of sustaining jobs here at home.

Since 1994, when President Clinton signed NAFTA, ushering in a new era of "free trade," life has gotten steadily worse for millions of Americans. As industrial corporations have relocated their production centers to Mexico—and eventually to countries beyond North America, where they could pay workers even lower wages—millions of good-paying union jobs have disappeared. China's full accession into the World Trade Organization (WTO) in 2001 wreaked similar havoc on the US working class. Economists at the Economic Policy Institute have concluded that China's demand for US exports may have supported 538,000 American jobs from 2001 to 2011, but Chinese imports into the US cost more than 3.2 million Americans their jobs—for a net loss of about 2.7 million jobs.[5] On top of that, to the extent those displaced workers were able to find new employment, the new jobs paid an average of 22.6 percent less than what they were earning before.

This kind of trade-driven displacement has gutted entire regions where manufacturing was the economic lifeblood of large numbers of communities; it has also forced great swaths of Americans into permanent, involuntary unemployment or a sinister cycle of low-wage service jobs. And it came against a backdrop in which neighborhoods and towns were already profoundly disrupted a decade earlier by corporate farm consolidation. These communities would go on to be pummeled again during the following decade via the China-related WTO trade shocks, during which many of the heralded consumer benefits of expanded trade with Beijing came with substantial adjustment costs in many regional labor markets in which the industries exposed to newly expanded competition from China were concentrated. Years later, the Great Recession of 2008 would deal another lethal round of job losses.

By the time Trump came to town in 2016, his fearmongering about migrants and scaremongering about the trade deficit found a receptive audience among workers already besieged by one economic calamity after another. Consequently, for many of these workers, there was seemingly nothing to lose by embracing Trump's call to arms: win at trade, bring jobs home, and *Make America Great Again*!

Meanwhile, the Democratic Party mounted a tone-deaf response. Hillary Clinton's campaign marketed blue baseball caps bearing the slogan "America Is Already Great."[6] Perhaps Secretary Clinton felt boxed into a corner, and so her campaign adopted a strategy of largely ignoring the voters who'd been crushed by America's trade relationships and the cumulative miseries associated with them. Rather than laying out a compelling plan to restore good-paying jobs and help struggling communities, top Democrats simply gave up on many working-class voters. For example, Senate Minority Leader Chuck Schumer argued, "For every blue-collar Democrat we lose in western Pennsylvania, we will pick up two moderate Republicans in the suburbs in Philadelphia, and you can repeat that in Ohio and Illinois and Wisconsin."[7] It was a losing strategy for the Democratic Party.

Having won the election in 2016, Trump has continued to stick with the message that the US is locked in a losing competition when it comes to trade. Even some of his presumptive opponents echoed those sentiments. Senator Bernie Sanders, for example, has tweeted: "It's wrong to pretend that China isn't one of our major economic competitors. When we are in the White House we will win that competition by fixing our trade policies." Certainly, Sanders aimed (and still aims) to fix trade policy by protecting workers and the environment. Yet there is a tinge of anxiety that progressives share with conservatives: fear of the trade deficit itself.

The truth is, a trade deficit is not in and of itself something to fear. America doesn't need to zero out its trade deficit to protect jobs and rebuild communities. As long as the federal government stands ready to use its fiscal capacity to maintain full employment at home, there is no reason to resort to a trade war. Instead, we can envision a new world trade order that works better, not for corporations seeking to exploit cheap labor and escape regulations, but for millions of workers who've received such a raw deal under previous "free trade" policies in the post-NAFTA era. Reenvisioning trade also can lead to better policies for developing countries and for the global environment.

Three Buckets

One way to think about trade imbalances is to add a third bucket to the model we used in the last chapter. Previously, we put Uncle Sam in one bucket and everyone else in the other. Whenever Uncle Sam spent dollars, there was only one place for them to go—into a collective bucket we called the nongovernment sector. That was a perfectly reasonable way to illustrate the fact that Uncle Sam's deficits poured dollars into "our" bucket. Now it's time to look more closely at the nongovernment bucket. Since this chapter is about international trade, we want to see how dollars flow between the US economy and the rest of the world. To do that, we need to split the nongovernment bucket into two separate buckets. When we do this, we end up with a three-bucket model. We still have the US-government bucket, but now we have a bucket that belongs to all US households and businesses (i.e., the domestic private sector bucket), along with one that belongs to the rest of the world (i.e., the foreign sector bucket).

As before, it's impossible for all of the buckets to be in surplus (or deficit) at the same time. If there's red ink in one bucket, there must be black ink in at least one other bucket. As Godley told me, "Everything must come from somewhere, and then go somewhere." For every payment that flows *out* of one bucket, a payment of equal size must be received *into* at least one other bucket. As a matter of accounting, that means that the balance across all three buckets must always sum to zero. Exhibit 8 captures these relations.

US government   US private sector   Foreign sector
financial balance   financial balance   financial balance

EXHIBIT 8. The Three Sector Accounting Identity

In the real world, dollars flow among the three buckets every day. If the US government buys some bulldozers from Caterpillar Inc. and hires some American workers to build a bridge, dollars will flow into the US private sector bucket as the government makes those payments. American workers and (most) US businesses also pay federal taxes, so Uncle Sam subtracts some of those dollars away from the private sector bucket.

To keep it simple, suppose, as before, that Uncle Sam spends $100 and taxes $90 away, leaving behind a surplus of $10 in the private sector bucket. Those dollars can spin around in the US private sector, changing hands as Americans pay for haircuts, theater tickets, and college tuition. They can also switch buckets, as Americans import products from abroad. Let's say Americans spend $5 buying goods and services from the rest of the world, while foreigners spend just $3 buying products from the United States. By importing more than it exports, the US is running a trade deficit. When all is said and done, the US trade deficit transfers $2 into the foreign sector bucket. Exhibit 9 nets all these payments out, showing that the US government's fiscal deficit (minus $10) is exactly balanced by the sum of the surpluses in the other two buckets ($8 plus $2). As long as the US economy remains at full employment, there is no inherent problem with this outcome.

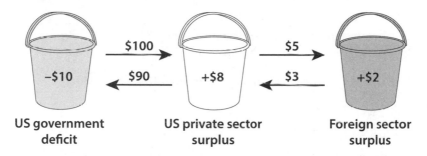

EXHIBIT 9.   US Fiscal Deficit Plus US Trade Deficit (Twin Deficits)

Since Uncle Sam is the *issuer* of the dollar, he never has to worry about running low. His bucket can manufacture dollars at will. But everyone else has to get the currency from somewhere. And the US private sector normally wants to accumulate more dollars than it spends—that is, to be in surplus. That's not to say that the private sector can't fall into deficit. It can, as it did during the late 1990s and early 2000s. But as Godley warned, that's usually an unsustainable situation because it often involves the private sector taking on too much debt.[8] (Remember, the private sector isn't a currency issuer, so it can't sustain deficits the way Uncle Sam can.) To keep the US private sector from falling into deficit, *someone* needs to supply that bucket with enough dollars to keep it in surplus. Right now, that "someone" is Uncle Sam. That's because the US runs persistent trade deficits (aka "stuff" surpluses), which cause dollars to flow out of the private sector's bucket and into the foreign bucket. As long as that remains the case, only Uncle Sam can supply enough dollars to keep the private sector in surplus. To do that, the government must run budget deficits that *exceed* the US trade deficit.[9] Exhibit 10 shows what happens if the government deficit becomes smaller than the trade deficit.

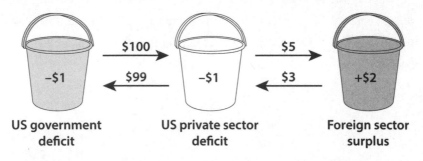

EXHIBIT 10. US Fiscal Deficit Smaller Than US Trade Deficit

In this example, the government has *almost* balanced its budget. But not quite. Uncle Sam is running a small deficit, spending $100 into the US economy and taxing $99 back out.[10] As a result, his deficit adds just $1 to the US private sector bucket. But the US is sending that dollar—and four more—on to the rest of the world. And foreigners are only sending $3 back. So the US is running a trade deficit, spending $5 on goods and services produced by the rest of the world but only collecting $3 for the things it sells abroad. Looking at all of these payments, the foreign sector accumulates a $2 surplus, while the government and the private sector each end up with a $1 deficit. A private sector deficit is the inevitable consequence of allowing the government deficit to fall below the trade deficit.

What would it take to return the private sector to its usual state of surplus? One option is for Uncle Sam to add more dollars to the private sector's bucket, either by spending more dollars into the US economy or taxing fewer dollars away. As soon as the government deficit gets bigger than the trade deficit, the private sector's financial balance will move back into surplus. Another way to eliminate the private sector's deficit is to try to shrink (or reverse) the trade deficit. There are a number of ways to try to do this. Sometimes, countries try to hold down the value of their currencies to make their goods more competitive on world markets. President Trump has routinely lashed out at China, accusing the Chinese government of manipulating its currency, the *yuan*, to gain an advantage over US producers. In December 2019, he accused Brazil and Argentina of "presiding over a massive devaluation of their currencies, which is not good for our farmers."[11] Some countries don't have the option to weaken their currencies. Nineteen countries in Europe, for example, have formed a currency union (the Economic and Monetary Union or EMU), making it impossible to alter the value of their currencies vis-à-vis one another (one euro equals one euro throughout the eurozone). When an *external* (i.e., currency) devaluation isn't an option, countries often pursue *internal* devaluation as a way to try to "win" at trade. The neoliberal term of art for this particular strategy is *structural reform*. It's the polite way of describing an agenda aimed at driving down labor costs (wages and pensions) to increase competitiveness by reducing the costs of production. Essentially, it means that a country uses weaker labor as a substitute for a weaker currency. When it comes to this strategy, Germany is Europe's poster child. After the German government committed to this strategy in the early 2000s, it was able to replace its long-standing trade deficits with massive trade surpluses.[12]

The thinking behind Trump's policy was to use tariffs (i.e., taxes on imports) to reduce the US trade deficit. By making certain foreign goods more expensive, Trump believes he is pursuing an America First strategy that will result in American consumers buying fewer imports and spending more money buying domestically produced goods. That would mean fewer dollars leaving the US private sector bucket and flowing into the foreign bucket. Trump sees that as "winning" because his entire worldview is shaped by cash flows. The one with the biggest bucket of money wins. MMT recognizes the importance of maintaining healthy financial balances but views the tariffs as largely counterproductive. That's because MMT recognizes that imports are *real* benefits. Viewed this way, Trump's tariffs are really a tax on US benefits. There are better ways to maintain a healthy balance in the private sector and, as we'll see, better ways to protect American jobs.

No Full Employment, No Fair Trade

Now that we understand the simple financial flows, we can return to thinking about the human and economic impacts of trade. Too often, the US doesn't just lose dollars to the rest of the world, it loses jobs, too. As we discussed above, most of the angst people feel when they think about US trade deficits appears to stem from pain—especially the pain that comes from unemployment as American businesses close up shop and ship jobs overseas. As MMT economist Pavlina Tcherneva has documented, unemployment resembles an epidemic: like a virus, it affects other people nearby, resulting not only in lost income but higher mortality and suicide rates and a permanent decline in well-being.[13] But it's easier to blame immigrant workers, foreign currency manipulators, or even global technology than to come to terms with the fact that joblessness is an official policy in the United States.

I have argued that one of the best answers to, "They took our jobs!" is, "Everyone gets a job!" The MMT solution to involuntary unemployment is to introduce a federal job guarantee that establishes a legal right to a good job at good wages with good benefits. This would address one of the most pernicious effects stemming from trade—the unemployment that is too often visited upon whole communities as jobs are lost to foreign competition. It's not enough just to provide training and other temporary forms of assistance to workers whose jobs are lost to foreign competition. Federal programs like Trade Adjustment Assistance (TAA)[14] are important, but something more is needed.

That something is a federal job guarantee. By no means is it a panacea, but at a minimum, it begins to tackle the problem of unemployment directly (as opposed to subsidizing the effects of unemployment).

Through the thick and thin of the business cycle, we leave tens of millions of Americans idle in the belief that this makes political, economic, and social sense. Consider the closure of the Harley-Davidson manufacturing facility in Kansas City, Missouri, the city in which I taught for seventeen years. The company's eight hundred workers were left stunned by the announcement that ultimately resulted in a net loss of 350 jobs.[15] The timing was particularly pernicious, coming as it did against the backdrop of a dividend increase for shareholders and an announcement that the company would spend millions buying back up to fifteen million shares of its own stock. Had a federal job guarantee program been in place, it would have mitigated the impact of the closure. At a minimum, it would have provided the workers whose jobs were lost with a way to remain employed right in their communities. But it would have done more than that.

The benefits of a federal job guarantee not only include the production of goods, services, and income. The guarantee also features on-the-job training and skill development; poverty alleviation; community building and social networking; social, political, and economic stability; and social multipliers (positive feedback loops and reinforcing dynamics that create a virtuous cycle of socioeconomic benefits). With a program like this in place, the government would have mitigated the localized devastation of communities that directly experienced the loss of well-paying US industrial jobs.

It may be hard to imagine an economy that doesn't allow millions to fall by the wayside. But that's because America has almost never achieved anything like true full employment. It's something we've rarely experienced, outside of wartime. One of the most important features of a job guarantee program is that it maintains a form of full employment by immediately rehiring the unemployed into public service work, providing them with income and the retraining required when they are displaced by trade shocks. In this way, the job guarantee can serve as the core of a response to both "free trade" and the "trade war." With a job guarantee, free trade is no longer a threat to full employment, and trade wars are no longer necessary to prevent unemployment.

Trade negotiations can then focus on labor standards and environmental sustainability, with the US using its market power to promote acceptable working conditions and environment standards worldwide.[16] Today, Chinese firms sell American households many environmentally unfriendly products. In addition, people all over the world currently endure unsafe and unsanitary working conditions in order to provide America its stuff surplus. If we want to prioritize the well-being of workers worldwide, communities, and the planet as a whole, then we need a new approach to global trade.

Especially in an era of global climate crisis, we should not be suckered by the simplistic rhetoric of countries "winning" and "losing" at trade. The *quality* of trade is at least as important as the *quantity* of trade. What ends and whose interests are our trade relationships serving? Just like with fiscal policy, the big scary number that is the trade deficit is not worthy of so much attention. As MMT reminds us, real resources, real social needs, and real environmental benefits are what matters most when it comes to trade policy.

At this point, it's important to understand a bit more about our trading partners around the world—and the United States' special privileges compared to other countries. So far, we've discussed how global trade affects the United States and how MMT can make the trade flows into and out of our own country more productive and humane. But what about Britain, France, Saudi Arabia, Turkey, Venezuela, and all the other nations out there?

The Special Position of the US Dollar

Since the 1970s, there has been a fundamental shift in the way our monetary system operates. This shift redefines how we should think about macroeconomics and the role of a national government that issues its own currency. Unfortunately, on the question of trade, as in so many other matters, policy makers remain locked in an anachronistic framework that belongs to the bygone gold standard era.

From the middle of the nineteenth century until the Nixon "gold shock" that ended US dollar convertibility in the early 1970s, the gold standard (in one form or another) served as the common monetary framework regulating domestic economies and trade between them. Although the framework's restrictions were gradually loosened, the overriding principle remained the same: in all countries, the monetary authority effectively tethered the value of its currency to gold by standing ready to buy or sell gold (or US dollars) to meet any supply or demand imbalance arising from international trade. To carry out these interventions, the central bank (or equivalent in those days) had to maintain enough gold (or US dollars) to back the circulating currency at a fixed exchange rate.

A gold standard is only credible if the government can make good on its promise to convert the currency into gold at a fixed price. Having enough gold was critical. And running a trade surplus was the surest way to build up a country's gold reserves. Conversely, trade deficits led to an outflow of gold, since countries used gold to pay for their imports. To try to prevent the loss of gold reserves, interest rates were frequently raised to draw the flow of gold bullion back into the country. The idea is that higher interest rates would slow down domestic demand sufficiently (meaning fewer imports and therefore less gold flowing out of the country) while the higher returns promised by increased rates would encourage more gold inflows. But raising interest rates to reverse an outflow of gold often meant that governments weren't free to keep interest rates low to support their domestic economies. Even when high interest rates succeeded in protecting gold reserves, the policy often had devastating consequences. That's because rising interest rates frequently triggered an economic slowdown, which meant that many of the citizens of the affected country had to endure domestic recessions and entrenched unemployment. So the gold standard created a recessionary bias in economies operating

with trade deficits. The inflexibility of the system prevented governments from focusing on full employment.

The gold standard system was suspended during World War I and
World War II, as the US (and other nations) needed expanded policy
space to run big deficits (creating lots of "green dollars") in order to
fight the wars. It was reestablished during the "interwar" years, placing
considerable stress on the global economy during the Great Depression. If we still had this kind of a system today, then Donald Trump's
desire to wipe out the US trade deficit would make far more sense.

After World War II, a new international monetary system was
born. The new system restored convertibility by replacing the old gold
standard with a new gold exchange standard. Instead of directly pegging currencies to a fixed price of gold, the system was replaced by
convertibility into the US dollar, reflecting the dominance of the US
in world trade (and the fact that the Allies won the war!). This new
system—known as the Bretton Woods framework—called for the US
dollar to be pegged to the value of gold. Moreover, all other currencies
in the system were then pegged to the US dollar's value. The exchange
rate applied at the time set the price of gold at $35 an ounce.

In effect Bretton Woods recreated a gold standard system, one
step removed, with the US dollar now providing the central link in
the monetary chain. Governments could now sell gold to the United
States Treasury at the price of $35 per ounce, and the US Treasury
had to honor the terms of that exchange. In 1971, following growing
trade deficits caused in part by the Vietnam War, other countries became concerned that the US gold holdings were no longer adequate to
cover the number of dollars in circulation at the fixed exchange rate.
To stem pressures on the dollar, President Richard M. Nixon shocked
the world by declaring a temporary suspension of the dollar's convertibility into gold. A second shock followed in 1973, when Nixon announced that he was making the "temporary" suspension permanent.
Nixon's move was brought about by the realization that the US needed
more policy space than was available under Bretton Woods.

Announcing the change in policy, Nixon declared: "We must create more and better jobs; we must stop the rise in the cost of living; we
must protect the dollar from the attacks of international money speculators."[17] To achieve the first two goals, he proposed tax cuts and a
90-day freeze on prices and wages; to achieve the third, Nixon directed
the suspension of the dollar's convertibility into gold.

Ultimately, the resultant social instability throughout the world
caused the system to collapse. It had been under pressure in the 1960s
with a series of "competitive devaluations"—weakening one's currency
to improve competitiveness in the trade arena—by the UK and other
countries that were facing chronically high unemployment due to persistent trading problems. Richard Nixon delivered the coup de grâce
in 1971. This ended the gold standard. From this point on, most major
currencies were no longer on a fixed exchange rate. Abandoning fixed
exchange rates and floating the currency gave currency-issuing governments like the US expanded policy space to sustain full employment.

Notwithstanding the collapse of the Bretton Woods system of fixed
exchange rates, gold standard *thinking* still dominates our discourse
on trade policy, which is why so many politicians still regard trade
deficits as inherently dangerous. On a gold standard the government
can run out of gold.

With the end of the gold standard and/or fixed global exchange
rates, this kind of thinking is no longer valid. The only residual legacy
left from Bretton Woods is that the US dollar still plays a central role
in the global economy. When companies and governments around
the world engage in trade with one another, they write an enormous
portion of those contracts in US dollars—even when the country doing the buying and the country doing the selling don't use dollars as
their internal domestic currency! A handful of other major currencies, like the euro, play a role like this as well. But none come close to
dominating markets the way the US dollar does. Nearly 90 percent of
currency trading involves the US dollar.[18] This is the situation people
are referring to when they say the US dollar is the dominant global

currency.[19] Could that change? Yes, of course. Nothing lasts forever. As MMT economist L. Randall Wray put it, "the dollar will not always reign supreme, but it has a lot of life remaining as the most desirable asset to hold in portfolios."[20]

The Spectrum of Monetary Sovereignty

Monetary sovereignty is key to understanding MMT. Governments need a high degree of monetary sovereignty in order to exercise policy autonomy—that is, to be able to run their fiscal and monetary policies without fear of painful backlash from financial or foreign exchange markets. Many countries possess, but don't take full advantage of, their monetary sovereignty. In addition to the United States, countries like the United Kingdom, Japan, Canada, and Australia (to name a few) enjoy a high degree of monetary sovereignty. They all issue nonconvertible fiat currencies, and they largely refrain from borrowing in currencies that aren't their own. Generally speaking, countries that fit this set of criteria will have greater monetary sovereignty and, thus, more policy autonomy when it comes to managing their own economic destinies. They needn't agonize over government deficits or trade deficits, and they are free to focus their domestic policy agenda on achieving macroeconomic goals like full employment and price stability. Not every government enjoys this much policy flexibility.

Some nations have weakened their monetary sovereignty, either by pegging their exchange rates (e.g., Bermuda, Venezuela, Niger), abandoning their national currencies (e.g., all nineteen countries in the eurozone, Ecuador, Panama), or by borrowing heavily in US dollars or other foreign currencies (e.g., Ukraine, Argentina, Turkey, Brazil). Doing any of these things compromises a nation's monetary sovereignty and diminishes its policy flexibility.

Most developing economies are at the weaker end of the sovereignty spectrum. Even those that can issue a nonconvertible fiat currency usually can't afford to ignore fiscal and trade imbalances. That's because most poorer developing nations rely on imports to meet vital social needs (e.g., food, oil, medicines, technologies). And that means they have to worry about how they're going to get enough foreign currency (usually US dollars) to pay for imports. Many end up borrowing in US dollars and then struggling to repay those loans. For these, and other reasons, many countries around the world are stuck in a situation where they can't rely on their own currency-issuing powers to build a good economy for all of their people. Developing countries may receive aid from the international community, or loans from institutions like the International Monetary Fund (IMF), but it never seems to be enough to help them escape the trap of needing to rely on foreign currency for their survival.

By running trade deficits, the US allows these countries to build up their US dollar reserves. Those dollars are a lifeline to the food, medicines, and other critical imports that many developing countries depend on for survival. They also help many indebted nations earn the currency they need to repay loans to the IMF and other foreign lenders. In a very important sense, America's trade deficits are not optional. Much of the world simply *must* run trade surpluses with America.

Even developed countries (e.g., Korea, Taiwan, Japan) end up stockpiling US dollars. These dollars are usually held in the form of US Treasuries. When foreign countries run trade surpluses with the United States, the US pours dollars into the foreign bucket. Just like anyone else with green dollars, foreigners can recycle them into the yellow dollars we call US Treasuries. That makes some people nervous as they interpret it as a sign of weakness on the part of the US. To them, it looks like the US is dependent on foreign lenders to pay its bills. (Remember that Barack Obama said that the US had taken out "a credit card from the Bank of China.") But that's not what's really happening. In fact, if you look closely at the major international holders of US Treasuries, you discover that nearly all of them are *net exporters* to the United States (including China, Japan, Taiwan, Hong Kong, and the world's major crude oil producers).[21] It is true that the US government pays interest on those yellow dollars, but as we have learned, bond sales are always optional in a country like the United States. Giving oreigners access to Treasuries simply grants them the same option available to any holder of green dollars. The rest of the world likes this for the same reason you and I might like having the option to hold some of our money in a checking account and some of it in a savings account. The point is, we are not dependent on foreigners in the way many fear.

In short, just as Uncle Sam's budget deficit arises from American businesses' and households' desires to accumulate a surplus of US dollars, America's trade deficit arises from the rest of the world's desire to accumulate a surplus of US currency. The global hunger for dollars is largely why we've been running a trade deficit nonstop for decades. In this regard, the United States does sit in a powerful position compared to the rest of the world—for both good and ill.

Thanks to the US dollar's unique role as a global reserve currency, Uncle Sam never has to borrow in anything but his own currency (and he doesn't even have to do that!). This gives the US something of an advantage, but it does not mean that the United States is the only country with the power to carry out its domestic policy agenda. Any country with a high degree of monetary sovereignty has the ability to pursue a domestic policy agenda aimed at keeping its economy operating at full employment. As we'll see, even developing countries can enhance their monetary sovereignty and open up enough policy space to allow them to pursue domestic full employment.

Many advanced economies enjoy a high degree of monetary sovereignty. They have many high-value-added production sectors (a point we'll return to below). They boast enormous opportunities for those eager to invest in their economies, buying stocks, real estate, and more. Since investing in those domestic assets requires obtaining the countries' respective currencies, demand for their currencies remains high across the globe. (In economic jargon, they have deep capital markets.) Just as MMT argues that domestic demand for the US dollar is driven by the need to pay federal taxes—and this demand supports the dollar's value—the international need for investment assets drives demand for both the US dollar and other major currencies, helping to stabilize their value. Like the US, these other advanced nations float their currencies, meaning they don't try to tie the value of the currency to anything else. That way, they don't have to defend the peg by buying, selling, or borrowing currencies they don't control. This is another reason they enjoy very high degrees of monetary sovereignty.

Many countries weaken their monetary sovereignty by continuing to peg their currencies to the US dollar (e.g., Saudi Arabia, Lebanon, and Jordan), or go even further and use the US dollar as their official domestic currency (e.g., Ecuador, Panama, and El Salvador). In both cases, making a much bigger effort to accumulate and stockpile dollars becomes a necessity.[22] Pegging your currency can also worsen your monetary sovereignty over time as your private sector grows increasingly accustomed to borrowing in the currency you're pegging to. Meanwhile, governments themselves may have to get deeper and deeper into US dollar debt, which reduces their monetary sovereignty even further.

Further down the spectrum, another choice that strips countries of monetary sovereignty is joining a currency union. Nations like France, Spain, and Italy, despite being advanced economies with deep capital markets, cannot operate as currency issuers. That's because they are all members of the eurozone, using a currency that can only be issued by the European Central Bank (ECB). That relegates all eurozone members to mere currency users. This point is crucial to understanding Greece's seemingly endless debt crises, for example.

Finally, at the opposite end of the monetary sovereignty spectrum from the US are the poorer developing countries of Africa, Asia, and Latin America. We should close out this chapter by discussing their situation in some detail because, despite the damage done by trade policy to the American working class, the United States is far from the most abused victim of the modern international trade order.

Out of the (Bretton) Woods,
into the Free-Trade Fire

Developing countries, more or less by definition, don't have the diverse and mature industries that advanced, developed countries do. Countries such as Bangladesh, Vietnam, or Ghana generally have to provide the rest of the world with cheap manufacturing labor or natural resources, like oil, metals, or minerals, and those export industries tend to dominate their economies. To get high-tech and high-value items like computers, cars, medicine, or advanced manufacturing robotics, developing countries have to import them from more developed economies. Many developing countries also lack the ability—or have been told they don't have the ability—to produce enough food, energy, and medicine to meet their own domestic demand. So, they rely on developed countries to supply them with imports of food, energy, and medicine. And, as we've discussed, they almost always need US dollars to pay for those crucial imports.

As MMT economist Fadhel Kaboub has argued, this position at the bottom of global supply chains brings fundamental economic problems—many of them arising from the historical legacy of colonization itself.[23] Exporting cheap labor and commodities, while importing expensive high-value items, tends to leave developing countries with perpetual trade deficits. The problem is that there isn't a robust, permanent appetite for developing countries' financial assets or real estate. Economists say that they lack deep capital markets. While investors will speculate in emerging markets, buying financial assets denominated in a developing country's local currency, they don't make the kinds of long-term investments that would allow developing countries to gain durable access to currencies like the US dollar. As long as the rest of the world refuses to accept the currencies of developing countries in payment for critical imports, developing nations will be forced to borrow US dollars and other foreign currencies they don't control. Not only does this undermine their monetary sovereignty, it can leave developing nations mired in a cycle whereby they sell domestic currency to get the foreign currency they need, driving down the value of the domestic currency and making those critical imports more expensive—which can easily lead to import-led inflation and even political turmoil, as we've seen in Venezuela, Argentina, and in Professor Kaboub's native Tunisia.[24]

Since less developed countries don't have advanced industries or deep capital markets, they're vulnerable to a wide variety of unpredictable outside risks. For example, dollar-starved economies often experience a burst of investment from speculative Western investors, who swoop into a country, feverishly investing in those economies and driving up the value of the local currency, only to get cold feet and suddenly pull their cash back out, causing the local currency to collapse.[25] Or maybe global demand for a country's key exports suddenly collapses, leaving the country scrambling to earn enough foreign currency to finance its imports. That happened to Venezuela and Russia when the natural gas (fracking) boom in the US drove oil prices sharply down. And it's what happened in Argentina when the price of soybeans collapsed, depriving the country of a critical source of US dollars. In the case of both investor panic and market collapse, the bottom drops out of the developing country's currency, leading to inflation and upheaval.

When outside events like these happen, even countries that were theoretically running sustainable economic policies can wind up in financial peril, forced to renegotiate foreign-denominated debt, seek aid from lenders like the IMF, or simply default.[26] Because many developing countries run trade deficits or have debts denominated in US dollars (or other foreign currencies), they can get into real trouble when something compromises their ability to earn (or borrow on affordable terms) enough foreign exchange to finance their imports and repay their foreign debts. Countries with greater monetary sovereignty—the US, the UK, or Australia—don't face these same risks.

In fact, the US dollar's role as the currency hegemon means the whole world is exposed to the United States' control over dollar interest

rates. Decisions taken by the Federal Reserve can have profound consequences for developing countries, and yet countries often have few
ways to defend themselves. For example, beginning in 1979, former
Federal Reserve chairman Paul Volcker initiated a series of substantial
interest rate hikes, believing that this was the only way to tame the
double-digit inflation that was roiling the US economy. When that
happened, Latin American countries that were indebted to the United
States, and sub-Saharan African countries that were indebted to former European colonizers, suddenly found themselves facing much
higher borrowing costs. They were already exporting so many low-
value-added manufacturing goods that they were reliant upon those
richer countries for more crucial imports. At the same time, rising
interest rates in the US raised the dollar exchange rate by stoking demand for US investment assets. This delivered a double gut punch to
developing countries who not only saw the value of their currencies
drop precipitously but also faced borrowing costs on a growing pile of
debt denominated in foreign currency. In the end, Volcker's rate hikes
drove many developing countries into crisis, fueling a rapid economic
downfall from which some countries have yet to fully recover.[27]

Back when Bretton Woods was still in effect, the system established
a host of international organizations, including the IMF, the World
Bank, and the General Agreement on Tariffs and Trade (now the
World Trade Organization or WTO). Within the Bretton Woods system, these organizations focused on actively governing the conditions
of trade among countries. This involved a variety of tools, like tariffs
and capital controls, aimed at keeping trade flows stable and national
economies at least somewhat insulated from one another.

When Bretton Woods ended, the global institutions it created remained. But over time, their governing philosophy shifted: the religion of free trade took over, and the tariffs and capital controls were
relaxed in the name of trade liberalization. Western elites decided that
fully exposing developing countries to global trade and to the in- and
out-rushes of investor money would discipline their economies into

becoming better. *Protectionism* and *government intervention* became dirty words. The champions of this new framework insisted that free trade would eventually bring full employment and harmonious trade relations across each participating country's economy.[28]

Nothing like that has happened, of course. The IMF, WTO, and World Bank, often run by bankers and diplomats from wealthy countries, have no commitment to full employment around the world. Instead, they tend to recommend a familiar package to developing countries hit by crisis: drastic cuts to government expenditures (i.e., fiscal austerity) and tight monetary policy (very high interest rates) to raise the value of their currency and lure investors back. And, of course, more free trade. They also frequently recommend that developing countries peg the value of their currency to a stronger currency, like the euro, yuan, or US dollar. This policy mix amounts to recommending that the developing country forsake any effort to enhance its monetary sovereignty.

Whatever the intention, the actual results from this package are perverse: when countries sacrifice monetary sovereignty but cannot acquire sufficient foreign currency to defend the target exchange rate, their currency pegs collapse, potentially causing a downward spiral, as governments, businesses, and even households cannot favorably convert domestic currency to repay debts denominated in foreign currency.[29] Hyperinflation can set in, as the exchange rate plummets, and the cost of crucial imports skyrocket in price. Then the recommended austerity and tight monetary policy crush the domestic economy, driving up unemployment and poverty, all in the name of luring in another batch of Western investors who will start the whole cycle over again.

And that's not all. Historically, international organizations (like the IMF) have recommended that developing countries, especially those that have achieved independence from colonial powers after World War II, focus on producing and selling just a few goods to richer countries.[30] This suggestion comes from an idea that a nineteenth-century

English economist, David Ricardo, called *comparative advantage*. Essentially, Ricardo recommended that countries should specialize in producing whatever goods and services they are most adept and efficient at. But many influential economists take the idea of comparative advantage to extremes. For instance, they argue that developing countries should focus on what they can produce most cheaply in the short term, rather than developing new industries that would enhance their monetary sovereignty over time.

In other words, international Western elites have told poorer countries they should *not* indulge in development strategies that focus on job creation, energy independence, or any goals aside from specialized production. In effect, it's a recommendation that keeps developing countries forever "developing," never achieving the kind of advanced, diversified economies of the modern West. That recommendation is the *opposite* of the historical path taken by the United States, Japan, and most other powerful economies. They often focused on producing crucial goods at home rather than importing them from abroad. For example, as a giant country with many diverse real resources, China has developed significantly simply by increasing internal trade, as the United States did, by hook or by crook, for centuries. As one would expect, the Chinese government has also severely limited the role of finance, insurance, and real estate in the industrial process.[31]

Good-bye, Trade War—Hello, Trade Peace?

While MMT certainly doesn't have all the answers, it can be a useful tool in untangling the knots that all of us—the United States, the advanced West, and the developing world—are entangled in.

To reform the global trade order, the US must take the largest strides in making it happen. In many ways, it has the furthest to go. This doesn't mean winning or losing a trade war. It simply means recognizing what I hope this chapter has demonstrated: trade is not about competition among countries but about power relationships among specific interests within specific countries.[32] Indeed, if we want a world that is safe for everyday people and the planet, we need to think a little less about trade war and start envisioning something a little more like trade peace.

First off, we have to stop treating trade as something that we "beat" other countries at by running a trade surplus. One country's surplus is another country's trade deficit, so by definition not everyone can win in that way at once. But it doesn't follow that the deficit country has to sustain real economic loss if it gets its policy matrix right. The Trumpian approach to trade creates strife and a zero-sum race to the bottom over too few globally available jobs. Already, President Trump's tariffs have failed to revive American manufacturing, raised prices for US consumers, invited retaliation from China, and contributed to a slowdown in the global economy. All in subservience to the trade deficit myth.

Instead, we must recognize that the US government can supply all the dollars our domestic private sector needs to reach full employment, *and* it can supply all the dollars the rest of the world needs to build up their reserves and protect their trade flows. Instead of using its currency hegemon status to mobilize global resources for its own narrow interests, the US could lead the effort to mobilize resources for a global Green New Deal, keeping interest rates low and stable to promote global economic tranquility.

Obviously, the US and other advanced countries with high degrees of monetary sovereignty can run their own job guarantee programs. But what about the middle-income and developing countries? Could Mexico, for instance, implement a job guarantee and end some of this human suffering? Perhaps. When it comes to direct job creation, history suggests developing countries may face fewer barriers than the international elite say they do.

For example, Argentina is usually cast as a poster child of financial problems. But during the country's inflationary crisis in 2001, Buenos Aires dramatically shifted to a domestically oriented growth strategy.[33]

First, it stopped pegging its exchange rate and hoarding US dollars. Instead, policy makers chose to default on foreign debt and invest in their own people. Argentina then created a massive direct job creation program that guaranteed work for poor heads of households. As MMT economists L. Randall Wray and Pavlina Tcherneva reported, Plan Jefes y Jefas de Hogar Desocupados (Plan for Unemployed Male and Female Heads of Households) created jobs for two million participants, roughly 13 percent of the labor force. Comprised mostly of women, the participants focused on community-based projects like gardening, renovation of social centers, running food kitchens, or teaching classes on public health.[34] This program, which helped Argentina avoid many of the problems associated with reliance on foreign capital, perhaps provides a clue as to how we can all move toward a more prosperous, sustainable, and peaceful planet.

Ultimately, as Tcherneva has suggested, we'll need something like a global job guarantee.[35] As I write this book, the International Labour Organization estimates that almost two hundred million people around the world are involuntarily unemployed.[36] Export-led growth may be framed as an employment policy for various countries, but it rarely succeeds. Moreover, we need a preventive full employment policy—an arrangement that avoids accepting unemployment as natural in the first place. Employment should be a human right as envisioned by the United Nations' Universal Declaration of Human Rights, not something that just floats in the winds of global market forces.

The United States can't run domestic policy for the rest of the world's governments. But we can run the dominant currency in a way that makes global full employment something everyone could actually achieve. With decent jobs guaranteed for all, workers can engage in a public-led industrial policy aimed at producing sustainable infrastructure and a wider array of public services.

Closer to home, when one considers the disparate living standards in Mexico vis-à-vis the United States, it is hard to make a case that Mexico has taken advantage of its trade relationship with the US, as

Trump has argued.[37] Unlike China and Japan, Mexico has often followed the militant neoliberal reforms proposed by the United States
and the international organizations. As part of NAFTA, for example,
Mexico lowered barriers to US and Canadian financial capital and,
perhaps even more importantly, agricultural products. Although
many US companies picked up their manufacturing jobs and took
them south of the border, the influx of US farm products into Mexico,
especially corn, displaced millions of rural Mexican workers. And that
drove many of them to cross the border for jobs in the United States.[38]

This brings us to the question of so-called free-trade agreements,
which will need to be rethought from the ground up.

Right now, those agreements favor wealthy investors around the
world, while leaving workers—not to mention the environment—
behind. Many current trade deals include investor-state dispute
settlement (ISDS) mechanisms, for example. These mechanisms provide corporations with a parallel system of justice that allows them
to sue democratically elected governments for adopting policies—
restrictions, regulations, or other protections—that the corporation
views as a threat to its bottom line. Instead of handling these disputes
in domestic courts, ISDS relies on private arbitration before an international body that is seen as more favorable to corporate interests.
Then there's international intellectual property enforcement, which,
among other things, allows corporations to charge exorbitant prices
and fees to developing countries before permitting them to manufacture affordable generic pharmaceuticals. For AIDS patients in the
world's poorest countries, the patent provisions in free-trade agreements like the Trans-Pacific Partnership are a death sentence.

Such "free trade" agreements entrench global divisions between
rich and poor. They shoehorn poor parts of the world into fossil fuel
extraction, helping to hasten climate change. They give developing
countries little choice but to submit to export-led growth—which, in
reality, means exploitative labor conditions to assemble cheap goods
on behalf of the wealthy and advanced nations. They even expand

the monetary sovereignty of rich countries at the expense of poorer countries.

The US can act as a global leader in reforming these trade arrangements, by setting standards in the deals it helps to craft. It can demand strict ecological standards of its trading partners, as well as robust labor protections, like a job guarantee, geared toward helping poorer nations achieve food and energy sovereignty. It can insist that its trading partners share green technology and intellectual property with other countries in a way that truly lifts all boats. A revamped WTO could mandate these sorts of provisions in trade agreements as well, rather than entrenching existing privileges for powerful multinational corporations, as it does today.

Meanwhile, as Fadhel Kaboub recommends, South-South trade partnerships could help developing countries grow complementary industries and escape their current position in the global production chain, where they're stuck importing high-value finished goods and exporting cheaper intermediate goods. Otherwise, we will need a system that transfers these productive resources and technological know-how from the developed world to the developing one.[39] That would deliver poorer parts of the world the industrial capacity they need to build up their (renewable) energy and (sustainable) food sovereignty—and thus escape the trap we discussed earlier of being dependent on imports to access critical resources.

In theory and practice, lack of food and energy sovereignty are solvable problems. Even major food importing countries with mostly desert climates can adopt a sustainable agriculture program by investing in more water efficient hydroponic and aquaponics food production. And even countries with no oil or natural gas reserves can adopt a renewable energy program by installing solar and wind farms, and by investing in energy efficiency for housing and transportation. And to the extent that we encourage a global effort to contain the effects of climate change, policies that help the developing world to decarbonize their economies not only lessens their dependency on US dollars to purchase fossil fuels, but also enhances global cooperative efforts to reduce harmful carbon emissions that continue to threaten our planet's long-term survival.

As long as most developing countries have to import basic necessities, they will remain "developing"—caught in a desperate scramble to acquire the currencies of the rich world. Corporations around the world will keep feverishly chasing short-term profits, extracting scarce natural resources, polluting precious ecosystems, and ruthlessly firing desperate people, all in the name of maximizing shareholder value. Left unchecked, the situation is an open invitation for demagogues like Trump to come along, blaming "foreigners" and exacerbating tensions among the world's people.

In addition to South-South trade agreements, developing countries need to return to regulating financial transactions across borders. They may not be able to implement the classical form of capital controls that ruled during Bretton Woods and relied on global cooperation but they can certainly do better than they are now. Foreign investors should be limited in the ways they can invest in domestic assets and in their ability to sell out and create downward pressure on the exchange rate market. This will reduce the need to accumulate dollar reserves and help developing countries realize the benefits that a flexible exchange rate system can provide. In other words, regulating international capital flows shouldn't be looked at as a short term "stopgap" measure but a permanent policy to help nations reach higher and higher degrees of monetary sovereignty.

We share only one planet. Our current trade system is not up to the task of meeting the social and economic challenges of global poverty and joblessness. Meanwhile, we need a global all-hands-on-deck effort to deal with climate change. Trade peace isn't simply something we can achieve; it's something we can't afford not to achieve.

6

You're Entitled!

MYTH #6: "Entitlement" programs like Social Security and Medicare are financially unsustainable. We can't afford them anymore.

REALITY: As long as the federal government commits to making the payments, it can always afford to support these programs. What matters is our economy's long-run capacity to produce the real goods and services people will need.

For decades, we've been told that we should panic about the cost of entitlement programs like Social Security, Medicare, and Medicaid. We're told that they're growing too quickly, that they're eating up the federal budget, and that they're unsustainable. We're told that they'll go broke and take the whole government down with them unless we make drastic changes.

The problem seems obvious to most people: sooner or later, these programs will cost more than the government can afford. In anticipation of looming financial shortfalls, many have argued that the only practical solution is to scale these programs back and start "living within our means." Others say we need to fix the solvency problem by bringing in more money.

Both sides are wrong. These are *federally funded* programs. The money can always be there.

The deficit myth has warped our understanding of all government spending. Entitlements have fared especially badly, however, partly because of early decisions that were intended to protect them. When Franklin D. Roosevelt established Social Security, he tried to protect it by setting up some special rules about how it would be paid for. That turned out to be a mistake. It put the political emphasis on the source of the program's finances, when what we should be talking about is our values, our priorities, and our nation's real productive capacity.

Before we move to the debate over the so-called financial crisis facing these programs, let's start with a more basic question about entitlements: Who is entitled to them and why?

Who Are You Calling Entitled?

Entitlement is the term for any government program that guarantees benefits to certain groups of people, including the elderly, the disabled, and the poor. The US Senate website defines it this way:[1]

> entitlement—A Federal program or provision of law that requires payments to any person or unit of government that meets the eligibility criteria established by law. Entitlements constitute a binding obligation on the part of the Federal Government, and eligible recipients have legal recourse if the obligation is not fulfilled. Social Security and veterans' compensation and pensions are examples of entitlement programs.

In other words, if you meet the criteria, you're in. You qualify for these programs because you belong to one of the groups they're meant to serve. That's it. You're legally entitled to receive its benefits, and no one can deny them to you. The government pays them automatically at that point.

Entitlement programs will help most of us at one time or another. Almost every American will benefit from Social Security and Medicare when they retire. The people receiving those benefits today may be our grandparents, parents, neighbors, or ourselves.

Social Security also provides disability insurance, which protects all of us should we become disabled in our working years. As of 2018, nearly ten million disabled Americans were receiving disability benefits through Social Security.[2] That includes people like Shaun Castle, the deputy executive director of the *Paralyzed Veterans of America*, who provides moving personal testimony about the way Social Security kept him from being homeless. Castle suffered a spinal cord injury while on active duty as a military police officer, an injury that led to paralysis after he had returned to civilian life. As Castle has explained in interviews[3] and in congressional testimony,[4] he relied on Social Security Disability Insurance (SSDI) to make ends meet while he was waiting for his military benefits to be approved.

Social Security also helps the dependents of people who die during their working years. I was reminded of that a few years back when a friend of mine died at an early age. She was a working professional, and the loss of her income put a terrible burden on the family. Her husband, now a widower, had to find a way to raise two children on his own. It was terrible for everyone, especially the kids. But at least the family had help with its financial needs because Social Security sent a check every month to cover a portion of her lost income. That money helped her husband care for the children until they turned eighteen.

Many of us will need help from an antipoverty program, too. Nearly six out of every ten people in the United States will experience at least one year of poverty between the ages of twenty and sixty-five.[5] Nearly one child in five already lives in poverty.

Receiving entitlement benefits isn't a moral failure or a sign of weakness. After all, basic financial security shouldn't be limited to those who can set aside a sizable nest egg for a rainy day. Obviously, it's good to save. But millions of people are struggling to make ends meet and can't afford to set aside money for the future. Everyone deserves to know they'll have medical care when they need it, financial security when they become old or disabled, and assistance if they lose a job or fall on hard times.

At least, that's how it's *supposed* to work. But America's entitlement programs—a category that includes Social Security, Medicare, and Medicaid and antipoverty programs like food assistance, housing vouchers, and tax credits—have been under attack for decades. Some of those attacks are motivated by self-interest, since wealthy individuals and corporations often fight against programs that could lead to calls for higher taxes. Some opponents are motivated by an ideology that sees these programs as redistributing income from the deserving rich to an undeserving class of poor and lower-income families.

The debate can get ugly. The day-to-day realities of aging, disability, and economic hardship haven't stopped some entitlement critics from engaging in personal attacks on the people who benefit from them. Senator Alan Simpson, who was appointed by President Obama to co-chair a deficit commission, referred to retired people as "greedy geezers" in what appeared to some to be an attempt to stir up resentment and divide younger and older people. Simpson also called pro–Social Security feminist activists "Pink Panthers" and told one of them that Social Security was like "a milk cow with 310 million tits." He told the same advocate for older women's rights, Ashley B. Carson, to "call when you get honest work!"[6]

Personal attacks on beneficiaries didn't begin with Simpson. They're as old as entitlements themselves. An 1882 magazine cover caricatured a veteran as "The Insatiable Glutton," grabbing public money with the help of his many "arms," each of which was a shady stereotype of a pension claimant.[7] A twenty-first-century cartoon with the caption "Top US Threats in 1991, 2001, and 2011" showed Saddam

Hussein, Osama Bin Laden, and an elderly woman with a sign reading "Entitlements."[8]

Attacks on entitlement programs, and the people who benefit from them, are sometimes motivated by resentment or by a hostility to government. Sometimes, people have simply been misinformed. Whatever the motivation, misguided economic thinking plays a huge part in the entitlement debate. Fortunately, MMT shows us why we don't have to pit one group against another in some desperate—and unnecessary—attempt to solve a "financial crisis." It tells us why looking at the sustainability of entitlement programs in *financial* terms misses the point, and why the biggest challenges facing these programs have nothing to do with affordability.

The Great Social Security Mistake

We can learn a lot about the corrosive effects of the deficit myth by studying the history of Social Security.

Social Security is one of the federal government's great success stories. It lifts millions of people out of poverty every year and provides some measure of economic security for millions more. It helps the elderly and the disabled. It's also the nation's largest child assistance program.[9] Because it delivers such important benefits to so many, it's not surprising that Social Security consistently enjoys high levels of support from the American people.[10]

So why is this popular and successful program under constant political attack? To answer that, we need to go back to 1935, the year it was born.

Roosevelt had ambitious plans that went well beyond Social Security as we know it today. He saw his 1935 bill as the first part of a much broader system that would provide financial security for everyone in this country, protecting Americans "from the cradle to the grave."[11] When he signed the Social Security Act of 1935, Roosevelt called it "a cornerstone in a structure which is being built but is by no means complete."[12]

The name itself, Social Security, gives us a clue to what Roosevelt had in mind. In his 1944 State of the Union address, FDR defined his broader vision in terms of economic rights—including the right to what he called a "useful and remunerative job," as well as the right to an adequate income, a decent home, adequate medical care, and protection from economic hardship caused by old age, unemployment, accident, or other misfortunes.

"All of these rights," said Roosevelt, "spell *security*."

Some of those expanded programs have come to pass since FDR first laid out his goals. The Social Security Act of 1935 encouraged states to establish unemployment insurance programs. In 1965, a broader vision for health care began to take shape with the passage of Medicare for the elderly and disabled and Medicaid for lower-income people. (Disabled people under sixty-five became eligible for Medicare in 1973, further broadening its mandate.)

Roosevelt knew that Social Security would face ongoing opposition from some quarters. He was right. To his opponents, FDR was a "socialist," and Social Security was just another big-government assault on freedom. But, in trying to protect it for future generations, Roosevelt made a fundamental mistake. That mistake endangered the program and reinforced the deficit myth, with consequences that go beyond Social Security.

To reinforce the idea that Social Security was self-supporting, the Social Security Act of 1935 tied the payment of benefits to a payroll tax that was meant to show how the program would be "paid for." Working people would contribute a portion of their wages and collect benefits later. Most people believed (and still believe) that the payroll tax generates the revenue that is used to pay benefits.

The first Social Security trust fund was created soon afterward. Money that was not "needed" to pay benefits in any given year was invested in US Treasuries and placed in the trust fund for safekeeping. This reinforced the belief that payroll taxes from working people—rather than the federal government as whole—were supplying the cash that kept Social Security afloat.

Roosevelt had another reason for funding the program this way. He wanted people to see that they were paying into it so that they would feel entitled to the benefits they'd eventually receive. If you're working now, you've undoubtedly noticed the payroll tax deduction that comes out of your paycheck each month, which shows up as a FICA (Federal Insurance Contributions Act) withholding. By making this contribution visible, FDR reasoned, each of us would develop such a strong sense of entitlement that "no damn politician can ever scrap my social security program."[13]

Roosevelt did something else that made the program more politically vulnerable. In the Social Security Act Amendments of 1939, which established the trust fund, he also gave the program a board of trustees. The trustees are now expected to evaluate the program's fiscal solvency by projecting program receipts and expenditures seventy-five years into the future. The only way to do that is by making a lot of assumptions about the various things that determine how much money will be paid into Social Security and how much will be paid out in the years ahead. Among other things, the trustees have to answer questions like: How many people will be working in seventy-five years and in the years in between? How fast will the economy grow, and how much will wages increase? How long will people live, on average, as we approach the twenty-second century? How many people will become disabled? What will happen to inflation rates? How many babies will be born?

Nobody can know for sure, of course, so the board's experts make the best predictions they can. According to their 2019 report, their best guess is that the program's main trust fund will be exhausted— that is, that its balance will run down to zero—by 2035.[14] Workers will still be paying into Social Security, but the trustees expect that the amount of money being withheld from workers' paychecks will fall short of what will be required to pay full benefits. If that were to happen, federal law says that the government must cut spending accordingly. That would force a 22 percent cut in benefits.

FDR thought that his political foes would have a hard time attacking the program as long as everyone could "see" that the money to pay benefits was there. And therein lies the problem. Today, everyone can see that the money *isn't* there. The surplus withholdings that are credited to the trust funds will keep the system together for a while. Eventually, however, the fund accounts will be empty (unless something changes), and this will trigger benefits cuts—not because the government can't afford the payments but because Congress wrote a law that says that it will not pay full benefits if the balances of the trust funds ever fall below zero.

An op-ed by Marc Goldwein, senior vice president of an organization called the Committee for a Responsible Federal Budget (CRFB), deploys some of the rhetoric commonly used against Social Security. First, Goldwein claims that the program is facing a "crisis" and headed toward "catastrophe." Why? Because, he says, "under current law, we cannot promise full benefits to even the average new retiree, to say nothing about current or future workers."[15]

What Goldwein fails to mention is that Congress could change current law with a single vote and the "crisis" would disappear forever. After all, it was Congress, acting at FDR's behest, that set up Social Security this way in the first place. As MMT shows, a currency-issuing government like the US is never financially constrained. As long as the payment obligations are denominated in its own unit of account—US dollars—the federal government can always afford to support these programs. What it lacks is not the *financial ability* to pay but the *legal authority* to pay.

So why not just change the law? Perhaps because the idea has never been seriously debated. Instead of challenging the funding structure itself, defenders of Social Security have mostly sided with FDR in thinking that the best way to protect the program is to show that there are ways to shore up the trust funds so that the trustees can report that the program is fully funded over the seventy-five-year forecast horizon.[16]

But even if Social Security was considered fully funded over the next seventy-five years, it would still be vulnerable to attack from some critics. Economist Laurence Kotlikoff is notorious for urging lawmakers to use an even longer time horizon to evaluate the program's fiscal sustainability. How long? Kotlikoff wants us to think as far as humanly possible (and beyond!) by trying to predict how much money will be paid into and out of Social Security over the indefinite future. The whole exercise is truly ridiculous, but many lawmakers have taken Kotlikoff seriously, inviting him to testify in House and Senate committee hearings. Channeling his inner Buzz Lightyear, Kotlikoff tells members of Congress that Social Security's unfunded obligations—that is, its future shortfalls over an infinite time horizon—add up to $43 trillion.[17] Evaluated this way, Social Security isn't just in trouble, it's bankrupt "to infinity and beyond!"

Social Security's funding setup has led to benefit cuts before. In the early 1980s, projected shortfalls led Congress to effectively cut benefits in several ways. It delayed the annual effective date of cost-of-living increases, which slightly lowered overall benefits, and taxed benefits for high-income recipients. Most importantly, the retirement age was gradually raised from sixty-five to sixty-seven.

People don't just work longer when the retirement age is raised; their benefits are cut, too, because they receive less over the course of their retirement. Those who retire early, often because they're no longer able to work, receive less because the benefit formula reflects lower total payouts. In fact, by raising the retirement age by just two years, Congress imposed a 30 percent reduction in total benefits for people retiring earlier than sixty-five.[18] The adjustment also affects people who start collecting benefits after the official retirement age.

But Social Security's funding structure doesn't just leave it open to attack from conservative Republicans. It has led many Democrats to propose cutting one of their party's signature programs. Some reports say that President Bill Clinton tried to broker a compromise deal in 1997 with then House Speaker Newt Gingrich to cut Social Security and Medicare, but the impeachment inquiry prevented it from going forward.[19]

When he ran for president in 2000, Al Gore used the idea of a lockbox to talk about how he would protect Social Security from future cuts. At the time, the federal budget was in surplus, and Gore believed that the government should lock those surplus dollars up in the trust funds so that Social Security would be in better financial health. He repeated the idea over and over like a mantra during the first debate of the 2000 presidential election with George W. Bush.

The lockbox metaphor, however well-intentioned, was another example of misguided economic thinking. That thinking was rooted in the idea that Uncle Sam only has a limited amount of dollars to work with and that locking some of them in a trust fund would somehow make it easier for the government to afford to pay benefits in the future. Gore's lockbox metaphor backfired politically. George W. Bush mocked the use of the phrase, telling voters that Social Security's trust funds were nothing more than a "cabinet full of IOUs." A Ponzi scheme, really. As president, Bush outlined a proposal to begin privatizing Social Security. Fortunately, he was not successful.[20]

Gore's heart was in the right place, but imagine how much better it would have been if he had simply said, "Social Security is safe. No major changes are necessary. The federal government can keep every promise it has made because it can never run out of money." Unfortunately, no politician has (yet) offered those kinds of assurances to the American people.

In 2013, President Obama proposed a benefit cut of his own, using something called the chained CPI. That's a fancy term for a simple idea: increase Social Security benefits more slowly than inflation, so that their actual value gets smaller over time. As the Center for Economic and Policy Research explains: "For the average worker retiring at age 65, this would mean a cut of about $650 each year by age 75 and a cut of roughly $1,130 each year at age 85."[21]

The chained CPI would cut benefits for the oldest retirees (who tend to be the poorest retirees) by nearly 10 percent.[22] A fairer approach would be to use something like the CPI-E (the E stands for "elderly"), which gives added weight to changes in cost for things that make up a greater percentage of living expenses for older people and the disabled, including medical care and transportation.[23] Indexing to CPI-E would help struggling seniors by increasing benefits rather than cutting them.

People have also proposed raising the retirement age again, as was done in the 1980s, this time to age seventy or even higher. For every year the retirement age is increased, benefits are cut by 6 to 7 percent.[24] Raising the retirement age also worsens inequality.[25]

Sometimes, lawmakers make the case for means-testing Social Security, reducing or eliminating benefits for people with higher incomes. At first glance, this may seem reasonable. Why should the government pay Social Security benefits to people like Bill Gates or Oprah Winfrey? These folks are set for life! There are two answers. First, FDR established Social Security as a universal program. That decision helped to sustain broad public support for the program over nearly a century. Means testing would undermine support by turning it into a welfare program that provides benefits only to a subset of the population deemed "needy" of public assistance. The other problem is that means testing, like so many other changes—chained CPI, increasing the retirement age, and so on—conflates an accounting problem with a financing problem. Finding ways to leave more dollars trapped on an accounting ledger for a longer number of years will extend the program's legal authority to pay out benefits, but it does nothing to enhance the government's financial ability to pay. It's an undue burden, imposed by a previous Congress, which has made Social Security (and parts of Medicare) vulnerable to attack for decades.

One way to see how the trust-fund approach leads to confusion over program sustainability is by comparing the treatment of Social Security's trust funds (there are two of them) with the trust funds that have been established for Medicare (there are also two). Every year, the Social Security and Medicare Boards of Trustees each publish an annual report that examines the current and projected financial status of Social Security's trust funds (Old-Age and Survivors Insurance [OASI] and Disability Insurance [DI]) and Medicare's trust funds (Supplementary Medical Insurance [SMI] and Hospital Insurance [HI]). For years, a summary of the reports has concluded, "Both Social Security and Medicare face long-term financing shortfalls under currently scheduled benefits and financing."[26] Specifically, the OASI, DI, and HI trust funds are all considered to be "in crisis."

According to the 2019 report, the OASI trust fund will be exhausted in 2034, DI will run out of money in 2052, and the HI fund will be depleted by 2026. Unless something changes, these programs will cease to be authorized to pay full benefits. But there's one trust fund that isn't in trouble: SMI (aka Medicare Parts B and D). Why is this one healthy while the others are projected to run out of money? The answer is simple: SMI has the legal authority to pay full benefits if the trust funds are ever exhausted, and the others don't. "For SMI, the Trustees project that both Part B and Part D will remain adequately financed into the indefinite future because current law provides financing."[27] That keeps SMI financially secure to infinity and beyond!

It's that simple. Social Security's programs and Medicare's Hospital Insurance are considered fiscally unsustainable because the government isn't committed to making payments, while Medicare Parts B and D get a clean bill of health because Congress has granted the legal authority to make the payments no matter what else happens.

Congress could in fact change the current law so that the same language applies to the other programs. That it hasn't done so is a political choice, not an economic one. You wouldn't know that by reading most newspapers, however, or by listening to most pundits. All we hear is that Social Security is going broke.

The near-constant fearmongering is taking a toll on younger people. I teach university classes. Each year I ask my students how many of them think they'll be able to collect Social Security when they retire, and each year fewer hands go up. That's consistent with a survey by the Transamerica Institute, which found that "80 percent of millennial workers [born 1981–1996] say they're worried Social Security won't be there for them."[28]

That's terribly sad because there is absolutely no reason that Social Security can't be there for future generations. What's even more unfortunate is that these attacks on Social Security are taking place just as the nation faces a growing retirement crisis—one that makes Social Security more important than ever.

People used to talk about retirement as a three-legged stool. The three legs were supposed to be a pension from your job, personal savings, and Social Security benefits. Unfortunately, for millions of Americans, two of those legs have been sawed off. Savings have been hurt by wage stagnation for working Americans, and employers are cutting back on reliable pensions.

The *Washington Post* told the story of workers at a McDonnell Douglas plant in Tulsa who lost their jobs, and their pensions, when the company closed the plant down.[29] That wasn't an accident: when the workers sued, court documents showed that McDonnell Douglas chose to close the Tulsa plant because many employees were approaching retirement age, when they could collect a full pension.

By closing the plant, the company was able to pay them only a fraction of their full pensions. The employees won their lawsuit, but the awards (which averaged $30,000) amounted to much less than the value of their pensions. The result? Instead of enjoying retirement after a lifetime of work, many were forced to keep working. To make ends meet, one ex-employee, a seventy-nine-year-old man, went to work as a greeter at Walmart, standing on his feet eight hours a day. Another worked the midnight shift, loading trucks at the age of seventy-three. A seventy-four-year-old took a job as a crossing guard, and a seventy-six-year-old started buying and selling junk to earn extra cash for his survival.

While their situations are extreme, these employees are not alone. Corporations around the country have cut costs by reducing pension benefits. That's one of the reasons so many older Americans are in trouble. One study concluded that 40 percent of middle-class Americans will experience downward mobility in retirement—falling out of the middle class—and 8.5 million people are in danger of falling into poverty or near poverty.[30] For many of these retirees, Social Security is the only thing keeping them from becoming impoverished.

Employers have cut back dramatically on defined benefit pension plans that guarantee a fixed payment every month after retirement. Instead, many employers now offer defined-contribution plans, like 401(k)s, that create special savings accounts for retirement. In 1975, nine out of ten workers in private companies had a defined-benefit pension plan. These pensions were often the result of labor negotiations, before unions lost bargaining power. By 2005, that number had dropped to one in three.[31]

While it's better than no retirement plan at all, the money in a 401(k) plan has to last throughout a person's retirement. These plans rarely provide the level of monthly income retirees might expect from defined benefit plans. The shift has hurt lower-income workers. As a report from the Economic Policy Institute (EPI) explains, "higher-income workers (with their greater capacity to make contributions) are more likely to participate in defined-contribution plans."[32]

The same report also finds that "the shift from defined-benefit to defined-contribution plans has exacerbated racial and ethnic disparities," has posed "particular challenges" for single people and women, and has widened the gap between workers who have college degrees and those who don't.

Millions of other working Americans have no employer retirement program at all. As the EPI report concludes: "For many groups— lower-income, black, Hispanic, non-college-educated, and unmarried Americans—the typical working-age family or individual *has no savings at all* in retirement accounts, and for those that do have savings, the median balances in retirement accounts are very low" (emphasis in original).

The retirement crisis is linked to the broader crisis of wage stagnation, along with the rising cost of education, health care, and other basic needs. In this light, retirement's three-legged stool looks more and more like a pile of useless sticks.

Today's workers aren't the only ones who would suffer from Social Security cuts. Currently, Social Security lifts fifteen million older Americans and one million children out of poverty.[33] Many of them remain close to the poverty line. The average retirement benefit was $1,409.51 per month in 2018, and women typically received about 20 percent less than that. The federal poverty level for individuals that year was $12,140 per year.

We should be looking for ways to increase benefits under these circumstances, not cut them. The program will not run out of money if we do. The constraints around Social Security are political, not economic, in nature.

Other Entitlements Are Also in Danger

I've spent a lot of time talking about Social Security because its financial structure illustrates how the deficit myth leads to poor decision-making and can undermine social goals. But the arguments over Social Security's finances have also helped reinforce misguided thinking about other entitlement programs, especially the persistent belief that they're becoming increasingly unaffordable.

It's true that entitlements make up a large percentage of federal spending today, but this isn't the first time that's been true. After the Civil War, the federal government provided pensions to disabled, impoverished, and elderly Union veterans and their families. By 1910, 28 percent of all men over sixty-five and more than three hundred thousand widows were receiving federal benefits.[34] In the three decades between 1880 and 1910, the federal government spent more than one-fourth of its budget on entitlements. This early entitlement plan has had a long life. As of 2017, the daughter of one Civil War veteran was still receiving her benefits![35]

Federal entitlements grew again during the Great Depression, with the creation of Social Security and programs to address widespread unemployment and poverty. There were alarmists then, too. Senator Daniel Hastings said that Social Security "may end the progress of a great country and bring its people to the level of the average European"[36]—an ironic statement today, given Western Europe's stronger safety net.

When Medicare was created in 1965, during the postwar economic boom, the debate focused less on government spending and more on fears of socialism raised by Ronald Reagan[37] and others. Medicare was also mocked as overly generous by opponents like Republican senator and presidential candidate Barry Goldwater.[38] "Having given our pensioners their medical care in kind," said Goldwater, "why not food baskets, why not public housing accommodations, why not vacation resorts, why not a ration of cigarettes for those who smoke and of beer for those who drink?"

Goldwater's questions were rhetorical, of course. Others raised more legitimate concerns. "Will there be lines of old folks at hospital doors," a *New York Times* reporter wondered, "with no rooms to put them in, too few doctors and nurses and technicians to care for them?"[39] As it turned out, there were no lines of old folks wrapped around the hospital doors, but it's always important to think about whether our economy has the productive capacity to deliver the real benefits—such as doctors, nurses, hospital beds—needed to adequately handle the demand created by government programs.

As the fiscal debate moved rightward, Medicare's opponents increasingly shifted their objections to the program's financial affordability. A 2012 op-ed offers many of the typical arguments. "If we do not reduce the growth rate of health-care costs," an investment banker wrote, "they will consume the federal budget. We risk a debt crisis rivaling the 2008–09 crash."[40]

Gail Wilensky, a former adviser to the first President Bush, claims that Medicare "is not sustainable in its current form," adding that "aging baby-boomers," along with "any increase from the historically low spending per capita will require some combination of benefit cuts, eligibility changes, cost-sharing increases, tax increases and reductions in payments to providers."[41]

Financial columnist Philip Moeller writes: "Despite the lack of big short-term changes, both Medicare and Social Security remain on unaffordable financial paths that will, without serious reforms, soak up ever-larger shares of government spending, according to annual report cards released by the programs' trustees on Monday."[42]

Diana Furchtgott-Roth of the conservative Manhattan Institute declares flatly that "Medicare is clearly unsustainable." She concludes: "As it stands now, Medicare cannot keep its promises to future seniors. It is the job of those elected politicians who said they would tackle the deficit to offer alternatives for debate and discussion."[43]

All of these arguments are misguided because all are grounded in the deficit myth. As long as we have health providers and facilities to meet demand, Medicare will be sustainable in the only terms that matter—our nation's real productive resources.

Entitlement programs also come under attack because of something called the dependency ratio, which compares the number of people currently working with the number of people receiving benefits. For

Medicare and Social Security, the concern is expressed in terms of the age dependency ratio. An article in the *Wall Street Journal*[44] offers a typical example of this argument:

> In 1980, there were 19 US adults age 65 and over for every 100 Americans between 18 and 64. But there has been a rapid shift since then. By 2017, there were 25 Americans 65 and older for every 100 people in their working years, according to new census figures released Thursday that detail age and race for every county.

These shifts in the age dependency ratio are usually presented as alarming and unexpected. (They're neither.) They're even used to argue that the current system amounts to a betrayal of the young by older people, as when a conservative author told the *Wall Street Journal*, "the failure to face what's evident, right in front of our eyes, is a form of generational theft."[45]

By this logic, the elderly are selfishly allowing the government to provide them with benefits in limited dollars, when they should be sacrificing their own interests so that those dollars are available for future generations. As we've seen, this is exactly the wrong way to think about government spending. It leads us to making decisions that are not only harmful to older people but to everyone.

Such criticisms are often accompanied by the claim that Americans are living longer. Unfortunately, that's not true. *Some* people are living longer, but a 2018 report from the Centers for Disease Control showed overall life expectancy had declined in the United States for the third year in a row.[46] So-called deaths of despair—from drugs, alcoholism, and suicide—play a large role in these declining figures. Other factors included a rise in flu deaths and increased deaths from chronic lower respiratory disease and strokes.

The real issue surrounding life span is one of fairness. Life expectancy is closely tied to income, and the statistics on that score are shocking. A study in the *Journal of the American Medical Association* found that the wealthiest men in the United States live nearly fifteen years longer than the poorest, while wealthy women live ten years longer than their poor counterparts.[47]

Entitlement critics may get the facts wrong, but they can be very good at political rhetoric. Word choice becomes important when you're attacking popular programs. No wonder they call their efforts entitlement *reform*, rather than entitlement cutting or entitlement elimination.

Even the word itself, *entitlement*, has taken on a loaded political meaning. As *The New Yorker*'s Hendrik Hertzberg noted, policy makers originally described these programs as "earned entitlements." Over time, the phrase disappeared. Then, in the mid-1970s, writes Hertzberg, it "reappeared, minus the 'earned,' bubbling up in the works of a pair of prominent conservative academics, Robert Nisbet and Robert Nozick."[48]

It was a clever move. They dropped the word *earned*, which sounds like a good thing to most people, and emphasized the word *entitlement*—which by the 1970s had taken on negative connotations, as when we say that a spoiled or privileged person acts entitled. As writer Richard Eskow observed, the term even appeared in the *Diagnostic and Statistical Manual of Mental Disorders* (DSM) to describe a symptom of narcissistic personality disorder:[49] "Has a sense of entitlement, i.e., unreasonable expectations of especially favorable treatment or automatic compliance with his or her expectations."

Hertzberg notes that Reagan originally used neutral expressions like *social safety net* in his early speeches but soon followed Nisbet and Nozick's lead and began using the term *entitlements*. The business press soon followed his lead. The word subtly stigmatized people who participate in entitlement programs, but sometimes the stigmatization isn't so subtle. Reagan famously attacked welfare recipients with the vicious and racist welfare queen stereotype. (Most welfare recipients are white, not that it should matter.)

When Obama established his National Commission on Fiscal Responsibility and Reform (the deficit commission) and named Alan Simpson as co-chair, the other co-chair was a Democratic political operative and investment banker from North Carolina named Erskine Bowles. While Simpson took the rhetorical lead, the more low-key Bowles was able to draw on valuable relationships dating back to his days as deputy chief of staff in the Clinton White House.

Yet no one did more to campaign against entitlements than Peter G. Peterson. Peterson passed away in 2018, but his work in this area—and, more importantly, his money—survive him. Peterson's name was never well known to the general public, but the billionaire budget hawk funneled as much as $1 billion[50] into a public relations campaign whose agenda included undermining support for popular social programs.

Peterson had been CEO of Bell & Howell, Richard Nixon's secretary of commerce, and head of Lehman Brothers before making billions as the cofounder of an investment fund and hedge fund called the Blackstone Group. He funded a wide array of think tanks, conferences, and hokey PR campaigns and invested both money and time into cultivating leading lights from both political parties. His annual fiscal summits have featured both Republican and Democratic politicians (Bill Clinton was a favored speaker for years), while leading television news figures served as (presumably well-paid) hosts, emcees, and moderators.

Peterson, along with the politicians, pundits, and policy advisers he supported, spent decades trying to convince the American people that government spending, especially on entitlements, is sending the economy over a cliff. The more radical among them, like Paul Ryan, have advocated for the full privatization of Social Security. Since Social Security is running out of money, the argument goes, it's better to put all our retirement eggs in the Wall Street basket. Whether they're ignorant of how government finance works or are engaged in a more nefarious scheme to funnel more of our money to Wall Street, they

are using the deficit myth to jeopardize the financial security of millions of Americans.

When Barack Obama decided to emphasize debt reduction with
his Deficit Commission, he seemed to misread the public mood of
a country still reeling from the financial crisis. The commission did,
however, provide a platform for Peterson's ideas. In an unorthodox
arrangement, it also relied on Peterson for funding and resources. As
the *Washington Post* reported in April 2010:

> (Deficit Commission) Executive Director Bruce Reed, who is on leave
> from the Democratic Leadership Council, said the commission will
> partner with other groups to get the word out, including the Peter G.
> Peterson Foundation, which will hold a fiscal summit Wednesday fea-
> turing former president Bill Clinton. And in June, commission mem-
> bers plan to participate in a 20-city electronic town hall meeting on the
> budget organized by the nonprofit America Speaks.[51]

America Speaks received more than $4 million from the Peterson
Foundation during the same period.[52] Peterson's foundation also paid
the salaries for two of the commission's staffers.[53] (A liberal group
also contributed a staffer to the Deficit Commission, per the *Post*, but
found the group unreceptive and concluded that "the commission had
gone off the rails.")

The commission's members were unable to agree on a plan, so
the co-chairs promptly produced one of their own along Peterson-
approved lines. It met with immediate praise from Peterson[54] and was
publicized with the help of the CRFB.[55] (The CRFB is one of a large
number of groups funded by Peterson.)

The cozy relationship between Peterson's organizations and
Obama's Deficit Commission reflected Peterson's long-standing influence with the political establishment. So did his 2012 Fiscal Summit,
which was organized while the Obama administration was trying to
negotiate a "grand bargain" on the budget with House Speaker John

Boehner. Speakers that year included both Boehner and Obama Treasury secretary Tim Geithner, two principals in those negotiations, as well as Bill Clinton, Paul Ryan, and Alan Simpson.[56]

While Simpson was vilifying millions of Americans in his official role, other Republicans were making exaggerated claims about fraud in the Social Security disability program.[57] That, too, was a form of demonization. Tellingly, the Senate Republicans who asked for a count of overpayments did not ask for a tally of *underpayments*.

Contrary to what Senate Republicans suggested, the disability program is neither generous nor rife with fraud. It's extremely difficult and time consuming to qualify for Social Security disability payments and even harder to appeal a denial. The average wait time for a hearing was 535 days in 2018 and was over 700 days in many cities. By the end of that year, 801,428 people were waiting for a hearing; 8,699 people died in 2016 while waiting for a hearing they never received.[58]

The goal of such demonization is to make people ashamed for receiving their benefits and to make other people resent them for it. The injustice of these attacks was underscored for me in the early 2000s when I spoke about Social Security to an audience of union members in Wichita, Kansas. A gentleman who looked like a biker came up to me afterward and shook my hand the best he could, since he could barely raise his hand or form a grip after years of manual labor. He thanked me for my talk and said he was looking forward to his coming retirement.

That man, and other workers like him, don't deserve to be insulted for wanting to retire and collect benefits after a lifetime of hard and painful work.

Welfare recipients were the targets of harsh language from Reagan and other Republicans. But it was a Democratic president, Bill Clinton, who signed the so-called welfare reform bill of 1996. That bill aspired to help people get back to work. What it really did was force people off the assistance rolls, reducing many families to poverty. A study by the National Poverty Center[59] concluded that "the prevalence of extreme poverty rose sharply between 1996 and 2011," largely as a result of this "reform."

There's strong evidence that the premises behind welfare reform—the myth that cash assistance discourages work, for example, or encourages unwed motherhood—are false and unfair to poor people. Eduardo Porter of the *New York Times*[60] cited a study showing that, even before the 1996 welfare cuts, "some four in 10 Americans on welfare were on it for only one or two years. Only about a third were on it for five years or more." Porter also cited a 1995 study showing that, even before benefits were eliminated for nonworking mothers, "welfare payments did not increase single motherhood. And the experience over the next 20 years," he adds, "suggested that ending welfare did not reduce it."

Constant attacks haven't succeeded in undermining public support for entitlement programs, but they have undermined public confidence in their long-term financial viability. The anti-entitlement crowd loves to congratulate itself on its courage. But there's nothing brave about attacking programs for the elderly, disabled, and poor, especially when there are rich campaign donors and billionaire-funded think tanks willing to reward them for their "bravery."

How We Should Talk About Entitlements

By now, I hope you're convinced that we've been thinking and talking about entitlements all wrong. And while I've focused on the US in this chapter, this misguided thinking has also hurt a lot of people around the world. It has led to cuts in vital social programs, such as the National Health Service (NHS) in the United Kingdom and critically underfunded pensions in Japan.[61] In these and other countries, the deficit myth has deprived people of improved public services because governments are convinced that they don't have the money to sustain programs that care for their people. That doesn't just force misery on the people whose lives would otherwise be improved by these programs; it hurts all of us. Our social safety nets strengthen our social bonds with one another and help to support the economy as a whole. Just think about all the grocery cashiers, truck drivers, shopkeepers, and others whose jobs depend, at least partly, on people spending their "entitlement" benefits in communities all around the country.

That's one reason the rhetoric around these programs is so misguided. The federal government shouldn't try to manage its budget "like a family sitting around the dinner table." We don't need to tighten our belts with shared sacrifice and fiscal restraint. (Ever notice how some people use the phrase *shared sacrifice* when somebody else will be doing all the sacrificing?)

So how should we talk about entitlements? The most important thing to remember is that there are three distinct issues, and we must keep them separate whenever we talk about programs like Social Security and Medicare. Those issues are: (1) the government's financial ability to pay, (2) the legal authority to pay benefits, and (3) our economy's productive capacity to deliver real program benefits.

As we have learned, MMT emphasizes the role of the government as the issuer of the currency. For countries like the US, the UK, and Japan, the government's financial ability to pay can never be in doubt. That's good news because it means that citizens should never be forced to suffer harsh austerity on the grounds that the government lacks the ability to pay for health care or to pay benefits to retirees or the disabled. But that does not mean that there are no limits to what these governments can responsibly afford to spend. Funding ever more generous entitlement programs could push the economy beyond its real resource constraint (i.e., full employment), fueling inflation, which is harmful to all. This is a critical part of the messaging that is almost completely absent from our contemporary debates.

I'll never forget the time I heard someone with a lot of clout try to explain this to a member of Congress. It was a remarkable moment that took place on the floor of the House of Representatives. It began with a question from Paul Ryan, the now-retired Speaker of the House of Representatives. Ryan was a self-professed deficit hawk who spent much of his time in Congress trying to privatize Social Security. He repeatedly urged lawmakers to join him in turning it from a guaranteed retirement program into a system of privatized personal retirement accounts that would put Wall Street money managers in charge of workers' retirement income. For years, Ryan made speeches and appeared on television, pitching his privatization scheme like a seasoned salesman. He talked up the benefits of choice and freedom, claiming there was an urgent need to act before the current system collapses under the weight of unsustainable financial commitments.

One day in 2005, Ryan decided to promote his scheme before a special congressional witness. After laying out his position regarding the so-called financial crisis facing Social Security, Ryan asked the witness whether he agreed with that assessment. As the witness began to answer the question, Ryan's face lost all color. It wasn't the answer Ryan was looking for. It did, however, separate two of the most important issues regarding entitlements: the government's financial ability to pay and our economy's productive capacity to deliver promised real benefits.

The witness was Alan Greenspan. As many readers will know, Greenspan was chairman of the Federal Reserve from 1987 to 2006. Appointed by Reagan, Greenspan was hardly what you'd call a progressive. Teeing up a question about the need to "deal with entitlements" with the Fed chair must have seemed like a safe move. Ryan almost certainly assumed that Greenspan, a fellow libertarian, would agree that Social Security's financing was unsustainable and that moving to a system of personal retirement accounts was a good idea. So, Ryan lobbed Greenspan the following softball question, expecting him to dutifully knock it out of the park.

"Having personal retirement accounts is another way of making a future retiree's benefits more secure for their retirement," Ryan asserted, before putting his lengthy, rather tortured question to Greenspan:

> Do you believe personal retirement accounts as a component to a system of solvency does help improve solvency because when you have a personal retirement account policy, if it is accompanied with a benefit offset, with that feature in place do you believe that personal retirement accounts can help us achieve solvency for the system and make those future retiree benefits more secure?[62]

Put simply, Ryan was asking Greenspan whether he agreed that Social Security was in financial trouble and that moving to a system of private, Wall Street–managed retirement accounts would help address the crisis.

To his credit, Greenspan didn't swing at that pitch. Instead, he leaned forward into the microphone and told Ryan something that shocked him: the truth. Greenspan started by dismissing the entire premise behind Ryan's question. "I wouldn't say that the pay-as-you-go benefits are insecure," he said, "in the sense that there's nothing to prevent the federal government from creating as much money as it wants and paying it to somebody."[63]

Let that last line soak in: "There's nothing to prevent the federal government from creating as much money as it wants and paying it to somebody."

It was exactly the right response, and it undermined Ryan's entire premise about the government's *financial* ability to pay. Uncle Sam can always pay! That was Greenspan's point. Because, when it comes to the federal government's financial capacity to pay benefits, money is no object. As chairman of the Federal Reserve, Greenspan knew that the Fed would clear any payment that had been authorized by Congress, just as MMT shows. All Congress had to do was commit to funding the program, and the money would always be there.

Ironically, Greenspan never pointed any of this out when he chaired the commission that cut Social Security benefits in 1983. Back then, he accepted the premise that Social Security was facing an inescapable funding shortfall. In response, the Greenspan Commission "rebalanced" Social Security's finances by gradually raising the retirement age and increasing payroll taxes to provide "advance funding" to cover future payments. The entire motivation for these changes was rooted in the faulty belief that the only way to keep Social Security afloat was to devise a plan to generate enough tax revenue to cover promised benefits.

The truth is none of the benefit cuts or other changes recommended by the Greenspan Commission were necessary to preserve the program, and Greenspan should always have known that. But Greenspan got it right when he answered Ryan that day, and he didn't stop there. The second part of his response was even better. It zeroed in on one of the other key issues we should be talking about. The relevant question wasn't the one Ryan asked. Instead of talking about the program's finances, Greenspan told Ryan that the issue he should be thinking about was: "How do you set up a system which assures that the real assets are created which those benefits are employed to purchase?"[64]

In other words, we are an aging society. Millons of people who are currently working to produce the real goods and services that we all need to survive will be leaving the workforce and heading into retirement. As a result, programs like Social Security and Medicare will be serving more and more Americans in the years ahead. When we think about entitlements, we should be thinking about how to make sure our economy will remain productive enough to supply the material goods—health care and consumption goods—that it will take to provide for the needs of future beneficiaries.

I'm not sure Ryan fully appreciated Greenspan's point. When we talk about whether entitlements are *sustainable*, we need to think in terms of our economy's *real* productive capacity. We need to think about how the economy will absorb those dollars, not where those dollars will come from. Coming up with the money to pay benefits is the easy part. The real challenge involves managing any inflationary pressures that might arise as that money gets spent into the real economy.

No wonder Ryan was surprised. In other settings, Greenspan often spoke as if the major challenge facing Social Security was its *financial* viability. But on that day, responding while under oath in the US Capitol, Alan Greenspan told the truth, the whole truth, and nothing but the truth: Social Security will be fine as long as the government is committed to paying promised benefits.

It's not easy to find experts who are willing to speak so honestly about the fact that the so-called crisis facing Social Security is a manmade, political problem and not a financial one.

I first came to understand this in 1998, after reading an article called "Save Social Security from Its Saviors."[65] It was written by Northwestern economics professor Robert Eisner, a pioneering, respected, and truly courageous voice in the world of economics. Eisner was fearless, and he was one of the first to see through the Social Security deficit myth. He was unafraid to call out anyone, left or right, who misdiagnosed the problem.

Much like Greenspan, Eisner rejectd the idea that Social Security was becoming financially unaffordable. He wrote:

> Social Security faces no crisis now or in the future. It will not go bankrupt. It will "be there," not only for those of us now enjoying it or looking forward to it in the near future, but for the baby boomers and the "Generation Xers" following them. All this is true as long as those who would nibble away at Social Security or destroy it in the name of "privatization" do not have their political way. But they very likely will not, since the elderly—and their children—vote, and will vote sensibly as the full implications of the issue become apparent.

Eisner's article focused on the other important issue we need to keep in mind when talking about Social Security and other entitlements—that is, the self-imposed rules that constrain the government's legal authority to pay certain benefits. Like Greenspan, Eisner understood that the federal government always has the *financial ability* to pay promised benefits. It is the *legal authority* to pay benefits that is muddying the waters and making it appear that programs like Social Security are going broke. Eisner's article was a brilliant attempt to provide a clearer picture of the issues that matter (and those that don't).

While nearly every politician is obsessed with the long-range projections that show the eventual depletion of Social Security's trust funds, Eisner reminded us that the trust funds are "merely accounting entities" and that maintaining positive balances in OASI and DI doesn't actually alter the government's financial ability to pay benefits. Keeping the trust funds loaded up with enough positive spreadsheet entries maintains the *legal authority* to pay benefits, but Social Security would be perfectly viable with or without these accounting entries, as long as Congress was committed to making payments. As Eisner put it, "The accountants can just as well declare the bottom line of the funds' accounts negative as positive—and the Treasury can go on making whatever outlays are prescribed by law. The Treasury can pay out all that Social Security provides while the accountants declare the funds more and more in the red."

Wait a minute. Am I telling you that a widely respected professor of economics thought that the solution to the "crisis" facing Social Security was for Congress to simply commit to making the payments regardless of the balance in the Social Security trust funds? Well, yeah. After all, that's exactly how it already works with SMI.

You and I could never run our finances that way. But that's because we're currency users, not issuers of the currency like Uncle Sam. Eisner understood that. Unlike the rest of us, "our government and its Treasury will not, indeed cannot, go bankrupt," Eisner explained. His message was, basically, stop fretting over a projected drawdown on some ledger and just keep your promise. After all, people are legally entitled to their benefits under law.

If it's really that easy to keep Social Security running smoothly, why are Democrats and Republicans always fighting over the program's finances? Why is it that almost everyone is focused on cutting benefits or raising taxes as a way to shore up the system? Why isn't there a vocal group of experts weighing in to calm the waters the way Eisner (who died in 1998) attempted? According to Barry Anderson, the top civil servant in the White House's Office of Management and Budget (OMB), "very few if any of the academics or analysts who comment on Social Security have the guts (or perhaps the knowledge) to recognize this fundamental fact."[66]

For those who lacked either the courage or the knowledge to champion the simple solutions—just grant OASI and DI the same legal authority that's already given to SMI—Eisner offered another way forward. It was nothing more than an accounting trick, but it would prevent Social Security from ever facing cuts due to insufficient trust fund balances. With enough accounting entries, the trustees would report a healthy long-range outlook, the legal authority to pay benefits would remain intact, and the *perceived* crisis would disappear. It wasn't his preferred solution, but if adding more numbers to the ledger will make everyone sleep better, Eisner showed that there are any number of "simple, painless remedies for this accounting problem."

While Democrats often focus on ways to beef up the trust funds by increasing the payroll tax, subjecting nonwage income to payroll tax withholdings, or lifting the cap so that all wage income is subject to FICA withholdings, Eisner showed that there was a more painless solution.[67] Since the trust funds comprise almost entirely nonmarketable, interest-bearing government bonds, why not make sure those bonds pay enough interest to keep the trust fund balance as large as necessary to satisfy the accountants? If the bonds paid out 25, 50, or 100 percent interest, the trust fund balances would explode, and the whole "problem" would disappear forever. It's obviously an account-ing trick, but Eisner didn't care. He was just showing lawmakers that there was an easy way to protect the program from facing cuts due to insufficient trust fund balances. After all, he wrote, "it was not God but Congress and the Treasury that determined the interest rate to be credited on the non-negotiable Treasury notes of the fund balances." The important thing to understand is that, from Eisner's point of view, filling the trust funds with as much money as needed is both incredibly simple and entirely unnecessary.

Since Eisner's time, few economists outside the MMT community have challenged the conventional narrative along similar lines. Al-though MMT didn't exist when Eisner published his paper, his main argument was entirely compatible with the MMT viewpoint. He knew that the currency issuer could always insert the spreadsheet entries that would keep the program in good (accounting) health.

We need to talk about entitlements with the understanding that MMT provides. Ultimately, the debate should stay centered on our priorities, our values, and our real productive capacity to care for our people. MMT gives us the lens we need to have an intelligent debate.

Greenspan was concerned about the demographic changes that are leaving the US with a smaller number of workers to produce our na-tional output. The dependency ratio is a legitimate concern here, not because there won't be enough money but because we might struggle to make enough of the real goods and services that people will want and need in the coming years. Greenspan understood that it's not enough to pay monetary benefits to future retirees. The value of that money matters, too. To guard against the age-old inflation problem of "too much money chasing too few goods," we need an economy that is productive enough to supply the mix of goods and services we'll need. How do we do that?

First, we must decide what our priorities are. Polling suggests that entitlements rank high on our list of social goals. Second, we should think about how to achieve them, while at the same time making sure our economy is productive enough to meet them without causing inflation.

Take retirement. Most of us would probably agree that a system that provides financial security for retired people is a good thing. We want a society that doesn't turn its back on seniors after they move out of the labor force. Social Security and Medicare are there to help ensure that people have basic protections as they enter a phase of life that isn't oriented around employment. They exist because we want people to be able to get the medical care they need and have the security of a stable income supplement so they can afford to live a decent life.

The federal government spent $1 trillion on health programs in 2017. Three-fifths of that was spent on America's largest federal health insurance program, Medicare. The rest was spent on Medicaid, children's health, and premium subsidies for the Affordable Care Act. Another $945 billion was paid out in the form of Social Security benefits to the elderly, their dependents, and the disabled. All told, these so-called entitlement programs cost nearly $2 trillion, or roughly half of the entire federal budget.[68] Those are big numbers. But, as we've learned, that's all they are: numbers. We can afford it. But what about real resources?

Record numbers of baby boomers, born between 1946 and 1964, are leaving the workforce. Over the next eighteen years, an average of ten thousand Americans will turn sixty-five every day. Many will continue to work for a few more years, but all of them will become eligible for Medicare as soon as they turn sixty-five. By 2030, for the first time in its history, the US will have more people sixty-five and older than children under the age of eighteen.[69] Boomers will make up one-fifth of the population.

We need to be prepared. A seventy-year-old consumes more health care and less childcare than a thirty-five-year-old. That means the economy will need to produce more of some things and less of other things. And, absent a surprise increase in the size of our future labor force—like another baby boom or a new influx of immigrants—we'll have to meet those needs with a shrinking workforce.

We should start preparing now. We need to train more doctors and nurses, build more assisted-living housing, and invest in infrastructure, education, and research and development (including automation). With the right investments, we can boost our economy's long-run productive capacity and avoid the inflationary pressures that could result from increased competition over a dwindling supply of real goods and services.

MMT doesn't pretend that the government's currency-issuing power gives it the ability to do whatever it wants. Instead, we focus attention on the real limits we face, so we can find the best possible solutions. That's the way the debate should work—by making real-world decisions based on real-world resources.

The proposals to cut entitlements strike me as inhumane. Maybe you feel the same way. The elderly, the disabled, and the poor are entitled to decent lives and financial security because they're human, not because some trust fund says there's enough money to care for them. These programs, and the values they represent, should be part of the fabric of our society. But even if you disagree with me, we should have that conversation with a proper understanding of government finances.

When we look to the future and think about how best to meet our needs, we should stop asking the question, How will we pay for it?, and start asking, How will we *resource* it?

We don't live in a perfect world. Our real resources aren't infinite. If we want to do something to make our lives better—provide medical care for all, or ensure that everyone can retire with financial security, or protect every citizen from poverty—there will be times when we have to choose between these and other goals.

We need to prepare today, by investing in those things that can make us productive enough to meet our goals without causing inflation. Everything that helps us do that—including automation, better infrastructure, access to education, research and development, or improvements in public health—is a smart investment in the future.

We could afford our entitlement programs after the Civil War, we could afford them in the twentieth century, and we can afford them now. The war on entitlements is rooted in outmoded thinking about the nature of money and the real purpose of taxation. It prevents us from having a deeper debate about our priorities, the kind of society we want to live in, and the resources needed to build it.

Our big challenge isn't cost. It's making sure that our economy is producing the right output mix over the coming decades. The problem isn't a lack of bits and bytes on some electronic spreadsheet. The problem is a lack of vision. There are many ways to improve life for all of us, even in a world of limited resources, if we're smart enough to imagine them and brave enough to try.

7

The Deficits That Matter

As long as there is plenty, poverty is evil. Government belongs
wherever evil needs an adversary and there are people in distress.
—JOHN F. KENNEDY

I came to Washington in 2015 to join the staff of the Democrats on
the Senate Budget Committee.

By that point, we were well into the grinding recovery from the
Great Recession.

For decades, America has placed trust and power in a global network of financial and political elites who have profoundly failed to
address the economic concerns of most people on the planet. The economic meltdown presented a brief opportunity to rethink our priorities. President Obama had been elected in the immediate aftermath
of the crisis, with a mandate for change and solid majorities in both
chambers of Congress. But by the time I arrived, Republicans had
taken control of both the House and the Senate, and the status quo of
senseless prudence and caution around deficit spending—at least for
social programs—had returned with a vengeance.

The Democrats were in the minority, which left Republicans to
call the shots and set the agenda. That left us playing defense. As I sat
through meetings and helped prepare talking points, I imagined the

possibilities of being in the majority: focusing the agenda on the myr-iad challenges facing the American people and writing a budget that would help millions lead more secure, productive, and happier lives. But with Democrats in the minority, I had little power to do much of anything.

And in truth, it may not have mattered much. For all the rancor between the parties, everyone was pretty much on the same page when it came to how the federal government "gets" the money it spends into the economy. Democrats and Republicans alike looked at the federal budget the way they looked at their own household budget—through the lens of a currency user rather than a currency issuer. The two sides broadly agreed that the nation faced a looming fiscal crisis and simply traded barbs over the root cause of the problem: Democrats focused on tax cuts and costly wars, while Republicans blamed overspending on programs like Social Security, Medicare, and Medicaid.

Even if we'd been in power, I suspect Democrats would have bowed to the deficit myth. With Senator Sanders at the helm, the focus would have veered toward a Robin Hood approach: taxing the rich (or cut-ting defense) to pay for more generous spending elsewhere. But given the political realities, avoiding any increase in the deficit likely would have remained a top priority.

Here I was in the halls of power, the chief economist for the Dem-ocrats, where I should have been able to make the insights of MMT heard. Instead, I doubted whether my ideas could make any impact at all. I couldn't bear the thought that I had taken a leave of absence from my teaching job, moved away from my friends and family, and taken up residence in Washington, DC, only to be surrounded by peo-ple who spent most of their time worrying about the budget deficit. I spent much of my own time drowning in frustration.

Then it struck me: a deficit is merely a gap between what we have and what we need. *Merriam-Webster's Collegiate Dictionary* literally defines a deficit as a "deficiency in amount or quality" or "a lack or impairment in an ability or functional capacity." Our government's fiscal deficit wasn't cause for concern, but America faced other deficits that mattered enormously: deficits in good jobs, in access to health care, in quality infrastructure, in a clean environment, in a sustainable climate, and more. If the senators on the Budget Committee wanted to talk about deficits so much, why not talk about those deficits instead?

As luck would have it, the director of the Congressional Budget Office (CBO)—Doug Elmendorf at the time—was scheduled to make an appearance before the Senate Budget Committee. It was a routine thing, and I knew just what to expect. Elmendorf would arrive in a buttoned-up suit, wearing spectacles and carrying a copy of the CBO's latest long-term budget outlook. He would start by walking the committee through the report's major findings, calling attention to projected budget shortfalls and warning of the potential risk of a debt crisis if the government failed to get its fiscal house in order. Then, the various senators would take turns grandstanding or arguing about whether we needed to cut spending or raise taxes to fix the deficit problem. I couldn't bear the thought of sitting through such a pointless exercise. So, I hatched a plan.

My boss was the ranking member of the committee, and it was customary for him to offer prepared remarks immediately following the chairman's opening statement. The staff had been asked to draft those remarks. I decided that this was my entry point—my one chance to force an entirely new conversation. I proposed to the staff that we ignore the fiscal deficit completely and talk instead about the deficits that really matter.

Fortunately, Senator Sanders listened to and cared deeply about ordinary people. He looked at the federal budget the way I did—as a moral document and an expression of our national priorities. We both believed that, rather than a nation of rugged and atomized individualists, Americans shared an interconnected destiny; that we all rise or fall together as a people. With that spirit as our shared foundation, Bernie, his staff, and I agreed to recraft his opening remarks: instead of discussing, yet again, how to bring down projected fiscal deficits, we should speak to our other deficits—in infrastructure, jobs, education, health and so on.

It fell to Bernie himself to sell the shift in focus. And he delivered: after the hearing, a headline in *The Hill*—the industry publication for Congress—declared, "Bernie Sanders flips the script with 'deficits' plan."[1]

The deficits that we identified are the ones that affect ordinary people the most, and they had been ignored for far too long. They are what lie at the core of any decent society. Our national infrastructure is crumbling. The cost of a college education is increasingly out of reach, and forty-five million Americans are saddled with more than $1.6 trillion in student loan debt. Income and wealth inequality are near record highs; average workers have seen their real wages increase by just 3 percent since the 1970s. Nearly one in four Americans say they will never be able to afford to retire. Our health-care system is inadequate, to say the least, with eighty-seven million people uninsured or underinsured. "Flipping the script" is as necessary now as it was then.

At the most basic conceptual level, America's federal budgeting process is a complete mess, utterly unable to grapple with these compounding crises. It's a process that assumes the government is cash constrained rather than a currency issuer. By its very nature, it blinds its participants to any ultimate goal other than "balanced" fiscal budgets over the long run. It's a process designed by technocrats to shackle policy options, to elevate the needs of abstract ledger entries over the needs of flesh and blood human beings.

Now, as much as ever, we must talk about the deficits that matter. So, let's do that.

The Good Jobs Deficit

Rick Marsh had put in twenty-five years at the GM plant in Lordstown, Ohio, when it closed down in the early months of 2019. Marsh's father, an elected union official, worked there before him. It was, as the *New York Times* noted, "the only real job he ever had."

Marsh owns a house and has a daughter with cerebral palsy. He could get a job in the natural gas fields of western Pennsylvania for about half the pay he made at GM. Or he could use his seniority to try to transfer to a GM plant elsewhere. But he and his wife are loath to take either option, as it would mean giving up the extensive network of support—at school, through local services—they've painstakingly built up for their daughter.[2]

Marsh's story is a common one. America's manufacturing employment remains well below the levels seen before NAFTA, the WTO agreement, and the other corporation-friendly trade deals that kicked the legs out from under Marsh's industry and so many others. The financial crisis didn't help either. Americans lost 212,000 telecommunications jobs and 122,000 manufacturing jobs in the eight years following 2008. Jobs in the public sector—work that has generally provided living wages as well as good benefits—have also declined. State and local governments cut some 361,000 jobs, while the US Post Office shed 112,000 workers.

Yes, the economy has been slowly recovering since the 2008 collapse and continues to create jobs as of this writing. Unemployment was at 3.7 percent at the start of 2020, way down from 10 percent at the height of the Great Recession. Yet that job growth has been overwhelmingly concentrated in low-skill, low-paid occupations. That's why millions of people are trying to cobble together enough income to survive by working two or three jobs. "It is impossible to live on $8.25 an hour," Rocio Caravantes told the *Chicago Tribune* in 2014.[3] At the time, Caravantes had to work two jobs scrubbing floors and cleaning toilets in downtown Chicago's luxury hotels, just to scrape together $495 every other week. Her rent was $500 a month, she had to travel an hour on public transit every day to reach her jobs, and she couldn't afford to miss a single day of work. Caravantes told the *Tribune* that she thought if she was a good worker her pay would increase. "I was wrong," she said. Meanwhile, $8.25 an hour remains the minimum wage in Illinois. The federal minimum is a mere $7.25 an hour.

No less than 40 percent of Americans say they would be unable to come up with $400 in an emergency.[4] And make no mistake: poorly paid work is why. If there were many good jobs out there, that wouldn't be the case. If the labor market was really healthy and strong, employers would be forced to raise pay to attract workers.

We may have revived the quantity of jobs available, but the quality of the new jobs is much lower. The food service sector, for example, has added 2 million jobs, while retail added 1.2 million. According to an "Economic News Release" by the US Department of Labor, the average annual median salary for retail workers is $28,310, while food service and prep workers received even smaller income—averaging just over $22,000. In fact, nearly three-quarters of the jobs gained since the 2008 crisis have paid no more than $50,000 annually, with most paying significantly less. Inflation-adjusted wages for the average worker have grown only 3 percent from the 1970s to 2018. Workers in the bottom fifth of the income ladder have experienced a decline in wages during the same period.[5]

There's no inherent reason why jobs in retail or food service should pay worse than the jobs that came before. But these are industries where unions have never been able to achieve the foothold they gained in midcentury manufacturing; they're industries where employers hold all the leverage and use every trick in the book—from outsourcing to franchising to hiring contractors rather than full-time workers—to keep pay and benefits as low as possible.

There's also a geographic aspect to all this: the places where jobs can be found aren't the same places as before. Several decades ago, during the recovery from the 1990–1991 recession, rural markets and small towns in the heartland had some of the highest rates of job creation in the country. But that ability to bounce back has declined since: In the recovery from the Great Recession, the highest rates of employment growth happened in urban areas and big cities like LA, New York City, and Houston. Jobs in less-dense areas and rural regions grew at less than a third of their previous rate.[6] In some places, effectively, there was no recovery from 2008. The job market just pulled up stakes and left.

Cairo, Illinois, used to be a bustling town at the intersection of the Mississippi and Ohio Rivers, with shops and drive-ins and clubs. But deindustrialization and the depredations of racism—Cairo is mostly African American—hit it hard. Now the town has two Dollar Generals and a few other stores to its name. When author and photographer Chris Arnade asked Marva, a forty-seven-year-old local teacher, why she stayed, her answer was simple: "[Cairo] is my home. It is a small community, and it is my family. You can't just abandon the people you grow up with."[7] There is something cruel in how the modern US economy often forces people to choose between their roots and their livelihood. And even when people do prefer to leave, moving to a whole new city is often expensive, difficult, and risky.

Meanwhile, for Americans lucky enough to live in the places where jobs are growing, they still often have to take worse jobs than before. This phenomenon—where people are laid off from good-paying work and can only replace it with poorly paid work that isn't commenserate with their skills and education—is what economists call underemployment. For example, Lisa Casino-Schuetz, a mother of two, earned a master's degree and once had a steady job with a six-figure salary. Then the crash came, the job disappeared, and Casino-Schuetz had to take a job at a sports medical facility for $15 an hour. Then that job laid her off, and she found work doing customer service for Amazon. Then that gig vanished, too. "You ask: 'Why me? What did I do wrong?'" she said.[8]

Underemployment affects such a broad array of people that writer Andrea Thompson devoted a whole blog to collecting their stories.

That even includes Thompson's own sixty-four-year-old grandmother:
A cook all her life, Thompson's grandmother faced a string of medical
surgeries and is now an underpaid lunch lady at the local high school.
Recently diagnosed with diabetes, she can't afford the health-care
costs associated with her condition.

This rampant sense that everyone is disposable affects Americans
in all sorts of ways beyond employment and pay. In a 2018 survey
by the American Psychiatric Association, two-thirds said they worried about meeting their expenses. The only comparable concerns
were for their personal health and the safety of their families—both
of which are affected by financial status. As the APA website notes:
"Nearly three-quarters of women, nearly three-quarters of young
adults (eight to twenty-four) and nearly four in five Hispanic adults
are somewhat or extremely anxious about paying their bills." A 2017
survey in the *Journal of Community Health* showed that one in three
working Americans believe their job is not secure.[9] The experience
of that vulnerability is correlated with significantly higher chances of
obesity, poor sleep, smoking, lost work days, and worsening health in
general. Economists Susan Case and Angus Deaton studied the steep
rise in mortality among middle-aged white Americans since 1999
and found the big causes were suicide, drugs, and alcoholism—the
so-called deaths of despair. These deaths were driven primarily by
economic anxiety.

Workers in the United States aren't the only ones facing these
challenges. David N. F. Bell and David G. Blanchflower found that,
in the aftermath of the 2008 financial crisis, underemployment pulled
down wages in most of the twenty-five European countries they studied.[10] But American workers have an even harder hill to climb than
their European peers. Employment in the US compares unfavorably
to many European countries. Moreover, the US is the only developed
country that doesn't require its employers to offer paid maternity
leave—in fact, it's the only one that doesn't require employers to offer paid leave of any sort. Some American employers step up on their

own, of course. But as a group, US workers get little more than one-fourth the vacation time of workers in Britain, France, or Spain.

There has been much talk of well-paid manufacturing jobs moving abroad and the impact that's had on the American dream. In the industrial Midwest, Trump eked out a win in 2016, promising a return to greatness and a time when it was possible to hold down a manufacturing job and live a stable and rewarding life. My guess is that what people really long for are the days when a single breadwinner could support a family, buy a home, put two cars in the garage, send the kids to college, take the family on vacation once a year, and retire with a decent pension. It comes out as "bring back manufacturing jobs" or "make America great again." But it's really about replacing the lost sense of job security and what a middle-income job was once able to provide.

Ultimately, the good jobs deficit comes down to the way money flows through the economy. Right now, those flows grant good pay and great benefits to a small portion of fortunate Americans, and meager pay and little-to-no benefits to a great many more. But money, as MMT notes, is the one resource the federal government can't run out of. There's no reason every job—all the way down to retail clerk or fast food worker or janitor in a luxury Chicago hotel—can't be a good job, with dignified pay, hours, security, and benefits.

The next chapter will explain how MMT's proposal to create a federal job guarantee can set a minimum standard for all employers to meet, with a livable wage and benefits package for anyone who wants it. MMT also offers other tools to tackle the problems of paid leave and vacation time, so that our quality of life can improve and with it our health and our sense of well-being. These ideas can deliver true full employment, lifting incomes for those at the bottom and spreading the benefits up the income ladder, effectively eliminating America's deficit of good-paying jobs.

As we transform our economy for a greener, safer, and more secure future, we can give Americans the quality of work they deserve.

The Savings Deficit

The good jobs deficit has all sorts of ripple effects through American society. The loss of good jobs means the loss of good pay, which means the inability to save. There was a time when, for many Americans, it was reasonable to hope that one college degree would lead to a well-paying job that offered security, decent (if not great) health benefits, and the ability to look forward to a stable retirement. But not anymore. Instead of saving for their golden years, workers are still paying off student debt into their forties and even fifties. They wonder how they'll ever have enough to retire. If they have children, they stress about paying for an education.

Enter the savings deficit.

In fact, it's fair to say the typical working American has no money put away for retirement. One study found the median retirement account balance among people of working age in the United States is . . . zero.[11] Other surveys find the portion of Americans with nothing saved for retirement ranges from 21 percent[12] to 45 percent[13]—and the portions get even larger than that when you include people with only $5,000 to $10,000 saved. By far the biggest reasons people give for their lack of savings are insufficient incomes and the cost of paying bills. No less than 66 percent of Americans believe they'll outlive what they have saved up.[14] There are slightly more than 200 million working age Americans, and over one hundred million do not own any form of retirement assets—meaning employer-based 401(k)s, individual accounts or pensions.[15] Low-income workers are, predictably, even worse off: 51 percent have no retirement savings.[16] The workers who do have retirement accounts have an average balance of $40,000. Still, 77 percent of Americans do not have adequate retirement savings for their age and income level. In June 2019, one in five people over the age of sixty-five were working—if not actively searching for a job.[17] Another 2019 poll from the Associated Press–NORC Center for Public

Affairs Research found that nearly one-quarter of Americans expect to never retire at all.

It was not always that way. The baby boomers came of age in relatively tranquil periods of economic growth. Their parents, the so-called Greatest Generation, were born into the Great Depression, but experienced periods of progress. Social Security was created, the GI bill was enacted, unemployment insurance was expanded, and the economy experienced a decades-long boom after World War II. To be sure, that growth was unequal, African Americans were largely excluded by segregation, and some of these periods were marked by political strife. But these generations typically expected to do better than their parents. The American dream was alive and mostly well, at least for the majority. Life expectancies and other health outcomes were improving overall, and productivity gains were shared between employers and employees. Sears, which recently filed for bankruptcy, shared the fruits of its profits with workers through the 1960s and '70s. Stock options, profit-sharing programs, and pensions were enjoyed by all employees, from janitors to top executives.

As we've already covered, the doom and gloom scenarios about Social Security are merely perpetuations of the deficit myth. But a big change that really has wrecked Americans' retirement security is the disappearance of defined-benefit pension plans.

Those kinds of plans—which guaranteed a set payment of income in retirement—used to be a staple for the immediate postwar generation (not to mention comprehensive health benefits and, in many cases, a union card). But around 1980, employers began replacing pensions with defined-contribution plans, such as 401(k)s, in which how much retirement income the plan pays out depends on how much employees are able to sock away into the plan over the course of their working lives. These days working people are generally expected to save for their retirement. But they can't save when they're struggling to make ends meet.

Many families now reflect the title of Senator Elizabeth Warren's book, *The Two-Income Trap: Why Middle-Class Parents Are Going Broke*, coauthored with her daughter, Amelia Warren Tyagi. With pay stagnating, and costs for health care and college tuition rising, both parents are forced to work to cover basic costs, struggling to keep their families in the middle class, while experiencing high levels of insecurity about the future. Though published in 2004, the book's central premise—the hollowing-out of the middle class—has only become more urgent and pervasive today. Rising educational costs mean they have to pay more for their children's college tuition, while rising health-care costs and reduced employer health benefits further erode saving power. The gradual disappearance of defined-benefit pensions robs individuals and families of income security, increasing the need to save even as it became harder to put away money.

The savings deficit has persisted through the "recovery" from the Great Recession. A recent *Wall Street Journal* article outlined how families, rather than saving for the future, are going into debt through unsecured personal loans and other forms of financing in order to stay, precariously, within the middle-income range. Debt, apart from housing mortgages, spiked by $1 trillion between 2013 and 2019, the rise mainly attributed to surging levels of student debt, auto loans, and unpaid credit card balances. In one example, a young couple in West Hartford, Connecticut, both twenty-eight years old, earn $130,000 between them working tech jobs. They have $51,000 in combined student debt, $18,000 in auto loans, and $50,000 in credit card debt. Add to this a $270,000 mortgage and the costs associated with a baby daughter and day care. They no longer go out to eat and had to go deeper in debt after a car accident. A Seattle area couple, both thirty-four years old, with a combined income of $155,000, have $88,000 in student debt and $1,200 dollars per month in day-care costs for their son. They pay $1,750 in rent per month because they can't afford to buy a two-bedroom house in Seattle, where the median home value is nearly $750,000. Both these couples, even with their relatively high joint incomes, can't afford to buy a home, let alone save.[18]

Not surprisingly, the savings deficit plays out differently among racial and ethnic groups. An Economic Policy Institute study that tracked retirement savings of families headed by someone aged 32 to 65 found severe disparities among whites, African Americans, and Hispanics. While 65 percent of white families had some savings as of 2013, only 26 percent of Hispanic families and 41 percent of African American families had anything set aside for retirement. And these numbers represent decreases of 12 percent for Hispanics and 6 percent for blacks from the number of families who had savings before the Great Recession. Among those black and Hispanic families that do have savings, the amount they have pales in comparison to that of whites. The median savings for those white families who had retirement accounts was $73,000, while only $22,000 for black and Hispanic families. And again, unlike white families, the retirement accounts of blacks and Hispanics did not rebound after the Great Recession: while the median savings for whites increased $3,387 from 2007 to 2013, the median savings for Hispanics decreased $5,508, and for blacks it decreased $10,561.

Economic injustice also persists between men and women. As the Economic Policy Institute notes, "At every education level, women are paid consistently less than their male counterparts, and the average wage for a man with a college degree is higher than the average wage for a woman with an advanced degree." Women head more households than ever before, so pay discrimination makes it even harder for them to save. So, too, does the absence of affordable childcare.[19]

The savings deficit may seem insurmountable. But we saw in Chapter 6 that there's no reason to doubt Social Security's fiscal solvency, and there is every reason to call for expanded Social Security benefits and a more robust public retirement system. MMT also gives us the tools to make good-paying jobs available to all Americans again, not to mention immediately erase student debt and make childcare affordable or even free, both of which would free up thousands of dollars families could use to shore up their retirement savings or build equity through buying a home. Working families should save, but first we must build an economy in which they can.

In order to make that happen, one of the most significant problems we need to address is our health-care deficit.

The Health-Care Deficit

We are paying for the American health-care deficit with our lives. In 1970, the United States had the highest life expectancy of any developed country. By 2016, it lagged behind the average for most developed countries—that is, the members of the Organization for Economic Co-operation and Development (OECD). Today, America has the lowest life expectancy of the most advanced and long-term developed OECD members. The infant mortality rate in the US is more than twice the average for all developed countries—only Chile, Turkey, and Mexico have higher rates.

Our health-care deficit doesn't merely play out between America and the rest of the world: longevity among Americans differs significantly based on factors like socioeconomic status and race. From 1980 to 2010, life expectancy for the wealthiest American men rose dramatically, to 88.8 years. Meanwhile, for the poorest American men, it actually fell slightly over that same period, to 76.1 years. For women, this "life gap" was 91.9 years for the wealthiest and 78.3 years for the poorest.

Or we can take a specific place, like Baltimore, as an example: In the city's low-income areas, life expectancy is nearly 20 years less than it is in the wealthiest areas. In the neighborhoods like Madison-Eastend, which are 90 percent black, the life expectancy rate was less than 69 years; while in the nearby Medfield, Hampden, Woodberry, and Remington neighborhoods, which are 78 percent white, life expectancy is 76.5 years.[20]

It's not that the US doesn't spend money on health care. We actually spend a lot more than any other developed country: $10,586 per capita according to OECD data. That's more than double Canada's per capita spending of $4,974, for instance. Spain spends $3,323 and is forecasted to have the highest life expectancy rate by 2040 at 85.8 years. The US is predicted to be ranked sixty-fourth by that time, with the average individual expected to live 79.8 years. So, what's the problem? If we're spending more money, why aren't we living longer, healthier lives?

Roughly 28.5 million Americans still lack health insurance, which means far more people go without health-care coverage in the United States than in any other similar country. In fact, the number of people with health insurance here in the US is actually on the decline because of Republican efforts to weaken the Affordable Care Act. Moreover, even people with health-care coverage often strain to afford the care they need, due to the inadequacy of the coverage offered. That's called the underinsurance problem. And when you combine it with the people who are completely uninsured, the total number of Americans who don't have the health-care coverage they need reached 87 million in 2019.[21]

Plenty of people with health insurance plans—even "good" employer-based coverage—are often forced to pay thousands of dollars in deductibles and copayments out of their own pocket if they need medical care. Under the Affordable Care Act, for example, the average individual deductible was over $6,000 for a bronze plan in 2017, and the average family deductible was nearly $12,400.[22] In an unexpected medical emergency, those individuals or families would have to pay up to $6,000 or $12,400, respectively. And remember how 40 percent of Americans report they'd have trouble finding an extra $400 for a sudden crisis?[23] According to the Census Bureau, health-care-related expenses forced 8 million people into poverty in 2018.[24]

Research indicates that 137 million Americans have faced tough choices due to medical debt in just the past year.[25] Moreover, medical debt is the top reason people give for cashing out their retirement accounts—linking the health-care deficit back to the savings deficit.

Nearly one American in four reported skipping doctor visits due to costs, and nearly one in five did not purchase prescribed medications for the same reason. As a result, many people who are considered insured must go without the care they need. The typical insurance also often doesn't cover certain crucial forms of care, like vision, hearing, or mental health, and many other people go untreated because their health conditions fall into those holes in their coverage.

Another telling example of the underinsurance problem comes from the policy analyst Matt Bruenig. His findings show that if the Republicans had succeeded in annulling the Affordable Care Act in 2017, 540,000 people would have died over the next decade because they would have lacked health-care coverage—but an additional 320,000 would die from lack of coverage even if the Republican effort was unsuccessful. That's an important point: even under Obamacare, millions of Americans are still uninsured.[26]

Add it all up, and it shouldn't be surprising the US still lags well behind similar developed countries in access to care, even after passage of the Affordable Care Act in 2010. Our health-care deficit leads to lost time for work and for play, but also to the worst lost time of all: the years with friends and loved ones that so many people lose because they die too soon.

At the very least, we know from MMT that our failure to provide proper insurance and care for every American isn't because the government can't "afford" to cover the cost. By settling for a system that provides coverage through a fractured web of private insurers, employer plans, and patchwork government programs, we've created a system of bottlenecks in which hospitals, providers, drug companies, and the private insurance companies can squeeze us for every last dollar—and in which bigger profits lie in making it harder for people to access care. If we're going to set up a system where everyone has a right to the health care they need, we'll have to make sure we have the real resources to do it. Financing isn't a constraint; real resources are. Closing the health-care deficit will require more primary care doctors, nurses, dentists, surgeons, medical equipment, hospital beds, and so on. To properly care for all of our people, we'll have to build more hospitals and community health centers, invest more heavily in medical research, and create an economy where training the next generation of doctors and nurses won't bury Americans in debt—which leads us to yet another deficit in US life we need to solve.

The Education Deficit

We have disparities in education that start in preschool and persist through high school and beyond. We have a credentialing system that lures students into a seemingly endless pursuit of college degrees—and this ties into the good jobs deficit, as employers demand higher education backgrounds for more and more jobs that used to not need them.[27] The savings deficit also bleeds into the education deficit: millions of students can't afford spiraling college costs, and the giant mountain of student debt that results is a huge drag on our economy.

Our education deficit begins early, starting with preschool. Some parts of the country make efforts to provide for their citizens. New York City, for instance, is attempting to offer free preschool for some of its residents.[28] But overall, preschool is a significant strain on the typical working family, costing $9,120 annually or $760 per month. The Obama administration made some headway on this issue by proposing Preschool for All and creating a federal-state partnership to fund high-quality preschools for four-year-olds from low- to middle-income families. Through the Preschool Development Grant Birth Through Five program, over 28,000 students were served in improved preschool classroom settings in eighteen states.[29] Additionally, Obama signed the Every Student Succeeds Act (ESSA) in December 2015, a bipartisan law that brought help to high-need students and families while solidifying the previously mentioned investments in high-quality preschools.[30] Unfortunately, Trump has repeatedly talked of overturning the ESSA and cutting the Obama-era education programs.

At the K–12 level, most funding for schools comes from local property taxes. And this has created enormous disparities in the quality of education. Property tax revenue in poor rural Mississippi is obviously vastly different than in Greenwich, Connecticut, and the quality of the schools in both places reflect this. Obviously, this deprives many students of the opportunities and resources they need in traditional academic areas like reading and mathematics, leaving them dispirited. But the damage even extends to sports programs. Sports are supposed to be a great leveler, but the *New York Times* recently examined how large city schools in Iowa are routinely trounced by their richer, suburban neighbors, who have the money for better training and equipment. In the last decade, Des Moines public high school teams had a record of 0–104 against their counterparts in the wealthy suburbs. Seventeen-year-old senior Dustin Hagler commented: "It's hard when you lose. But it's not just losing. It's hard not to feel beaten down. Like the odds are stacked against you." That makes football a metaphor for American schooling writ large, and Hagler's sense of defeat likely describes how disadvantaged kids across the country feel when they simply don't have the same resources available to their peers in wealthier school districts.[31]

The deficit in our education system continues into higher education. In the 1987–1988 school year, tuition for a private four-year institution was $15,160; by 2017–2018, that cost had more than doubled. Tuition for public institutions shows similar trends: in 1987–1988 it was $3,190, but it had risen to $9, 970 in the 2017–2018 school year.[32]

Tuition hikes have led to a national student debt crisis: the average borrower from the class of 2017 now owes $28,650. For Americans attending private not-for-profit colleges and universities, the average amount of debt is $32,300; for those attending for-profit institutions,

the average is $39,950. Students of color are disproportionately af-
fected as well. On average, black students in 2012 borrowed $3,500
more dollars than white students. And this disproportionate burden
leads to increased dropout rates among African Americans across all
types of higher education: at for-profit four-year colleges and universities, 65 percent of black borrowers dropped out compared to 44 percent of white borrowers. Overall, 39 percent of black students with
debt dropped out in 2009—with two-thirds of them citing high costs
as their reason for leaving.[33]

In total, our higher education deficit has left forty-five million
Americans burdened with student debt, curtailing their freedoms and
preventing them from contributing fully to society and the economy.
The official figure for delinquent student loans reached $166 billion
in the fourth quarter of 2018, but the Federal Reserve Bank of New
York estimates that as much as a third of a trillion dollars in student
loans ($333 billion) may have gone delinquent during that time. As
Bloomberg's Alexandre Tanzi points out, that figure is close to the
$441 billion the government gave out under TARP (the Troubled As-
set Relief Program) after the 2008 financial crisis.[34]

Finally, while the average student debt for the class of 2017 was
around $30,000, many people owe much more—some well in excess
of $100,000. Students generally pay between $350 and $1,000 a month
in principal and interest, and those payments often make it difficult
for them to get out of their parents' basements, start a family, buy a
car, or even go out to eat. It's worth noting that all those activities support jobs in our economy.

We have told young people that the way to climb the income ladder
is to go to college, that this is the pathway to higher lifetime earnings
and more financial security. That is no longer true. You need a college degree just to hold on to the rungs. Without it, you risk falling
down the income ladder. The problem is that earnings aren't rising
for people with college degrees; in fact, for 60 percent of college graduates, their wages today are lower than in 2000.[35] Basically, incomes

for college graduates are stuck (in real terms) where they were two to three decades ago, while the costs of attending college have risen dramatically (in real terms). So we're breaking our backs, and piling on debt, in the belief that this is how you get ahead. In fact, this is how you run in place.

What can MMT contribute as a way out of the education deficit? Most K–12 funding comes from local property taxes, which puts it outside the federal government's control. But we'll see in more detail in the next chapter how money can be channeled through grants from federal government programs, helping make state university systems tuition free, or at least much more affordable than they are now. MMT's lens also shows how we could easily and quickly retire all student debt through the federal government, freeing up income that could be spent back into the economy, creating millions of new private sector jobs.[36] Finally, the twin trends of stagnating wages coupled with increasing education requirements in job applications both result from employers holding all the cards. With MMT's tools, we can restore full employment and tight labor markets, helping return bargaining clout to workers.

As with the other deficits we've examined, when we stop asking, How are we going to pay for it? and examine the issue through the MMT lens, solutions—and hope—are not just possible but palpable.

The Infrastructure Deficit

Have you ever sat in a car on a congested highway or waited for what seems like an eternity at one or more of our nation's airports waiting for traffic to clear enough for takeoff? Wouldn't it be nice if we had cleaner, more efficient ways to get around? The *New York Times* ran a photo essay in 2019, "Your Tales of LaGuardia Airport Hell," about one of New York City's three major airports.[37] It's now undergoing an $8 billion facelift—but will still have no rail link into the city. How many of us get stuck in traffic daily because the highways we drive on have too few lanes, and of those that do have more lanes, one or more are regularly closed to fill the potholes that keep showing up? How many of us have been late for work, class, or an appointment because mass transit systems are running late or have broken down completely? How many times have you heard your kids exclaim, "The internet is out again!" How many of you have sat in the waiting room of your hospital's emergency room for hours waiting to be seen? Or worse, been admitted to care but remained on a hospital bed in the hallway waiting for an exam room to become available?

We all know a nation's infrastructure—roads, bridges, dams, levees, schools, hospitals, railways, power grids, broadband, waste and water treatment, and so on—keeps its society and economy functioning smoothly, every bit as much as a well-educated populace. But as we also all know, America's infrastructure is no longer up to that task. That's the infrastructure deficit.

We all share in this general frustration. But sometimes, the deficit becomes too tragically apparent: when a bridge fails, trains collide, a levee collapses, or a city's drinking water becomes poisonous. That's when people bear added financial costs, are injured, or lose their lives.

Recent flooding in the Midwest makes our infrastructure deficit glaringly apparent. In the summer of 2019, waters inundated Nebraskans and led to the loss of 340 businesses and over two thousand residences. Farmers and livestock workers were hit hardest—with estimates of losses surpassing $800 million in ranching and crops. The 1927-built Spencer Dam collapsed, taking Nebraskan Kenny Angel's home and his life. Although the dam was inspected in 2018 and rated "fair," the report from the Nebraska Department of Natural Resources declared, "deficiencies exist which could lead to dam failure during rare, extreme storm events." There are other levees and dams on the brink of failure.[38] According to the 2017 Infrastructure Report Card, 15,498 dams have been declared as "high-hazard potential," which is defined as: "A dam in which failure or mis-operation is expected to result in loss of life and may also cause significant economic losses, including damages to downstream property or critical infrastructure, environmental damage, or disruption of lifeline facilities." The number of deficient high-hazard potential dams has risen to 2,170 or more.[39]

We have fallen so far behind, in fact, that the American Society of Civil Engineers (ASCE) gives a D+ grade to America's infrastructure. They estimate it will take $4.59 trillion over a ten-year period to get it up to appropriate standards. That update would earn America's infrastructure a grade of B, which the ASCE defines as, "the system or network is in good to excellent condition; some elements show signs of general deterioration that require attention. A few elements exhibit significant deficiencies. Safe and reliable, with minimal capacity issues and minimal risk." The ASCE concluded that our most serious infrastructure weaknesses include aviation, drinking water, energy, waste management, levees, roads, schools, and other forms of infrastructure critical to our health, our well-being, and our future prosperity. In other words, the Flint water crisis, which occurred in 2014, is the tip of the iceberg.[40]

For example, in New Jersey, the city of Newark's drinking water had unsafe levels of lead in August of 2019,[41] possibly a result of filters distributed in 2018 not working properly. According to the ASCE data, the state of New Jersey received a D+ grade, consistent with the United States as a whole. The ASCE found the biggest threats to the adequacy of the water systems to be age and lack of reinvestment.

Left out of recent ASCE reports is, perhaps, our most basic infrastructure need: affordable, quality housing. Lying within the infrastructure deficit is also a national housing deficit.

Researcher Peter Gowan and journalist Ryan Cooper studied the problem of housing, particularly for people who rent, and found that the situation has become even worse since 2008. They wrote:

The number of burdened renters remains substantially above its pre-crisis level. In 2007, 8 million households spent 30–50 percent of their income on rent; in 2017, that number was at 9.8 million. In 2007, 9 million households spent 50 percent or more of their income on rent; in 2017, that number was at 11 million. These burdened renters (paying 30 percent of their income or more on rent) now account for 47 percent of all renters.[42]

This shortfall in basic infrastructure is robbing poor families of safe and healthy places to live. Most families who rent spend more than the recommended 30 percent of their income on housing. Local zoning and construction laws also hold back construction of new housing supply, raising prices in the process. On top of it all, families' inability to secure affordable housing even helps drive the education deficit: the wealthier the school district your home is in, the higher quality of school your children attend.

The housing deficit that historically affected African Americans also persists. Black homeownership in today's America is nearly the same as it was during times when housing discrimination was legal. That discrimination began in the 1930s when the government designed a plan to increase housing—but primarily for middle- and lower-income whites. Segregation was further promoted when the Federal Housing Administration (FHA) was established. The FHA began redlining— refusing to insure mortgages—in and around African American neighborhoods, while simultaneously subsidizing builders who were mass-producing subdivisions, as long as none of the homes being built were sold to African Americans. This was justified by the FHA's theory that if African Americans purchased homes in these suburbs, the property values would decline, and the whites' homes they were insuring would decrease in value. Americans' racism and Americans' desire to keep their home values up combined in a self-justifying feedback loop. The Fair Housing Act was passed in 1968, to permit African Americans to buy homes in these "white" neighborhoods. But in a 2015 statistic, the black homeownership rate was 33 percent for thirty-five- to forty-four-year-olds—lower than in the 1960s when housing discrimination was legal and segregation was still promoted by FHA policy. Any effort to address our housing deficit thus must boldly address the ugly legacy of racial discrimination, which has restricted access to affordable homes and better-funded school districts.

Simply put, we can do much more than what we are doing now. Carrying a grade of D+ is disgraceful for a nation that strives for greatness. We need to retrofit businesses and homes with sustainable sources of energy; build affordable housing for all our people; repair structurally deficient bridges; blanket the nation with high-speed rail; fix our airports; shore up our levees, dams, sewage, and water systems; and more. Building this infrastructure will increase our convenience, save lives, boost the nation's long-term productivity, and increase equality of opportunity—not to mention provide many of the good-paying jobs needed to close the jobs deficit.

MMT's new lens can empower our politicians to be more proactive when it comes to channeling investment. A good example is Senator Elizabeth Warren's affordable housing plan—proposed during her campaign to win the Democratic nomination for president—to invest $500 billion over the next decade in building, rehabbing, and preserving low-income units. Again, it is never money that the federal government lacks to address needs like infrastructure and housing; real resources are the actual constraint. And there's no reason to think American is on the verge of running out of concrete, steel, wood, or metals. In fact, when it comes to housing, we actually have far more empty homes than we have homeless Americans.[43] The materials are there; we have simply failed to send the money where it needs to go. And we've allowed the money to go where it isn't needed because we remain shackled by the deficit myth.

The Climate Deficit

All the deficits we've covered so far exist among us as Americans. But just as no man is an island, neither is any one country or society, or even the whole human race. Neither America nor the global community of nations can sustain themselves without a livable planet—without clean air and water, fertile soil, stable weather, dependable temperatures, or healthy ecosystems. Which brings us to the climate deficit.

The science indicates that, to avoid the worst climate change scenarios, we need to limit global warming over this century to 1.5 degrees Celsius above preindustrial levels. Current plans, however, would only limit the temperature rise to 3 or 4 degrees Celsius above that threshold.

What happens if we fail to close the gap between where we are and where we need to be? The latest reports from the Intergovernmental Panel on Climate Change (IPCC) paint a dire picture: rising sea levels, more drastic flooding, more severe droughts, stronger storms and hurricanes, and heat waves leading to many more deaths. Many coastal cities and communities around the world could become unlivable, and significant climate pattern shifts could upend crops and freshwater supplies, leading to hundreds of millions of new climate refugees. Disease, famine, infrastructure failure, and economic crises will all become worse around the world.[44]

Just the distance between 1.5 degrees of warming and 2 degrees would have major consquences. It would expose 37 percent of all human beings to extreme heat once every five years (as opposed to 14 percent under 1.5 degrees of warming[45]); rising sea levels would put an additional ten million people in danger;[46] and overall, several hundred million additional human beings would be at some climate-related risk by 2050. If we succeed in limiting warming to 1.5 degrees, we will still witness the death of an estimated 70 percent to 90 percent of all coral reefs around the world, as oceans absorb more of the carbon dioxide in the atmosphere and become more acidic. Should the planet warm by 2 degrees or more, essentially all of the coral in the world will die off.[47]

As for 3 degrees or more of warming, around 550,000 Americans in over 300,000 homes on today's coastlines could face "chronic inundation" by 2045—meaning flooding that happens more or less every other week. By the end of the century, those numbers would rise to 4.7 million people in 2.4 million homes, which is roughly the amount you'd get if you combined all the homes in Los Angeles and Houston.[48] To take a specific example: Charleston, South Carolina, could see tidal floods increase more than tenfold, from 11 per year in 2014 to 180 per year in 2045.

In July of 2019, Alaska's summertime heat hit an all-time record of 90 degrees Fahrenheit. If business-as-usual global warming continues, that kind of record breaker will become more commonplace. By 2050, certain regions and cities in America will suffer monthlong heat waves and stretches of summer days so hot it will be dangerous to go outdoors. Rainfall and precipitation will come in greater bursts and longer absences, instead of being more evenly spread out. California, for instance, has rocketed between flooding[49] and drought-fueled wildfires[50] just in 2019, and the whiplash between heavy rains and severe stretches of no rain at all is projected to become more intense.[51] This will put even greater pressure on water supplies that are already stressed. Research indicates 96 of the 204 basins supplying the US with fresh water could fail to meet monthly demand by 2071.[52] Meanwhile, half the global population will live in water-stressed areas by 2025, the World Health Organization estimates.[53] Imagine what would happen to local industries as diverse as agriculture and ski resorts if the weather patterns they've relied on shift drastically in the coming decades? Or what US cities and states that are already facing water shortages will do when supplies dwindle even further?

Across the world, heat waves and dust storms have gotten worse, colder weather areas have shrunk, deserts have expanded, and drought has expanded to another 1 percent of land every year from 1961 to 2013. Already, agriculture in Europe is getting hammered by heat waves, and American agriculture is enduring heavy spring and summer floods. If warming continues, major farming regions across the world could simultaneously endure "multiple bread-basket failure," according to

Cynthia Rosenzweig, a senior NASA scientist and a contributing author to one of the IPCC reports.[54]

Nathan Hultman at Brookings has a useful analogy: during the last ice age, when the global temperature was between 4 and 7 degrees Celsius colder than today, the city of Chicago was under half a mile of ice—meaning a few degrees of difference globally can lead to vast changes in climate and weather and ecosystems. If we don't deviate from our current course, the global population is going to experience a 3 or 4 degree change in the opposite direction. In other words, whatever the hotter-world equivalent is of a mountain of ice atop one of America's biggest cities, we're headed for the low end of the warming range that would make that world a reality.[55]

Careless human activity is punishing ecosystems in other ways as well, and climate change will exacerbate the damage. Thanks to overfishing, ocean wildlife of all kinds is already half as abundant as it was in 1970, according to a 2015 report by the World Wide Fund for Nature and the Zoological Society of London. Unabated climate change will kill still more, as ocean temperatures and acidity rise.[56] We also face a potential mass die-off in world insect populations, which are falling by 2.5 percent per year according to a 2019 analysis. A third of species are endangered, and 40 percent are in decline.[57] The main culprit is the clear-cutting and pesticide use involved in human agriculture—which itself links back to climate change through land use—but rising temperatures in various regions are also speeding along the deaths of insect species that can't adapt quickly enough. You can imagine the consequences for global biodiversity, farming, industry, and food supplies if sea life and insect life continue to collapse.

When burned, the fossil fuels that release carbon dioxide also release particulate matter (i.e., soot), ozone, and other pollutants, which kill significant numbers of people by exacerbating cardiovascular disease and other health effects. Particulate matter alone causes up to 30,000 premature deaths per year, as of a 2014 estimate.[58] Limiting emissions to 1.5 degrees of warming instead of 2 degrees would also prevent pollution from prematurely killing 150 million people world-wide by 2100, particularly in major urban areas of Asia and Africa.[59]

Finally, national and global inequality will put some people more directly in climate change's crosshairs. In the last two decades, 4.2 billion people have already suffered from weather-related disasters, and those in developing and low-income countries are the hardest hit. "Sadly, the people at greater risk from climate hazards are the poor, the vulnerable and the marginalized who, in many cases, have been excluded from socioeconomic progress," as former United Nations secretary-general Ban Ki-moon noted. Here in America, low-income African Americans endured the most hardships and losses when Hurricane Katrina hit New Orleans in 2005, and they had the hardest time recovering.[60]

Of course, global warming may not destroy human civilization. But the most likely business-as-usual scenarios do suggest global poverty reduction could be set back decades, which intrinsically means hundreds of millions of additional deaths.[61] But then, that's assuming the consensus of the IPCC reports isn't significantly underestimating the danger.[62] These are only the most *likely* scenarios; we may be underestimating the cascade effects and feedback loops, meaning there's a small but real chance that business as usual will lead to far more catastrophic results.

"We're already at 1 degree warming and seeing some significant impacts," Hultman wrote, summing up the IPCC's conclusions. "1.5 degrees is going to have more severe impacts; 2 degrees has more; and we probably don't want to test what happens above 2 degrees—although our current momentum appears to have us on a trajectory for about a 3 degrees or more world."

To hit the 1.5 degree target, the world will need to cut its fossil fuel use in half by 2030 and eliminate all fossil fuel consumption by 2050.[63] Stated bluntly, this will require a total overhaul of US and global civilization. The way we practice agriculture and use land, the way we generate energy, the way we design our cities and transit—all will require extensive changes. We will need to drastically increase the efficiency with which our homes, buildings, factories, transportation systems, and everything else use energy, which will require a sweeping deployment of the latest technologies, both here in America and abroad. On top of that, we'll have to completely revamp our national infrastructure to improve climate resilience and to electrify all forms of energy use, from cars to home heating to heavy industry. We'll also need a massive build-out of solar, wind, storage, and other investments, so that all of our electricity comes from renewables—done as fast as possible.[64]

The United States also bears special responsibility in this regard: we're the world's second-largest producer of greenhouse gas emissions—at 15 percent to China's 25 percent—while America's *per-person* emissions are more than double China's.

This sweeping renewal of American society is possible. The IPCC and other scientists conclude both the changes needed here in the US and globally can be accomplished more or less with technology already available. Again, if we realize the limit is real resources, not money or the "burden" of the national deficit, we can see that closing the climate deficit is possible if we act fast. Furthermore, all the work needed to close the climate deficit will help close the good jobs deficit, and efforts to shore up our communities and cities against the ravages of climate change would be part and parcel of closing the infrastructure deficit.

The Mercator Research Institute on Global Commons and Climate Change (MCC) runs a carbon clock, counting down the days until humanity has emitted all the greenhouse gases it can afford and still stay under 2 degrees of warming.[65] It's similar to the US National Debt Clock mounted in New York City, displaying the historical record of prior deficit spending.[66] But unlike the National Debt Clock, the MCC's carbon clock is tracking a deficit that actually matters.

As of this writing, and at current rates of emission, we have a little less than twenty-six years to solve our climate deficit.

The Democracy Deficit

You might think there couldn't possibly be any deficit more conse-
quential than the fate of the global climate that sustains human civilization. But there's one more gap in American life that, while not
necessarily greater in scope, cuts even deeper because this deficit is the
reason for all our other deficits. It's why we perpetually fail to generate
enough good jobs; why so many of us go without adequate health care
or education; why we've pushed our planetary ecology to the brink of
collapse, all seemingly without care. It's the deficit between the few
and the many; between the powerful and the powerless; between those
with voice and those without. It's our democracy deficit.

As much as democracy rests on rights and values and constitutions,
the democracy deficit begins, once more, with resources—with who
has money and wealth and influence and leverage and who does not.

Remember that MMT says the government deficit is always someone else's surplus. And in the US in recent decades, as the government
deficit has increased, dollars have flowed disproportionately into the
pockets of the wealthy, creating vast distances between them and the
rest of America. Such economic inequality is hardly new to America,
but in recent years, it's risen to heights not seen since the Gilded Age
and the robber barons.

Consider the Gini coefficient, a measure of income inequality that
economists often rely on. A Gini coefficient of zero would mean a perfectly egalitarian economy, while a coefficient of one means that one
person literally gets all the income generated. No country experiences
either extreme. But the World Economic Forum reports that, among
the advanced and long-term developed countries, none has a higher
Gini coefficient than the United States. And our rapidly expanding
disparities show no signs of abatement.[67]

Yet many might ask, what's the problem? The US economy seems
to be doing well by any number of other measures. Isn't inequality just
the way of the world? Isn't it a natural outgrowth of the dynamism and

creative power in our land of opportunity? Doesn't the lure of princely sums spur people to heights of creativity and achievement, benefiting us all in the process? In short, does inequality really matter?

Yes, it does. The economic realm is not separable from the social realm and the political realm. Income and wealth are both measures of the political power and social clout human beings possess—if the first is unequally distributed, the second is unequally distributed as well.

Income provides people material essentials, but decent pay and decent hours also give people time and stability to participate in family and community. A well-known fact in social science is that social capital—a technical term for communal bonds like member- ship in clubs, attending church, being married, interacting with one's neighbors—also increases noticeably with wealth and income. Re- search shows that overworked Americans are more likely to feel iso- lated and alienated as human beings.[68]

While the share of income going to the top 1 percent has doubled since 1980, the share going to the bottom 50 percent has fallen from more than 20 percent to just 13 percent. President Trump may boast of boom times, but the reality is that half of all Americans live pay- check to paycheck, while forty million live in poverty. One child in five lives in poverty.[69] Poverty, with its unending psychological stress, its food insecurity, and its exposure to pollution and lead and disease, does enormous damage to human beings of all ages—but especially to children, whose mental and physical development is permanently im- pacted, leaving them trapped in cycles of suffering that are very diffi- cult to escape.[70] Simply put, poverty strips people of the opportunities to flourish and to participate in the American dream.

Wealth is just as fundamental to questions of power and democ- racy as income. If you have significant ownership stakes in a company, for instance, you get to decide how it invests, whether it outsources, and whether it creates low-wage employment or quality jobs with good wages and benefits. If you own real estate in a neighborhood, you have immense power over whether people in that neighborhood can afford housing and their utility bills—not to mention sway over the course of the neighborhood's economic development. (Who does, and does not, own property—and thus who gets to decide what happens to the property—is really the heart of the gentrification problem, for instance.) People with great wealth essentially get to decide the fate of their fellow citizens' livelihoods. As of 2016, the wealthiest 10 percent of US households commanded more than 70 percent of all wealth in the country. Meanwhile, the top 1 percent controlled almost 40 percent[71]—a larger share than they've posted at any point since 1929, just before the Great Depression.

When they become extreme, inequalities in wealth and income begin to widen inequalities in the political realm. The rich and powerful can attend high-dollar fundraisers, maxing out political contributions that give them access and influence over the political process. Meanwhile, millions disengage, convinced that their voices (and their votes) don't even matter. More than 80 percent of Americans who make more than $150,000 a year voted in the 2012 election, but just 47 percent of those making less than $10,000 cast a ballot. This trend extends back through 2010 and 2008 as well.[72] About half of eligible voters did not participate in the 2016 election. Milwaukee, Wisconsin, for example, saw the worst turnout in sixteen years, and the falloff in voter participation from 2012 to 2016 was much more severe in the city's poorest neighborhoods. When the New York Times asked Cedric Flemming—a local barber scraping by and struggling with expensive health premiums—why so many didn't vote in the 2016 election, his response was blunt: "Milwaukee is tired. Both of them were terrible. They never do anything for us anyway."[73]

Drive around many major cities and you'll see struggling neighborhoods with people barely scraping by, rundown buildings, an absence of grocery stores, and so on. Travel a short distance and you might enter a neighborhood with multimillion-dollar homes or swanky apartments with uniformed doormen, its inhabitants living a completely different kind of life. Homeless people line the streets of New York,

San Francisco, and LA, on blocks where the bars and restaurants roar with money. Professional athletes sign multimillion-dollar contracts; every tweak and twinge in their bodies is instantly attended to by top specialists, while millions of Americans cannot afford even basic health insurance. CEOs who have failed miserably in their jobs are given multimillion-dollar severance packages, while ordinary people are left picking up the pieces of the economy these CEOs have destroyed.

Rural America, too, has been heavily impacted by our economic inequities. While oil companies, Walmart, Amazon, college football coaches, and televangelists have prospered, small towns have been gutted. Shuttered storefronts, unemployment, impoverished school districts, and drugs have become part of a tragic story of today's small towns and inner cities. A recent article in *The Nation* profiled rural America's "hidden homeless"—people like Holly Phelps, an ex-convict and single mother who landed in Marion, Illinois, with her two daughters. Phelps worked at a laundromat but couldn't afford a place to live. Her mother, an alcoholic, lived over an hour away. "I had no healthy place to go. I didn't know whether I was coming or going. I was keeping my stuff in a shed . . . and no one understood what I was going through," she says. Because she wasn't sleeping on the streets, or in a shelter, she was not considered homeless—even though her family had no secure place to sleep every night.[74]

After the 2016 election, Anthony Rice, an African American man living in Youngstown, Ohio, told journalist and photographer Chris Arnade that "most in this neighborhood" sat out the election: "We didn't have a dog in this fight." Rice said he voted for Clinton, but he "don't mind Trump." Nor did Trump's win surprise him: "Obama promised a lot and only a little came of it. Maybe New York City got delivered promises. This street here is still filled with homes falling down."[75]

"Nobody helps us out here. We get thrown in jail," another older gentleman in Bakersfield, California, told Arnade. "People we have in office are criminals and protect their big friends who are also criminals. We out on the streets, voters, we suffer."[76]

Americans who don't make a lot simply don't feel that their stories and struggles register with the policy makers and politicians in government or that participation in US democracy is even worth bothering with. And they may well be right: a striking political science paper in 2014 found that, while there's a fair amount of overlap between the political preferences of everyday Americans and the political preferences of rich elites, when the two sets of interests diverge, it's almost invariably the rich whose desires are served by the political system.[77] Functionally, the participation of most Americans in our democracy often seems irrelevant—which raises the question of whether meaningful democracy is even possible in a country with such vast economic inequities.

Democrats often complain that the problem with the wealthiest Americans is that they're not "paying their fair share of taxes." And taxes are definitely part of the story. But they're far from the whole story. MMT does not take the Robin Hood approach of taxing the rich to give to the poor. As we've seen, our federal taxes don't pay for anything, including raising anyone's standard of living. At the same time, the myth that Uncle Sam's deficit is cause for concern helps drive our very real democracy deficit: if our elected leaders believe they must either go begging to the rich before they can spend money on the public good—or that they must fight the rich for that same money—then of course the foibles and ticks and quixotic political desires of our richest citizens will become the primary obsession of our government.

But taxes are important in other ways. As the *World Inequality Report* notes, "the income-inequality trajectory observed in the United States" is partially explained by "a tax system that grew less progressive."[78] Taxes can be used to curb astronomical accumulations of wealth. That's important precisely because the wealthy use their money to amass power and influence over the political process: they've rigged the tax code in their favor; they've rewritten labor laws, trade agreements, rules governing patents and protections, and much more. They've remade public policy to serve their economic interests. This is *why* so many of our companies pay out enormous piles of cash to shareholders and upper management, smaller sums to the well-educated upper class, and a pittance to everyone else. It's why Silicon Valley has gleaming skyscrapers in downtown San Francisco, but working-class communities in Flint, Michigan, don't have access to water that isn't poisonous. It's why our welfare state and health-care system and retirement system are all in shambles, and why we're staring down the barrel of an unaddressed climate crisis. The profits and power wealthy elites can find in *not* addressing these problems are just so much greater than the profits and power to be found in addressing them.

During the widely shared economic boom just after World War II, when US inequality was at its lowest ebb, there were no fewer than *twenty-four* tax brackets. The top bracket, which applied to all individual or household income over roughly $1,900,000 (in 2013 dollars), was *91* percent.[79] The point of these tax rates wasn't to fund government spending, of course; it was to put a cap on the amount of money any one person or family could extract from the shared and interdependent economic activity of all Americans. Strengthening the progressivity of our tax code is a critical part of what is needed to reverse the decades-long trends in income and wealth inequality.

But taxing the rich isn't enough. These extraordinary concentrations of wealth and income threaten to tear society apart. To restore a more balanced distribution of wealth and income, we need policies to prevent a tiny handful of people at the very top from taking so much more than their fair share in the first place. As former labor secretary Robert Reich has written, we need a slate of policies aimed at predistribution at least as much as we need conventional taxation and redistribution.[80] We must thoroughly reform our labor laws to strengthen unions and do away with the capricious leverage employers wield over employees through things like mandatory arbitration and noncompete agreements. We can also remake licensing and intellectual property law, to cut down oligarchs' and corporations' use of those laws to stifle competition and siphon money from the rest of us. And we must drive workers' wages and benefits and bargaining power back up, by making it easier for workers to collectively bargain and by sustaining the kind of tight labor markets we saw during World War II—through things like a job guarantee and public investment and better macroeconomic policy.

Until we do so, the democracy deficit will leave us with "an education system in which you can buy admissions; a political system in which you can buy Congress; a justice system in which you can buy your way out of jail" and, "a health care system in which you can buy care others can't."[81]

Beyond the democracy deficit, there are practical economic consequences to America's yawning inequality chasm. Imagine if rising inequality continued unabated until only a tiny handful of people— literally—did have it all. The economy would collapse as there wouldn't be enough people with income to keep our businesses afloat. Companies would go under, and eventually only a few people would be employed building yachts for the wealthy, working as their groundskeepers or flying them around in their private jets. A 2015 study by the IMF already found that "an increase in the income share of the bottom 20% (the poor) is associated with higher GDP growth," while "GDP growth actually declines" when "the income share of the top 20% (the rich) increases."[82] If you increase the income of poor people, they generally consume more, spending that money right back into the economy. Conversely, we see that more income to the rich results in more stock-market purchases and savings, rather than the money flowing back into the economy. So much for trickle down!

For a quarter century after World War II, Americans' real hourly wages rose in tandem with increases in worker productivity.[83] This was reflected in widely shared prosperity, and an underlying sense that hard work and personal integrity were rewarded and that you could get ahead. Then the so-called Reagan revolution of 1980 inaugurated an era of unbridled greed—lowering taxes for the wealthy, cutting regulations on corporations, and accelerating war on workers' rights to organize and earn a livable wage. Particularly after 1980, a yawning gap has opened up between productivity and wages. Productivity continues on its steady upward trend, but wages do not—they grow modestly if at all. If the hourly pay rate had followed the same growth trend as productivity from 1973 to 2014, there would have been no rise in income inequality during that period.[84]

Where has all that increased productivity gone? It was skimmed off at the top. Back in 1950, the average S&P 500 CEO made 20 times as much as the average worker. By 2017, the average CEO at an S&P 500 corporation was making 361 times as much as the average worker.[85] Since 1980, the global 1 percent has captured twice as much growth as the bottom 50 percent.[86] Twenty-five people have as much wealth as 56 percent of the country's population.[87] Just three people—Bill Gates, Jeff Bezos, and Warren Buffett—own more wealth than the bottom half of Americans, some 160 million people.

Workers certainly created new wealth over the last four decades, but they did not get to share in it because the democracy deficit can be found *within* American companies as well. Many of our firms are now feudal economic fiefdoms, in which a small group of wealthy owners give orders to—and extract value from—the labor of vast numbers of everyday Americans.

By helping us see government spending in a new light, MMT gives us many more options when we think about how we might address economic inequality and the democracy deficit—not just by taxing the rich, but by investing in the kinds of programs that will actually raise the standard of living for low- and middle-income Americans. Democracy means that we all have a voice, that we all have a say, and that we all matter. We need a politics that recognizes that and restores the fundamental equation in a democratic society: one person, one vote. And we must restore it in the economic realm as much as the political realm because the two are ultimately inseparable.

The Constitution places the power of the purse in the hands of Congress, our elected representatives. But in practice, the fiscal deficit myth has prevented Congress from using that power to fix the real deficits hobbling our economy. By shifting the discussion of budgeting from its focus on debt and deficits to one that focuses on the deficits that matter, MMT gives us the power to imagine a new politics and a new economy, moving us from a narrative of scarcity to one of opportunity.

8

Building an
Economy for the People

I t was summer 2010 when Warren Mosler (whom we first met in
Chapter 1) traveled to Kansas City, Missouri, to join me for a meeting with Congressman Emanuel Cleaver. Cleaver was a United Methodist pastor and the first African American mayor of Kansas City. In
2004, he was elected to represent Missouri's fifth congressional district, a western-central part of the state that included the University of
Missouri–Kansas City (UMKC), where I had been teaching. Cleaver
agreed to meet with us as a favor to a mutual friend, a local politician
who happened to be working on a PhD at my university.[1] I'll never
forget that meeting.

The Great Recession (2007–2009) was technically over, but the
economy was still in shambles. Almost 10 percent of the labor force
was without work, and the African American youth (age sixteen to
nineteen) unemployment rate was nearly 50 percent. As Mosler and I
saw it, the $787 billion stimulus package, passed by Congress in Feb-
ruary 2009, hadn't done nearly enough to end the foreclosure crisis
and put millions of people back to work. Mosler believed that Congress
could essentially fix things in three easy steps.[2] First, he wanted a federally funded job guarantee to make sure that every unemployed worker
could immediately transition back into paid employment. Second, he

called for a payroll tax holiday that would have temporarily reduced the withholding for Social Security payroll taxes from 6.2 percent to zero. This would have been tantamount to a 6.2 percent pay raise for about 150 million Americans. For self-employed workers who pay both the employer and employee side of the withholding, it would have meant a 12.4 percent increase in take-home pay. At a time when consumer spending was weak, it would have improved the bottom line for millions of companies as well. Finally, Mosler recognized the profound strain the Great Recession had on state and local government budgets. To help these *currency-using* governments weather the sharp decline in tax revenues, he proposed $500 billion in aid, distributed on a per-capita basis to all fifty states, the District of Columbia, and US island territories. That would have protected tens of thousands of teachers, firefighters, police, and other public sector workers, whose jobs were on the line as state revenues dried up.

When we walked into the congressman's West 31st Street office, the fiscal deficit stood at $1.4 trillion. Lawmakers were in full panic mode. The Congressional Budget Office (CBO) had just published its *Long-Term Budget Outlook*, opening the report with the following sentence: "Recently, the federal government has been recording the largest budget deficits, as a share of the economy, since the end of World War II."[3] If nothing was done to stem the tide of red ink, the report continued, "higher debt would increase the probability of a fiscal crisis in which investors would lose confidence in the government's ability to manage its budget, and the government would be forced to pay much more to borrow money."[4] To address the *perceived* fiscal crisis, President Obama created a bipartisan commission and tasked it with finding ways to substantially reduce the deficit. Mosler and I were there to encourage Cleaver to embrace a set of policies that would *increase* the deficit, at least temporarily.

The congressman greeted us and invited us to sit. He smiled warmly, as he settled into his plush executive chair behind an impressive wooden desk. Mosler began by explaining that he wasn't worried about the CBO report or the federal government's ability to sustain fiscal deficits, however large they might become. The issuer of the currency could never run out of money, as President Obama had once claimed. What was needed, Mosler explained, was an ambitious mix of well-targeted tax cuts and additional spending to restore growth and usher in a new era of prosperity. Cleaver wasn't buying it. America was broke. Where was Congress going to find the money to carry out Mosler's proposals? The deficit was already sky high, and everyone in Congress was looking for ways to raise revenue and cut spending. I could tell he felt like the victim of some bad practical joke.

I watched as he squirmed uncomfortably in that oversized chair. The whole conversation ran much like the chapters of this book. Point-by-point, Mosler took Cleaver through a yawning narrative that began with the government imposing a tax in order to provision itself and ended with an explanation about why, contrary to popular belief, Social Security wasn't "going broke." I could tell that it was an excruciating experience for Cleaver. His body language said it all. For nearly forty-five minutes, he shifted anxiously in that big chair. He interrupted only once or twice and only to have Mosler respond that he had missed an essential part of the argument. He winced, as if experiencing physical pain, as Mosler explained that the purpose of collecting taxes is to regulate inflation, that we never need to retire the national debt, and that we should think of exports as real costs and imports as real benefits. I knew exactly how Cleaver was feeling, because I had had the same emotional response when I first encountered Mosler in the mid-1990s. I had also experienced what came next.

With only a few minutes remaining in our hourlong scheduled meeting, it happened. The Copernican moment. I recognized it immediately. Mosler's words had clicked. It was the breakthrough we had hoped for. For the first time, the congressman was seeing the world through an MMT lens, and things had just come into focus. From that moment, his entire demeanor changed. His eyes widened. His posture became confident. And then he leaned forward, clasped his hands, looked Warren in the eye, and softly said, "*I can't say that.*"

I've thought back on that conversation at least a hundred times. What was he afraid of? Why should a more realistic story about money, taxes, and debt be so unspeakable? There's a passage in the Bible (John 8:32) where Jesus finishes a speech at the temple by telling his listeners, "The truth will set you free." Reverend Cleaver had probably preached that verse to his own congregation at St. James United Methodist Church. But with us, on that summer day, while millions of Americans struggled to find work or fend off foreclosure on their homes, he decided that the truth could not be spoken. At least not by him.

Congressman Cleaver is a man of faith. But he's also a man of reason, working in a political arena that is thoroughly saturated by deficit myths. He might have been persuaded by Mosler's message, but he was not going to become a messenger.[5] It was just too risky. That's because there is only one acceptable way to talk about money, taxes, and the national debt, especially in and around Washington, DC. Taxes raise revenue for Uncle Sam, and it's taxpayer money that funds our government. Borrowing drives the nation into debt, which burdens our kids and grandkids. You can safely utter any of these phrases, and you will come across as a serious intellectual. But stray from the conventional wisdom, and you'll be sidelined by an inner circle of self-proclaimed budget wonks, lawmakers, and congressional staffers who, wittingly or unwittingly, spread the deficit myth. Preaching the virtues of fiscal restraint is always a safe play. Challenging these articles of faith is heretical. Cleaver understood that.

MMT is not a religion, and it's not looking for disciples to follow some screed. What it offers is a realistic description of how a modern fiat currency works, along with some prescriptive ideas about how to transform that understanding into better public policy. By helping us to see more clearly what the obstacles are (e.g., inflation) and aren't (e.g., running out of money), MMT opens the door to a new way of thinking about how we could run our economy. In almost all cases, it shows us that we have allowed myths and misunderstandings about money, debt, and taxes to hold us back. By tearing down these myths, MMT shows us that it's possible to build a stronger and more secure future for ourselves, our global partners, and future generations. So, how do we get there?

I believe that Congressman Cleaver is a good person. He wants what's best for his district and his country. After our meeting, he realized that Congress had the power to do much more, even if the CBO and the beltway pundits were preaching gloom and doom over the budget outlook. But he's just one person. And while his status as an elected member of Congress may appear to give him more power than the rest of us, he felt powerless in that moment. His hands were tied by the deficit myth's stranglehold on our public discourse. For that to change, the public's understanding of the economy has to change. No member of Congress is going to bring about that change. We are. It's like my former boss, Bernie Sanders, always says, "Change never comes from the top down. It always comes from the bottom up." If we're going to take advantage of the policy space that MMT opens up, it's going to be because enough of us—readers like you—help to shift the public debate in a new direction. Through the MMT lens, we can see an alternative and more hopeful set of possibilities. It's our future. It's our economy. And it's our monetary system. We can make it work for us.

The Descriptive Side of MMT

Even though we're talking about how to act on the insights of MMT, I don't want you to think of MMT as something that every government needs to adopt or implement. MMT does not come with a prepackaged set of policies to be rolled out across the global landscape. It is, first and foremost, a *description* of how a modern fiat currency works.

With an improved understanding of the monetary system comes the ability to distinguish artificial barriers from legitimate constraints. The descriptive side of MMT is about helping us break free of the myths and misunderstandings that have been holding us back. Getting an accurate picture of how the monetary system works is a necessary first step toward building an economy that works for all people. Reaching that better world will require moving beyond the descriptive side of MMT to its *prescriptive*, policy-making side. That necessarily means asking what role we want our public institutions—for example, Congress and the Federal Reserve—to play in supporting a policy agenda that advances our collective interests.

The descriptive aspect is like a doctor's diagnostic tool kit. Before medical interns can prescribe a course of treatment to an ailing patient, they must first establish a working knowledge of how the body functions. That means learning about the circulatory system, the digestive system, the nervous system, and so on. Only after interns have demonstrated competence in their understanding of how the human body works do we allow them to become doctors and write prescriptions for patients. The problem we have today is that economic policy is often prescribed by people who, despite holding advanced degrees in economics, possess no real understanding of how our monetary system works. By offering a better descriptive framework, MMT helps us to see a wider array of policy treatments that could make our economy stronger and healthier.

An MMT view of the monetary system changes the way we think about what it means for currency-issuing nations to "live within their means." It asks us to think in terms of real resource constraints—inflation—rather than perceived financial constraints. It teaches us to ask not "How will you *pay* for it?" but "How will you *resource* it?" It shows us that if we have the technological know-how and the available resources—the people, the factories, the equipment, and the raw materials—to put a man on the moon or embark on a Green New Deal to tackle climate change, then funding to carry out those missions can always be made available. Coming up with the money is the easy part. Managing the inflation risk is the critical challenge. More than any other economic approach, MMT places inflation at the center of the debate over spending limits. It also offers a more sophisticated array of techniques for managing inflationary pressures than what we have today.

What MMT describes is the reality of our post–Bretton Woods monetary system. We are no longer on a gold standard, and yet much of our political discourse is still rooted in that outmoded way of thinking. We see it every time a reporter asks a politician, Where will you find the money to do that? It's long past time we came to grips with what it means to be the issuer of a sovereign fiat currency. For the currency issuer, money is no object. Literally or figuratively. It doesn't exist in some scarce physical form—like gold—that the government needs to "find" in order to spend. It is conjured into existence from a computer keyboard each time the Federal Reserve carries out an authorized payment on behalf of the Treasury.

That might sound like a free lunch. It isn't. MMT isn't a blank check. It doesn't grant us carte blanche when it comes to funding new programs. And it's not a plot to grow the size of government. As an analytical framework, MMT is about identifying the untapped potential in our economy, what we call our fiscal space. If there are millions of people looking for paid work and our economy has the capacity to produce more goods and services without raising prices, then we have the fiscal space to bring those resources into productive employment. How we choose to utilize that fiscal space is a political matter, and here MMT can be used to defend policies that are traditionally more liberal (e.g., Medicare for all, free college, or middle-class tax cuts) or more conservative (e.g., military spending or corporate tax cuts).

The point is that we run our economy like a six-foot-tall guy who wanders around perpetually hunched over in a house with eight-foot ceilings because someone convinced him that if he tries to stand up tall he'll suffer a massive head trauma. For too many years, we've been crouching down when we could have been standing strong. Irrational fears about government debt and fiscal deficits caused policy makers in the US, Japan, the UK, and elsewhere to pivot away from fiscal stimulus toward austerity in the years following the global financial crisis. This forced immeasurable pain on tens, if not hundreds, of millions worldwide. Populist movements, on both the left and the right, found inspiration in these failings. Not everything can be fixed through a more generous application of the federal budget. Austerity has exacerbated many of our social and economic problems, but budget cuts are not the sole drivers of stagnation and rising inequality. Restoring economic security to the working class will require tackling monopoly power, sweeping reforms to our tax code, labor laws, and trade and housing policies and more.[6]

It will also require a new economic model. We must end the cruel and inefficient practice of relying on democratically unaccountable central bankers to target the "right" mix of inflation and unemployment. To build an economy for the people, responsibility for maintaining employment and income security must become the responsibility of elected representatives of the people. Congress, with its great power over the federal budget, must play an active and permanent role in stabilizing output and employment through time.

The Prescriptive Side of MMT

Recall the Peter Parker (aka Spider-Man) principle that "with great power there must also come—great responsibility." The prescriptive side of MMT moves us beyond the looking glass into a conversation about what fiscal and monetary policy might look like in an MMT-informed world. MMT urges us to demote monetary policy (at least in its current form) and elevate fiscal policy as the primary tool for macroeconomic stabilization. Congress holds the power of the purse, and we need to harness that power to build an economy that works for all of us. I know what you're thinking. Can we really trust the government with that kind of power? My answer is yes. And no.

I say yes, because we the people have already entrusted them with that power. MMT doesn't give Congress any new authority over our monetary system. We have a democratically elected government that unshackled itself from the gold standard nearly half a century ago. That decision gave Congress unfettered access to the public purse. Having the power of the purse means never having to ask, Where will we *find* the money? To cut taxes or spend trillions on endless wars, Congress just needs to find enough votes and—*voilà!*—the money will be there.

Today, the federal budget is about $4.5 trillion, roughly 20 percent of total GDP. If it wants to, Congress can write a $5 trillion budget. Or a $6 trillion budget. Or even more. It can pour trillions into education, infrastructure, health care, and housing. Any amount of spending that is authorized by Congress will take place. The Federal Reserve's elaborate network of primary dealers is there to guarantee it. That is the reality of the S(TAB) model, which decouples spending from the prior need to raise money by taxing or borrowing. The question is, How do we want the federal government to *use* its great power? How much should it spend? What should it fund? What about inflation? And taxes? Can we trust Congress to make the right choices, at the right time, making productive investments when there is fiscal space and exercising the necessary restraint as resources become scarce? Perhaps I'm too cynical, but I'd like some kind of insurance policy.

There are two parts to the federal budget. There's the *discretionary* part, over which Congress has, well, discretion to change the amount of money it puts into existing or new programs each year. Most of the money that gets spent on defense, education, environmental protection, and transportation comes from annual, discretionary budget appropriations. But there's also a *nondiscretionary* or mandatory part, which is more or less preordained by statutory criteria. Spending on programs like Social Security, Medicare, and Medicaid fall under this category. Unemployment insurance, Supplemental Nutrition Assistance Program (SNAP, formerly food stamps), interest on US Treasuries, and student loans are also binding commitments that cause spending to rise or fall independent of congressional action. When someone becomes disabled, retires, loses a job, turns sixty-five, invests in US Treasuries, or takes out a federal student loan, federal dollars are *automatically* released to meet those expenditures.

In total, mandatory spending accounts for just over 60 percent of federal expenditures, and interest accounts for nearly 10 percent.[7] That means that 70 percent of the federal budget is essentially on autopilot, leaving just 30 percent under the discretionary control of lawmakers.[8] Of course, with enough votes, Congress has the power to change any part of the budget. It could stop issuing Treasuries and leave it to the Federal Reserve to supply interest-bearing securities.[9] Over time, that would completely eliminate interest expenditure from the federal budget.[10] It could vote to pass a single-payer, Medicare-for-all bill that would substantially increase mandatory spending, while saving the rest of us trillions over time.[11] Or it could simply appropriate more discretionary funding for things like transportation and education. As we learned in the first chapter of this book, Congress is a legal body with the power to suspend or modify any self-imposed constraint (e.g., PAYGO, Byrd rule, debt ceiling, 302(a) allocation, no overdraft, etc.) that might otherwise prevent lawmakers from appropriating funding or stop the Federal Reserve from clearing authorized payments on behalf of the Treasury. Even the CBO and the House and Senate budget committees, which were themselves created through an act of Congress in 1974, could be dissolved or instructed to follow new protocols.[12] And, of course, the Federal Reserve is a creature of Congress, with a mandate that is subject to change.

Before we get to a discussion about how policy making might improve in an MMT-informed world, let me share a couple of stories that illustrate the dysfunctional way we do things today. One of the first things I remember, after becoming chief economist to the Democrats on the Senate Budget Committee, was a meeting to discuss a proposed trillion-dollar infrastructure bill. A dozen or so senior staffers gathered around a large conference table on the third floor of the Dirksen Senate Building. No one questioned the significant need for infrastructure investment. A trillion dollars, while ambitious, would have only taken a bite out of the problem. No one blanched at the price tag, but there was considerable debate about whether (and how) *to pay for it.*

Before I tell you about that debate, it's important to understand what those words mean to lawmakers and their staffers on Capitol Hill. In truth, there is only one way to pay for anything. All federal spending is carried out in exactly the same way—that is, the Federal Reserve credits the appropriate bank account(s). But in Washington speak, you "pay for" your spending by showing that you can "find" enough money to cover the cost of whatever it is you're proposing to spend. It's all a game, really, and it's rooted in the flawed mental model (TAB)S that holds back so much of our potential. To avoid adding to the deficit, lawmakers look for ways to cover the costs of their proposed spending *without borrowing.* That usually means they go looking for new tax revenue.[13]

So, back to the debate over the trillion-dollar infrastructure bill. The conversation began with staffers being asked whether we thought a so-called pay-for should be attached to the bill. It was my first week on the job, so I was relieved when another staffer spoke up first. "No," this person began, "I think we should just do it as a clean bill." A clean bill meant writing a spending bill that didn't include any language about how to pay for it. Another staffer agreed, and soon I echoed their sentiments. Our country desperately needed to make these investments. There was clearly enough fiscal space to do it, and infrastructure is one of the things that has traditionally enjoyed bipartisan support. Since the GOP was in control of the Senate, we reasoned, the bill would need at least some support from Republicans to pass. Proposing a tax increase would guarantee defeat. Not everyone agreed. Another staffer objected that the press wouldn't take the legislation seriously unless it specified exactly how it would be paid for. In the end, the bill included a proposal to raise revenue by closing a variety of tax loopholes that overwhelmingly benefit the rich. Needless to say, that legislation did not pass. Meanwhile, the latest ASCE report card shows how deferred maintenance is catching up with us, as the cost of our needed improvements has climbed to a whopping $4.59 trillion.[14]

Sometimes, lawmakers are willing to look the other way and vote to authorize spending without worrying about where the money will come from. Take defense spending, for example. Each year, Congress votes to approve a defense policy bill. In 2017, a 1,215-page bill, known as the National Defense Authorization Act, sailed through the Senate with a vote of 89–9. The White House had requested $700 billion, but the Senate authorized $737 billion, kicking in an extra $37 billion without a hint of concern about where to "find" the money.[15] They simply voted in an overwhelmingly bipartisan way to increase the Pentagon's discretionary budget.

That might seem like a double standard. As Congresswoman Alexandria Ocasio-Cortez put it, "We write unlimited blank checks for war. We just wrote a $2 trillion check for that tax, the GOP tax cut, and nobody asked those folks, 'How are they are going to pay for it?'"[16] She's right. Somehow, there's always money for war and tax cuts. For just about everything else, however, lawmakers are expected to show that they can "pay for" their spending. At least on paper.

With 535 members of Congress—100 in the Senate and 435 in the House of Representatives—this requires a steady stream of new funding options. During my time in the Senate, I learned about a one-stop shop that was created to provide lawmakers with ready access to a litany of so-called pay-fors. If a Congressman needed to find $10 billion, $50 billion, $500 billion, or more, Calvin Johnson had you covered. For years, Johnson, a professor of corporate and business law at the University of Texas Law School, helped to run something called The Shelf Project. Together, Johnson and other tax experts assembled a collection of different "proposals that can be pulled off the shelf when

Congress is ready to raise revenue."[17] Johnson's testimony before the Senate Committee on Finance in 2010 was titled "50 Ways to Raise a Trillion."[18]

In the summer, when lawmakers return home to their districts, the binders mostly sat on the shelves, gathering dust. But when Congress was in session and someone needed a plausible pay-for to attach to some piece of legislation, Johnson's phone was under constant pressure. He and his colleagues were deeply passionate about their work. They weren't cobbling together proposals simply for the sake of helping lawmakers jump through the pay-for hoop. For them, the project was about identifying ways to make the tax system fairer and more efficient. But in the eyes of many staffers, the Shelf Project was sort of like the filing cabinet in the fraternity house, where folders containing hundreds of old midterm exams are stored. In other words, it's where you go to cheat your way around obstacles like PAYGO.

Shopping for pay-fors went something like this: "Hi, I'm a staffer in Senator X's office. The senator needs $350 billion over ten years. What have you got?" Johnson might recommend a single change to some part of the tax code that would raise the full $350 billion. Or, he might pull down a few binders that, together, would generate the full amount. Six-of-one, half-a-dozen of the other. The goal was to find your boss enough revenue to play the game.

My own impression is that nearly everyone in Congress has at least some sense of just how crazy the pay-for game is. I first realized this in 2015, during vote-a-rama week.[19] Vote-a-rama is a frenzied circus during which all one hundred senators assemble to cast rapid-fire votes on a plethora of nonbinding budget amendments. One after another, senators rise to urge their colleagues to vote in support of their "deficit-neutral" amendment to expand Social Security, cut taxes, raise the minimum wage, and so on. I watched part of it from the back benches on the Senate floor, and I remembering laughing after hearing California senator Barbara Boxer tell one of her colleagues, "I voted for your amendment even though your pay-for is bullshit."

I couldn't have said it better myself. Her point was a simple one. We've got a really screwy way of drafting, evaluating, and passing legislation. We pretend that the federal government needs to budget like a household. We think of taxes as something the government needs (i.e., revenue) instead of remembering that taxes are there to subtract spending power from the rest of us so that the government's own spending doesn't push the economy beyond its full-employment limit. We hamstring legislation by demanding that the government "pay for" new spending, even when the economy could safely absorb that spending *without* the need for higher taxes. And we do all of this because we've decided that these household budgeting practices somehow serve the public interest. They don't.

What would it look like if the government overcame the deficit myths and started budgeting like a currency issuer instead of pretending that it needs to pay for its spending just like the rest of us? It might feel like the myths are there to protect us from politicians who would otherwise spend too much and tax too little. There may be some truth to that, but the bigger problem is that they also prevent us from spending enough. Somewhere between excessive spending and unwarranted fiscal restraint lies a better economy for all. To build that economy, we need a new plan. So, what's the MMT prescription? Is there a way to improve the well-being of our people without pushing things too far? Can fiscal policy really take over the economic steering wheel? What's left for monetary policy?

Transferring the economic steering wheel to the fiscal authority means relying on democratically elected members of Congress to relax the purse strings when bigger deficits can help support the economy and then tighten them back up as the economy reaches its full employment speed limit. This is the essence of the functional finance approach that was pioneered by Abba P. Lerner in the 1940s. Instead of obsessing over deficits and trying to force the budget into balance, Lerner wanted lawmakers to write a budget that would keep the economy in balance at full employment.

MMT draws inspiration from Lerner's work but with the caveat that we need to do more than simply ask Congress to take over the steering wheel from the Federal Reserve. We need to offer some guiding principles to help lawmakers wield this power responsibly and in ways that serve the broader public good. For that, we'll need to establish some new guardrails. And we'll need to provide lawmakers with clearly marked speed limits, a dashboard of indicators, and a driverless feature that takes over much of the steering. That way, fiscal policy can serve as a powerful stabilizing force even when our politics are at their most dysfunctional.

Mandatory Driverless Spending

Today, we rely on *monetary policy*—the Federal Reserve—to actively dial interest rates up and down in an effort to discover the invisible NAIRU that is supposed to keep the economy on an even keel. MMT considers *fiscal policy* a more potent stabilizer and one that can be used to target even broader measures of well-being. Lerner agreed that fiscal policy should sit in the driver's seat, but he assumed we could just hand over the keys and leave it up to Congress to figure out how to work the economic steering wheel. In contrast, MMT wants to make sure that both the car and the driver are well-equipped to steer fiscal policy in a responsible direction. Congress will always have the power to take discretionary action, but in an increasingly polarized political climate, we should make sure to include a hands-free feature as well. That way, fiscal policy will respond to changing economic conditions even when Congress is unwilling to act. Call it an insurance policy.

Having part of the budget respond automatically to changing road conditions is critically important. It's what prevented the Great Recession from developing into a second Great Depression. Yes, there was discretionary legislation—Congress passed the $787 billion American Recovery and Reinvestment Act in February 2009—but what really saved us were the fiscal adjustments that occurred automatically, without any need for legislative action. Those adjustments happened because of mechanisms known as automatic stabilizers, which are built into the government budget. They work like the shock absorbers in your car. In good driving conditions, you hardly notice them, but when the road gets bumpy, they make all the difference.

When the economy hit its rough patch in 2008, the automatic stabilizers created a "driverless" fiscal response that helped cushion the blow. Taxes fell off a cliff as millions of Americans lost their jobs and businesses struggled to stay afloat. At the same time, spending rose sharply, because millions of people automatically received support through unemployment insurance, food stamps, Medicaid, and other safety net programs. The result was a sudden spike in the fiscal deficit, one that added more than $1.4 trillion to the nongovernment bucket in 2009. The red ink that poured from Uncle Sam's bucket turned black as it entered the buckets of millions of struggling families and businesses. Looking back on this dynamic, Paul Krugman wrote:

> That's an interesting way to think about what has happened—and it also suggests a startling conclusion: namely, government deficits, mainly the result of automatic stabilizers rather than discretionary policy, are the only thing that has saved us from a second Great Depression.[20]

Although they saved us from a darker fate, the automatic stabilizers weren't strong enough to prevent an enormously painful recession. It took seven years to claw back all of the jobs that were lost in the aftermath of the financial crisis. Millions lost their homes. Some even lost their lives as a direct consequence of long-term unemployment. As the journalist Jeff Spross put it, "the damage done by long-term joblessness to mental and physical health is rivaled only by the death of a spouse."[21]

To better protect our economy—and more importantly, the people, families, and communities in it—MMT recommends the addition of a powerful new automatic stabilizer, known as a federal job guarantee. We first encountered the idea in Chapter 2, where it was shown that we could achieve genuine full employment—a job for every person who wants one. Today, the Federal Reserve defines full employment as a level of *unemployment* that leaves millions locked in a game of musical chairs, searching for jobs that don't exist. MMT resolves the problem by directly funding employment for those without work. Because it's a driverless stabilizer, the steering wheel will always turn in the right direction at the right moment in time.

To understand the economic logic behind the job guarantee, think back to Chapter 1 and the story of Warren Mosler's business cards. Remember that Mosler wanted a tidy house, clean cars, and a nicely manicured yard. To get these things, he subjected his kids to a tax, payable only in his own business cards. The purpose of the tax was to motivate the kids to perform the work that was required to earn the cards. Similarly, when a government demands that taxes and other obligations be paid in its own unique currency (e.g., the US dollar), it does so to motivate people to spend some of their time working to get the currency. It might want a standing army, a court system, public parks, hospitals, bridges, and so on. Unemployment is defined as people seeking paid work in the government's unit of account. The US dollar is basically a tax credit. MMT is the only macroeconomic approach that understands this, and the job guarantee follows directly from this understanding.

Once you realize this, it becomes clear that any currency-issuing government has the power to eliminate domestic unemployment simply by offering to hire the unemployed. If it decides not to exercise this power, then it is *choosing the unemployment rate*. As of this writing, the official unemployment rate (3.5 percent) is low by historical standards. A broader measure of unemployment, one that comes closer to capturing the true extent of the problem, is nearly twice as high (6.5 percent). This measure, known as U-6 by the Bureau of Labor Statistics, tells us that there are nearly twelve million Americans who are looking for a way to earn more currency, but the jobs just aren't there. The government could hire them all.

Currently, the federal government chooses not to do that. Instead, it provides unemployment insurance as a way to cushion incomes when people lose jobs. Assuming workers qualify to receive benefits, unemployment insurance replaces a portion of the wages that are lost when someone becomes unemployed. The average payout is $347 per week. This helps to cushion the economy when aggregate demand begins to fall off, but it doesn't protect the worker from a bout of joblessness. Some workers will find new jobs relatively quickly, while others will languish among the ranks of the unemployed for months or even years. In a deep recession, many will experience long-term unemployment, eventually seeing their benefits run out and their skills atrophy.

While unemployment insurance is considered the most important automatic stabilizer we have today, it is not the most powerful stabilizer we can design. Part of the problem is that not everyone who is unemployed is eligible to receive benefits. That's because not all work is covered by unemployment insurance. Some people are ineligible because they quit their jobs or are terminated for misconduct. Others aren't employed long enough to qualify, or they have previously exhausted their benefits. Even many eligible workers don't receive benefits. According to the government's Bureau of Labor Statistics, "In 2018, 77 percent of the unemployed people who had worked in the previous 12 months had not applied for unemployment insurance benefits since their last job. Of the unemployed who had not applied, 3 out of 5 did not apply because they did not believe they were eligible to receive benefits."[22] The federal job guarantee would eliminate the uncertainty by establishing a universal right of employment to all.[23]

Here's how it would work.[24] Instead of leaving millions jobless, the government would establish an open-ended commitment to provide job seekers with access to the currency in exchange for performing public service work. Participation would be purely voluntary. No one is required to work in the program. To ensure that we're not just

creating make-work jobs but *good jobs*, MMT economists have recommended that these jobs pay a living wage and that the work itself
should serve a useful public purpose.[25] Since the job guarantee would
establish a permanent commitment, it would become a mandatory
(as opposed to discretionary) federal spending program. As with
other mandatory programs—for example, unemployment insurance
or food stamps—spending would bounce up and down as people enter and exit the program. If the economy slips into recession, more
people will transition into public service employment, and the budget will automatically register higher spending to support those jobs.
When the economy improves and the private sector is ready to begin
hiring again, workers will move out of the program and the budget
will automatically shrink. This makes the job guarantee a powerful
new automatic stabilizer, one that would fortify the existing driverless
mechanisms in the federal budget.[26]

From a purely economic standpoint, the major advantage of the job
guarantee is its ability to stabilize employment over the business cycle.
This doesn't just benefit those who are able to quickly find new jobs.
It benefits all of us. As of 2020, the US is in the midst of the longest
expansion—that is, uninterrupted job growth—in recorded history.
But at some point, the expansion will come to an end, and the economy
will slip into recession. That's just the nature of capitalism. Businesses
hire and invest when they're swamped with customers. Eventually,
demand will slack off (often because people decide they've taken on
too much debt), and people will start to close up their wallets.[27] As
customers begin to disappear, businesses scale back production and
begin laying off some of their workers. If we had a job guarantee in
place today, it could employ many of the twelve million people who
are currently without the work they need, and it could catch many of
the people who would otherwise experience unemployment when the
next recession comes. It would weave stronger fibers into the existing
social safety net, catching people with new employment opportunities the moment they're laid off. Whether you own your own business

or work for someone else, your own economic security is probably closely tied to the income security of others.

Relying on unemployment insurance isn't good enough. Not everyone is eligible, and most states only pay benefits for thirteen to twenty-six weeks. When the Great Recession began (December 2007), there were already 1.3 million people experiencing long-term unemployment (more than twenty-seven weeks). In August 2009, after the recession had *officially ended*, 5 million Americans had been without work for twenty-seven weeks or longer. A year later, that number had climbed to 6.8 million. Even though Congress voted to extend the benefit period, those extensions eventually ended, leaving millions without jobs or income. Businesses and communities across America felt the blow. As the unemployed struggled to pay their mortgages, homes were foreclosed on, property values plummeted, revenue from property taxes shriveled up, state and local governments slashed spending on everything from education to transportation, classroom sizes swelled, infrastructure deteriorated, and on and on. The deep and protracted recession hurt us all.

Congress could have pulled the discretionary lever again, authorizing a new round of fiscal stimulus to sustain aggregate demand. But it didn't. By that point, lawmakers were more focused on fighting against the budget deficit than allowing bigger deficits to help heal the ailing economy. So, Congress left it up to the Federal Reserve to do what it could. That failure to act cost us.

Things would have been very different with a federal job guarantee in place. The economic steering wheel would have automatically turned in the direction of bigger fiscal deficits. Turning the wheel in the direction of even bigger deficits didn't feel right to Congressman Cleaver and his colleagues, but it was exactly what was needed in that moment. Think of it this way. Suppose you're driving through a winter storm and you hit an icy patch that sends your car skidding out of control. What would you do? Instinctively, most of us would probably turn the steering wheel in the opposite direction. If the car is drifting rightward, yanking the wheel to the left just *feels* like the right thing to do. It isn't. As they teach us in high school driver's ed class, we need to turn *into* the skid to regain control. It feels wrong, but it's the only way to avoid a potential collision. The job guarantee equips the federal budget with an automated feature that overrides lawmakers' natural impulse to turn against deficits when the economy is skidding off course. As the economy gets back on track, companies begin hiring workers out of the federal job guarantee program. When this happens, those workers fall off the government budget, and the steering wheel automatically adjusts to reduce the size of the deficit.

So, the job guarantee is a powerful economic stabilizer. By maintaining incomes and keeping people employed throughout the business cycle, future recessions would be shorter lasting and less severe. That's because people can enter the program as soon as the economy begins to soften and exit more quickly as hiring conditions improve, since businesses are reluctant to hire people who have been unemployed for long periods of time. Staying employed and building new skills while in the program improves the odds of getting recruited out of the program when the economic tides begin to turn.

What kind of work would these people do, and how can we make sure there are always enough jobs available for everyone who wants to work in the program? How much would workers get paid, and who would administer a federal program of this size? Has anything like this been tried before? There is an enormous MMT literature, spanning more than three decades, that answers these questions and many, many more.[28] A complete treatment is beyond the scope of this work, but we can answer the big questions and describe the broad contours of the program as laid out in a 2018 report coauthored by five MMT economists.[29]

What we envision is a highly decentralized Public Service Employment (PSE) program that offers paid work at a living wage (we recommend $15 per hour) with a basic package of benefits that include health care and paid leave. Both part-time and full-time work should be offered, and work arrangements should be sufficiently flexible to accommodate the needs of caregivers, students, older workers, those with disabilities, and so on. While funding must come from the top (federal government), the jobs themselves would largely be designed by the people living in the communities that will benefit from the work that is performed. As we explain in the report, "the goal is to create jobs in every community, and to create projects that are beneficial to every community, [so] it makes sense to involve local communities in these projects, from the proposal stage through to implementation, administration, and evaluation."

The program budget could reside within the Department of Labor (DOL), and DOL would specify the *general guidelines* for the kinds of projects that would qualify for funding. The goal is to provide jobs that fulfill unmet community needs. As we envision it, all of the jobs should be oriented around an overarching goal: building a care economy. We are an aging society in the midst of a climate crisis with more than enough useful work to be done. We can address our good jobs deficit by creating millions of good-paying jobs that care for people, communities, and our planet.

When it comes to creating those jobs, we think it's important to recognize that the federal government is not in the best position to identify the community's most pressing needs. The people who live and work in the community are. That's why we recommend that government agencies work with community partners to assess and catalogue unmet needs so that jobs can be tailored to meet the needs of the community. Together, states and municipalities would work with their community partners to create a repository of work projects. Think of it like a massively scaled-up Shelf Project, but instead of binders full of pay-fors, the shelves would be filled with a wide variety of available jobs. The idea is to keep the shelves stocked with enough potential work to allow people with different skills and interests to walk in without a job and walk out with one that fits them.[30]

By design, the demand for public service jobs will fluctuate over time. On average, we estimate that the program would harness the energies of approximately fifteen million people. Some will choose part-time work, but most participants will want full-time employment.[31] Suppose we end up with the equivalent of twelve million full-time workers in the program. Assuming two weeks of paid leave, that means these people are offering to devote *twenty-four billion hours* of time, annually, to public service employment.[32] Now imagine just *some* of the things we could accomplish by using twenty-four billion hours to address tangible deficits in our communities.

We could create a twenty-first-century Civilian Conservation Corps—one free of the racist and exclusionary practices of the New Deal era—that puts millions of people to work on projects aimed at caring for the environment.[33] The jobs bank should include a wide variety of available work, ranging from fire prevention to flood control and sustainable agriculture. We could care for blighted communities, which have suffered from decades of neglect and disinvestment, by cleaning up vacant lots, building playgrounds and community gardens, designing afterschool programs for young people, and providing apprenticeships and classes for adults. And we can care for one another, taking care of our aging population and ensuring that children have the resources they need to thrive in their infancy and early childhood.

In short, the job guarantee is the MMT solution to our chronic jobs deficit. Instead of trapping millions in unemployment as a sacrificial tribute to the "natural rate" of unemployment, the job guarantee ensures that everyone who wants to work can have a job. And as we learned in Chapter 2, it's also a better price stabilizer. It spends only enough to hire everyone who is prepared to work, and it maintains a pool of employable people from which the private sector can readily hire at a modest premium over the program wage. Further, by establishing the right to a living-wage job, the job guarantee strengthens the bargaining power of labor, reduces racial inequities, decreases poverty, and raises the floor on low-wage work while building stronger, more vibrant, more connected communities.[34]

Has anything like this ever been tried? No country has implemented a full-fledged job guarantee, but a number of countries have experimented with versions of the idea. In the 1930s, the US fought the Great Depression by directly creating millions of jobs under President Franklin D. Roosevelt's New Deal. The Public Works Administration (PWA) put hundreds of thousands of men to work building schools, hospitals, libraries, post offices, bridges, and dams. In its first six years, the Works Progress Administration created about eight million construction and conservation jobs as well as thousands of jobs for writers, actors, and musicians. The National Youth Administration created 1.5 million part-time jobs for high school kids and 600,000 for college students. As MMT proposes, the jobs were federally funded, but the programs weren't permanent, and they didn't guarantee employment to all.

Argentina's Jefes de Hogar plan wasn't a full-throated job guarantee either, but in 2001 it became "the only direct job creation program in the world specifically modelled after" the proposal developed by MMT economists.[35] The program was launched as an emergency measure following a financial crisis that plunged the economy into recession and drove the official unemployment rate above 20 percent. It was inspired by the work of Warren Mosler and designed in consultation with MMT economists—Pavlina Tcherneva, Mathew Forstater, and L. Randall Wray—as a way to quickly put people back to work. A first of its kind, the Jefes de Hogar plan created a federally funded, locally administered jobs program that guaranteed four hours of daily work in exchange for 150 pesos per month. As Tcherneva explains, jobs were limited to heads of households with "children under age eighteen, persons with disabilities, or a pregnant woman."[36] At its peak, the program employed some two million people, about 13 percent of the labor force. Almost 90 percent of the jobs were in community projects,

and 75 percent of the participants were women. Just six months after launching the program, extreme poverty had fallen by 25 percent.
Within three years, half of the participants had left the program, most
for jobs in the private sector.[37]

In 2003, at its annual Growth and Development Summit, South
Africa's government formalized a commitment to "more jobs, better jobs, [and] decent work for all."[38] The Expanded Public Works
Program (EPWP) grew out of that commitment. The program created "temporary work for the unemployed to carry out socially useful activities."[39] Two years later, the Indian government instituted the
Mahatma Gandhi National Rural Employment Guarantee Scheme
(MGNREGS). The program was motivated by a desire to narrow disparities between rural and urban incomes. To create opportunities for
those living where unemployment was high, the government guaranteed one hundred days of minimum wage work—with wages equal
for men and women—for any rural household. India's job guarantee
remains targeted (rather than universal), but it's one of the largest federally funded employment guarantee programs in the world. Studies
have shown that by establishing a uniform wage, India's rural employment guarantee helped to foster gender equality and female empowerment, while also improving transparency of the political process.[40]

So, yes, there are historical and even recent examples of governments adopting targeted forms of an employment guarantee. Most
were implemented as temporary measures to cope with a crisis of one
kind or another. MMT thinks differently about the scope and the ultimate purpose of the job guarantee. It's not an emergency measure
to be turned on during crisis and then shut down as private sector
job growth recovers. Instead, the job guarantee is a way to equip our
economy with a more powerful driverless stabilizer. Think about it
this way: you wouldn't have your mechanic remove the shock absorbers in your car just because the city fills some potholes or repaves
the roads. You want them there at all times because you know you
get a better ride with them than without. The same is true of the job

guarantee. Without it, we rely on weaker stabilizers that provide temporary income to the unemployed, while permanently trapping millions of people in an unemployed buffer stock. With the job guarantee in place, we can use full employment to absorb the inevitable bumps in the road.

Experience shows that creating jobs for the unemployed works. It brings a myriad of benefits that go well beyond simply providing income to those who would otherwise suffer bouts of unemployment. The idea is not unique to MMT. It's been called the forgotten leg of the New Deal.[41] FDR had hoped that Congress would enshrine a job guarantee in the form of an Economic Bill of Rights, but his party never carried through with a formal commitment after his death.[42] Still, the fight for guaranteed employment went on. It was an integral part of the civil rights movement, and it remains a cornerstone of international human rights law.[43] Many now also see it as a critical ingredient in the fight for greater economic equality and climate justice. It's an opportunity to transform tens of billions of hours of human idleness into a wide array of jobs that will help us build an economy that is both more resilient and more environmentally and ecologically sustainable.

Guardrails for Discretionary Fiscal Adjustments

It's important to recognize that MMT is not a panacea. It won't fix our broken politics or force lawmakers to invest public money in ways that best serve the public interest. The US Congress, along with the Japanese Diet, the British Parliament, and other governing bodies are full of public officials who should, but very often do not, budget for the people. The job guarantee offers a partial solution.[44] It forces the budget to respond automatically to changing economic conditions, and unlike tax cuts that never actually trickle down to those in need, the job guarantee targets communities that are hardest hit by unemployment. That means income goes directly into the hands of those who need it most.

But we can't just enable the driverless feature, recline the seat, and expect changes in mandatory spending to steer us forward. We need discretionary spending, too. Decisions about how much to spend on the military, climate change, education, infrastructure, health care, and other discretionary programs require serious deliberation. Today, those deliberations occur in the context of a budgeting philosophy that is antithetical to MMT. It's a philosophy that tells us that budgets are supposed to balance—at least over an arbitrary ten-year time period—and that lawmakers should demonstrate that they can pay for new programs without adding to the deficit. The coveted permission slip that allows legislation to move forward comes from a CBO that has itself fallen prey to the deficit myth. To get around the bevy of rules and conventions that constrain the budgeting process, lawmakers use budget gimmicks or simply waive the rules in an ad hoc and often partisan way. We can pretend the current process serves us well, but I think Senator Boxer had a more apt description.

What if we stopped trying to achieve a balanced budget and pursued an ambitious agenda to rebalance our economy instead? Budgeting through an MMT lens means never striving for any particular budget outcome. Bigger deficits should be just as acceptable as smaller ones or even fiscal surpluses. The number that falls out of the budget box at the end of the fiscal year isn't what's important. What matters is building a healthy economy so that all of us can thrive. Are there enough decent-paying jobs for everyone who wants to work? Do people have the health care and education they need? Can our seniors enjoy a dignified retirement? Does every child have enough food, clean drinking water, and a safe place to live? Are we doing everything we can to keep our planet habitable? In short, are we tending to the deficits that matter?

MMT teaches us that if we have the *real resources* we need—that is, if we have the building materials to fix our infrastructure, if we have people who want to become doctors, nurses, and teachers, if we can grow all the food we need—then the *money* can always be made available to accomplish our goals. That is the beauty of a sovereign currency. Contrary to Margaret Thatcher's dictum, *there is public money*, and we should not be wary of embracing it. As former Fed chair Alan Greenspan testified, "There's nothing to prevent the federal government from creating as much money as it wants and paying it to someone." His successor, Ben Bernanke, went further, describing how the government actually pays its bills: "It's not taxpayer money. We simply use the computer to mark up the size of the account." These are paradigm-shifting observations that should liberate us from the age-old question, How will we pay for it? The truth is, the federal government is already paying all of its bills using nothing more than a keyboard at the New York Federal Reserve. Taxes subtract spending power from the rest of us, but they don't pay the bills. It's high time we come to grips with what it means to live in a country where the government is the currency monopolist. No US president should ever again claim that the government has "run out of money," and no reporter should ever let such a claim go unchallenged. We all deserve to know the truth: a currency-issuing government can afford to buy whatever is for sale in its own unit of account. Uncle Sam's pockets are never empty.

The government's spending capacity is infinite, but our economy's productive capacity isn't. There are limits to what we can and should do. MMT urges us to respect our material and ecological constraints and to ask, How will we resource it? Budgeting through an MMT lens would have us replace the artificial budget constraint that tells us to live within our *financial* means with inflation constraint that tells us to live within our *biological and material* means.

As we've learned, every economy has its own internal speed limit. There is only so much demand that can be placed on our material resources—our workers, factories, machinery, and raw materials— before we push things too far. Once an economy reaches its full employment potential, *any* additional spending—whether it comes from the government, the domestic private sector (US households and businesses), or the rest of the world (foreign demand for our exports)—carries inflation risk. The good news is that because we chronically run our economy *below* its maximum speed limit, there's almost always room to rev up spending without risking an acceleration in inflation. And that's what matters.

There was a time when our political leaders had this figured out. For example, President John F. Kennedy sought the expertise of Nobel Prize–winning economist James Tobin, who served as an adviser to Kennedy's 1960 presidential campaign and then as a member of the president's Council of Economic Advisers. Tobin recalls JFK asking, "Is there any limit to the deficit? I know of course about the political limits. . . . But is there any economic limit?" When Tobin confessed that "the only limit is really inflation," the president replied, "That's right, isn't it? The deficit can be any size, the debt can be any size, provided they don't cause inflation. Everything else is just talk."[45]

Kennedy's intuition was right. It's not the size of the debt or deficit that matters. It's the strain we place on our planet and our productive resources that matters.

On May 25, 1961, President Kennedy delivered his moon-shot speech before a joint session of Congress. Before requesting a single dime to fund his ambitious space exploration program, Kennedy assured Congress:

> I believe we possess all the resources and talents necessary. But the facts of the matter are that we have never made the national decisions or marshaled the national resources required for such leadership. We have never specified long-range goals on an urgent time schedule, or managed our resources and our time so as to insure their fulfillment.[46]

Kennedy got it exactly right. Our material resources are scarce and must be managed. Time is the ultimate scarce resource. No one can squeeze more than twenty-four hours from a day. Human ingenuity is constrained by our existing technological knowledge and capabilities. Our technical capabilities and our material resources are the only things that can limit our possibilities. JFK understood that America would need to develop new technologies to carry out his ambitious space exploration program. Landing a man on the moon and bringing him safely back to earth would require substantial funding to facilitate scientific research and the development of new technologies. Kennedy told Congress that no part of his space exploration program "will be so difficult or so expensive." And then he asked Congress—and the American people—to support the mission.

> Let it be clear—and this is a judgment which the Members of the Congress must finally make—let it be clear that I am asking the Congress and the country to accept a firm commitment to a new course of action, a course which will last for many years and carry very heavy costs: 531 million dollars in fiscal '62—an estimated 7 to 9 billion dollars additional over the next five years.

Kennedy made no reference to taxes or taxpayers in his moon-shot speech. To fund the program, he simply asked "the Space Committees of the Congress, and the Appropriating Committees, that you will consider the matter carefully." He knew that Congress had the power to increase the discretionary budget to provide the billions of dollars he was requesting. Consistent with the teachings of MMT, Kennedy showed that finding the money was the easy part. The real challenge would come later, as Kennedy explained:

> This decision demands a major national commitment of scientific and technical manpower, material and facilities, and the possibility of their diversion from other important activities where they are already thinly spread. It means a degree of dedication, organization and discipline which have not always characterized our research and development efforts. It means we cannot afford undue work stoppages, inflated costs of material or talent, wasteful interagency rivalries, or a high turnover of key personnel.

To pull off his ambitious agenda, the government would need to command more of the economy's real resources—more scientists and engineers, more contractors and civil servants, more satellites and spacecraft and fuel boosters, and so on. Even though the official unemployment rate stood at 7.1 percent when JFK delivered his famous speech, Kennedy understood that the moon shot might require the government to compete for high-skilled labor and other real resources. To manage the inflation risk, his administration pressured unions and private industry, urging them to keep wage and price increases to a minimum to avoid driving inflation higher. It worked. The economy grew, unemployment fell sharply, and inflation remained below 1.5 percent for the first half of the decade.[47]

Eight years after that famous speech, NASA's Apollo 11 mission safely landed the first human beings on the moon. Today, almost all of us benefit in one way or another from that historic endeavor. As the economist Mariana Mazzucato put it, "the launching of Sputnik in 1957 by the Soviets led to an eruption of panic among US policy makers."[48] That panic gave rise to a space race that paved the way for the development of many of the things we now take for granted. The personal computer as well as "much of the technology in our smart phones today can be traced back to the Apollo program and related missions."[49]

Can You Imagine a People's Economy?

The challenges we face today are very different from those faced by Kennedy nearly sixty years ago, but no less daunting and surely far more important. To avoid global catastrophe, we need to limit the impacts of climate change and adapt to the degree of warming that is already inevitable. To do this, governments must make investments, in the US and elsewhere, that will dwarf in scale and duration the massive commitment of real resources required for the space program.

It is not melodramatic to regard our immediate future as a fight for survival, and in that sense the right analogy is World War II. In his important book, *How to Pay for the War*, John Maynard Keynes explained what Kennedy later understood: Coming up with the money is the easy part. The real challenge lies in managing your available resources—labor, equipment, technology, natural resources, and so on—so that inflation does not accelerate. If Kennedy had used the wrong lens, America might never have gone to the moon. If Keynes had used the wrong lens, the British war effort may very well have been too little too late. If our generation continues to use the wrong lens, we will not make the right investments at the scale and pace needed to avert ever-greater social and ecological crises. The good news is that we now have the right lens, and that lens is MMT.

A just and more prosperous world—one that combines ecological sustainability with full employment, human well-being, a lower degree of inequality, and excellent public services that meet the needs of all—is within reach. As we collectively expand our understanding of public money and shift our nation's focus away from an obsession with budget deficits, we can begin to build a better economy, one that works for all of our people.

Human imagination is incredibly powerful. Transformational moments in human history have come about when someone or some group of people were able to imagine a world that the rest of us couldn't see. In many cases, such as with our previous example of Copernicus, the shift was simply one of perspective, but once the shift came, it spawned an explosion of new discoveries and advances. MMT is in one sense a very simple way of seeing the big picture of modern economies from a different perspective, but we should not underestimate the profound change a simple shift in perspective can have. We have let our imaginations become far too limited, and it is holding us back. We have been too restrictive in public policy out of unwarranted fears about numbers recorded in government agency spreadsheets. We have held back progress in science, fought unnecessary wars, kept living standards too low, and lived with less beauty than we could have enjoyed.

Austerity is a failure of imagination—a failure to imagine how we can simultaneously improve living standards, invest in our nation's future, maintain a healthy economy, and manage inflation. Trade wars are a failure of imagination—a failure to imagine how we can simultaneously maintain domestic full employment, help poorer nations sustainably develop, lower our global carbon impact, and continue to enjoy the benefits from trade. Ecological exploitation is a failure of imagination—a failure to imagine how we can simultaneously improve living standards, maintain a prosperous economy, and transition human activity so that we are protecting people and the planet. MMT provides a profound tool kit for all countries to begin to reimagine how they can care for their local populations, preserve treasured cultural identities, rejuvenate unique ecosystems, redevelop sustainable and local agriculture, increase productive capacity, and encourage innovation.

Let's look at one example of how MMT can help us find alternative approaches to improving real outcomes. One of the main challenges facing policy makers in the US and around the world is the transition to sustainable and zero carbon energy production. The transition of our nation's electric infrastructure has begun, but there is a long way to go to scale up renewable energy, energy storage, and other technologies to replace fossil fuels as the primary means of electricity production. Under the old paradigm, the policy debate is often based on either government mandates or market incentives. A government mandate requiring power companies to generate cleaner forms of electricity could leave ratepayers (households and businesses) saddled with the extra costs. Though market incentives, such as giving tax credits to companies who develop more sustainable energy generation, can potentially stimulate a build-out of alternative energy sources, they can also slow adoption as developers wait for optimal economic conditions. As a result, utilities might wait longer before retiring existing coal plants.

How might an MMT-led approach introduce new options into the mix? One possibility might be that the federal government could allow electric utilities to sell to the government at book value any high-emission generator, no matter its age, in order to remove those costs from rates—a bit like the "cash for clunkers" program (Car Allowance Rebate System), which encouraged US residents to trade in their old, less-fuel-efficient vehicles for more-fuel-efficient ones, but aimed at grid decarbonization. This would free up private capital for a rapid transition to renewable energy and avoid burdening households and businesses with higher costs for electricity due to a change in public policy.

The federal government could go further and increase funding for research and development and scaled-up deployment of energy storage technologies. The US could have the lowest electricity costs in the world while rapidly transitioning to 100 percent renewable energy. That's good for businesses, the environment, and households. And it's financially affordable for the government. Note that in this example, the government is not taking over but rather is facilitating a public policy outcome via private sector energy markets. There are, of course, many other options.

What's important here is not whether this example is a good idea or not, but that we begin to imagine how the government's fiscal capacity can help deploy real resources effectively to achieve a clear public policy objective. As we rethink the kind of health care, education, urban planning, scientific research, agriculture, and housing we need for our future, how might our knowledge of MMT shift our focus to the real resources we need and suggest ways where a change in fiscal policy can help?

Can you imagine an economy where private enterprise and public investment all combine to raise living standards for everyone? Can you imagine an economy where every rural and urban community has sufficient health, education, and transportation services to meet the needs of the local population? Can you imagine an economy that can measure and continually improve human well-being, not just gross domestic product? Can you imagine an economy where human activity rejuvenates and enriches all ecosystems? Can you imagine an economy where nations trade in ways that enhance living standards and environmental conditions for all parties? Can you imagine an economy comprising of a strong middle class with service- and labor-based occupations that have good wages and benefits? Can you imagine an economy where all are ensured a carefree retirement, with all their food, housing, and health-care needs met? Can you imagine an economy where all manner of research is fully funded, with a steady stream of successful ideas commercialized or rolled out to serve the public?

In the United States, where we have an abundance of resources and labor, there is no reason we cannot embark on a policy agenda that results in provisioning our entire population with quality health services, providing each worker with adequate and appropriate advanced education and job training, upgrading our infrastructure to meet the demands of a low-carbon world, and ensuring adequate housing for everyone while redesigning our cities to be clean, beautiful, and nurturing of community spirit. We can be a global force for good, leading the way in decarbonization, providing assistance to countries with real needs, while ensuring our domestic economy thrives and no communities, from small towns to urban neighborhoods, are left behind.

With the knowledge of how we can pay for it, it's now in your hands to imagine and to help build the people's economy.

Acknowledgments

I COULD NOT have written this book without the support and emotional encouragement of my husband, Paul Kelton. He offered feedback on numerous drafts of each chapter and took on more than his share of the day-to-day responsibilities, freeing me to spend evenings and weekends holed up in front of a computer. That got me out of folding a lot of laundry and cooking my fair share of meals, but it also meant sacrificing many hours away from my children, Bradley and Katherine. I am grateful to all of them for giving me the space to work and for filling my life with so much joy.

I am also deeply indebted to my friend, Zachary Carter, a brilliant writer who steered me to the right agent—Howard Yoon—who believed in the project from the very beginning. When the time came to settle on the best publisher for the book, Howard advised me to think carefully about which of the possible editors would bring out the best in me as a writer. I chose to work with John Mahaney and have thanked my lucky stars ever since. John didn't let me write the book I originally set out to write. He rescued me from myself by flagging the overuse of technical jargon and by stripping the manuscript of charts and complex equations. "You're writing for everyone," he constantly reminded me. His mentoring made the book what it is.

Thanks also to Pete Garceau, who provided the cover art, and Patti Isaacs for turning my clumsy sketches into the beautiful illustrations that appear throughout the book. I also owe a huge debt of gratitude to Kate Mueller for her meticulous copyediting of the manuscript.

And then there are my parents, friends, and colleagues. I would not be where I am today without the love and encouragement of my parents, Jerald and Marlene Bell. I am also indebted to my undergraduate professor, John F. Henry, who not only exposed me to the great economists and philosophers of the past but also introduced me to L. Randall Wray, a present-day giant in the field of macroeconomics and leading MMT economist. Together, Mathew Forstater, Pavlina Tcherneva, Randy Wray, and I spent many years at the University of Missouri–Kansas City (UMKC), working together to build on the ideas of Warren Mosler. This book is a product of years of collaborative work with them. Major thanks are also owed to Scott Fullwiler, Rohan Grey, Nathan Tankus, Raúl Carrillo, and Fadhel Kaboub for enduring two years of constant contact in which I sought their input and expertise on a range of issues. I am also deeply grateful to Steven Hail, Marshall Auerback, Daniel José Camacho, Jesse Meyerson, Kenneth Wapner, Jeff Spross, and Richard Eskow for helping to improve the final product.

Thanks also to Zack Exley, Geoff Coventry, James Stuart, Max Skidmore, Ben Strubel, Samuel Connor, and Bill Goggin, all of whom demonstrated a commitment to MMT long before its rise to prominence.

And thank you to the incredible group of advocates who have formed reading groups, launched podcasts, and built websites to help introduce others to MMT. Thanks, also, to the many graduate and undergraduate students at UMKC, Stony Brook University, and the New School for Social Research, who helped me sharpen my ideas over many years. To Don St. Clair, Carolyn McClanahan, Patty Bruseau, and Stacy Pilcard for always checking in with an encouraging word: your thoughtfulness means more than you will ever know.

I must also thank some of the people who helped build an audience for this book by sharing their large, diverse platforms with me over the years: Harry Shearer, Chris Hayes, Joe Weisenthal, Sam Seder, Fareed Zakaria, Ezra Klein, Jon Favreau, Neil Cavuto, Nick Hanauer, Michael Moore, Mehdi Hasan, and many others. Thanks also to Congresswoman Alexandria Ocasio-Cortez for encouraging the press to help make MMT "a larger part of the conversation." Finally, I thank Amy, whose hope for a better future led her to phone NPR's *Planet Money* with some profound questions that help us see through the deficit myth.

Notes

Introduction: Bumper Sticker Shock

1. It is best to imagine monetary sovereignty as a continuum with some nations having a very high degree of sovereignty and others having less, little, or practically none. Countries with the highest degree of maximum sovereignty are those that spend, tax, and borrow in their own nonconvertible (floating exchange rate) currencies. Nonconvertible means that the state does not promise to convert the domestic currency into gold or foreign currency at a fixed price. Under this definition, the US, the UK, Japan, Australia, Canada, and even China are monetary sovereigns. In contrast, countries like Ecuador and Panama lack monetary sovereignty because their monetary systems are designed exclusively around the US dollar, a currency their governments cannot issue. Venezuela and Argentina issue their own domestic currencies, but they also borrow heavily in US dollars, which erodes their monetary sovereignty. The nineteen countries that operate with the euro also lack monetary sovereignty because they have transferred currency-issuing authority to the European Central Bank.

2. According to the Northwestern Institute for Policy Research, "more than eight million Americans lost their jobs, nearly four million homes were foreclosed each year, and 2.5 million businesses were shuttered." Institute for Policy Research, "The Great Recession: 10 Years Later," September 27, 2018, www.ipr.northwestern.edu/about/news/2014/IPR-research-Great-Recession-unemployment-forec.

3. Ryan Lizza, "Inside the Crisis," *The New Yorker*, October 12, 2009, www.newyorker.com/magazine/2009/10/12/inside-the-crisis.

4. Ibid.

5. Joe Weisenthal, "Obama: The US Government Is Broke!," *Business Insider*, May 24, 2009, www.businessinsider.com/obama-the-us-government-is-broke-2009-5.

6. CBPP, "Chart Book: The Legacy of the Great Recession," Center on Budget and Policy Priorities, June 6, 2019, www.cbpp.org/research/economy/chart-book-the-legacy-of-the-great-recession.

7. Dean Baker, *The Housing Bubble and the Great Recession: Ten Years Later* (Washington, DC: Center for Economic and Policy Research, September 2018), cepr.net/images/stories/reports/housing-bubble-2018-09.pdf.

8. Eric Levitt, "Bernie Sanders Is the Howard Schultz of the Left," *Intelligencer* (Doylestown, PA), April 16, 2019, nymag.com/intelligencer/2019/04/bernie-sanders-fox-news-town-hall-medicare-for-all-video-centrism.html.

Chapter 1: Don't Think of a Household

1. US Constitution, Article 1, Section 8, Clause 5, www.usconstitution.net/xconst_A1Sec8.html.

2. Other entities may create other financial instruments—for example, bank lending creates bank deposits, which can function like government currency in some instances—but only the US Treasury and the Federal Reserve can manufacture the currency itself. Brett W. Fawley and Luciana Juvenal, "Why Health Care Matters and the Current Debt Does Not," Federal Reserve Bank of St. Louis, October 1, 2011, www.stlouisfed.org/publications/regional-economist/october-2011/why-health-care-matters-and-the-current-debt-does-not.

3. A modest amount of external debt does not compromise a country's monetary sovereignty.

4. We should note that MMT does not consider monetary sovereignty a binary thing. It is best to think of a spectrum of monetary sovereignty, with some countries having more and others less. Because the US dollar is at the center of the global financial system—that is, it is the reserve currency—the United States has unparalleled monetary sovereignty. But countries like Japan, the UK, and Australia have a high degree of monetary sovereignty as well. Even China, which manages the value of the yuan, has substantial monetary sovereignty.

5. Margaret Thatcher, Speech to Conservative Party Conference, Winter Gardens, Blackpool, UK, October 14, 1983, Margaret Thatcher Foundation, www.margaretthatcher.org/document/105454.

6. Lizzie Dearden, "Theresa May Prompts Anger after Telling Nurse Who Hasn't Had Pay Rise for Eight Years: 'There's No Magic Money Tree,'" *Independent* (London), June 3, 2017, www.independent.co.uk/news/uk/politics

/theresa-may-nurse-magic-money-tree-bbcqt-question-time-pay-rise-eight
-years-election-latest-a7770576.html.

7. Since borrowing is off the table, lawmakers are left with two options: they can carve money out of some other part(s) of the federal budget or generate new revenue by collecting higher taxes. It's worth noting that the rule can be waived if lawmakers want to pass something but can't agree on spending cuts or tax increases that would keep it deficit neutral.

8. Warren Mosler, *Soft Currency Economics II: What Everyone Thinks They Know About Monetary Policy Is Wrong*, 2nd ed. (Christiansted, USVI: Valance, 2012).

9. Sometimes the textbooks recognize that the government can print money, but this method of financing is quickly dropped from the formal budget model on the grounds that printing money is inflationary, so the student is taught that governments must either finance their expenditures by collecting taxes or borrowing someone's savings.

10. David Graeber, *Debt: The First 5,000 Years* (New York: Melville House, 2011); L. Randall Wray, *Understanding Modern Money: The Key to Full Employment and Price Stability* (Cheltenham, UK: Edward Elgar, 2006); and Stephanie A. Bell, John F. Henry, and L. Randall Wray, "A Chartalist Critique of John Locke's Theory of Property, Accumulation, and Money: Or, Is It Moral to Trade Your Nuts for Gold?," *Review of Social Economy* 62, no. 1 (2004): 51–65.

11. There is an enormous literature that traces the history of state-issued currencies. Interested readers should consult works by Christine Desan, Mathew Forstater, David Graeber, John Henry, Michael Hudson, and L. Randall Wray.

12. Buttonwood, "Monopoly Money," Buttonwood's notebook, *The Economist*, October 19, 2009, www.economist.com/buttonwoods-notebook/2009/10/19/monopoly-money.

13. There is also the US Federal Reserve, which is "the issuing authority for all Federal Reserve notes." As the government's fiscal agent, the Fed makes most of its payments electronically, crediting something called a bank reserve account with digital dollars. See US Mint, "About the United States Mint" (webpage), www.usmint.gov/about.

14. Board of Governors of the Federal Reserve System, "About the Fed: Currency: The Federal Reserve Board's Role" (webpage), www.federalreserve.gov/aboutthefed/currency.htm.

15. Ale Emmons, "Senate Committee Votes to Raise Defense Spending for Second Year in a Row to $750 Billion," The Intercept, May 23, 2019, theintercept.com/2019/05/23/defense-spending-bill-senate/.

16. We could go deep into the weeds on all of this, and MMT has done just that. If you're interested in a rigorous look at the detailed reserve accounting, including the day-to-day coordination between the US Treasury and

the Federal Reserve, the broker-dealers, and so on, see works by Stephanie Kelton, Scott Fullwiler, and Eric Tymoigne.

17. Izabella Kaminska, "Why MMT Is Like an Autostereogram," FT Alphaville, *Financial Times* (London), February 22, 2012, ftalphaville.ft.com /2012/02/22/892201/why-mmt-is-like-an-autostereogram/.

18. Sally Helm and Alex Goldmark, hosts, interview Stephanie Kelton, "Modern Monetary Theory," *Planet Money*, NPR, September 26, 2018, 22:00, www.npr.org/templates/transcript/transcript.php?storyId=652001941.

19. It's important to remember that taxes are necessary for state and local governments. At the state and local level, your tax dollars *do help* pay for teachers, firefighters, police, local infrastructure projects, libraries, and so on.

20. When it comes to countering inflationary pressures, fiscal adjustments— cutting government expenditures or raising taxes—are not the only options. The government can also make use of nonfiscal powers, such as regulations to reduce demand and make room for government spending. And, of course, wage and price controls have played an important role. See Yair Listokin, *Law and Macroeconomics: Legal Remedies to Recessions* (Cambridge, MA: Harvard University Press, 2019).

21. Stephanie Kelton (née Bell), "Do Taxes and Bonds Finance Government Spending?, " *Journal of Economic Issues* 34, no. 3 (2000): 603–620, DOI: 10.1080/00213624.2000.11506296.

22. There is a big spike in tax payments around April 15 each year, but individual filers and many businesses also pay quarterly taxes, so there are literally trillions of dollars of tax payments being processed throughout the year.

23. There are also rules that currently govern some of the accounting practices that impact ways in which US Treasuries can be sold and how the Treasury's balance at the Federal Reserve must be managed. All of these were also imposed by Congress and, thus, can be altered at will. For more on all of this, see Eric Tymoigne, "Modern Money Theory and Interrelations Between the Treasury and Central Bank: The Case of the United States," *Journal of Economic Issues* 48, no. 3 (September 2014): 641–662.

24. Economists refer to this as trickle-down or supply-side economics. The idea is that tax cuts unleash enormous pent-up energies, spurring investment and innovation that juices the economy so much that the government actually ends up collecting more taxes even as it *cuts* taxes. In 2019, President Trump awarded the Presidential Medal of Freedom to Arthur Laffer, the economist who popularized this philosophy.

Chapter 2: Think of Inflation

1. Note that an increase in prices is a necessary but not sufficient precursor for inflation. An inflationary process requires continuously rising prices, so

the price level must be increasing over a number of time periods to constitute inflation.

2. John T. Harvey, "What Actually Causes Inflation (and Who Gains from It)," *Forbes*, May 30, 2011, www.forbes.com/sites/johntharvey/2011/05/30 /what-actually-causes-inflation/#3ea806e9f9a9.

3. Aimee Picchi, "Drug Prices in 2019 Are Surging, with Hikes at 5 Times Inflation," CBS News, July 1, 2019, www.cbsnews.com/news/drug-prices-in -2019-are-surging-with-hikes-at-5-times-inflation/.

4. Monetarism was built on the quantity theory of money (QTM), which took hold in the nineteenth century. The QTM transforms a simple truism known as the *equation of exchange*, MV = PY, into a story about the forces that give rise to inflation, wherein M is the quantity of money in circulation (a measure of the existing money supply), V is the income velocity of circulation (or the average number of times each money unit gets spent during a time period), P is the price level, and Y is real output (real goods and services). The equation of exchange is a truism because it's simply an accounting iden- tity that states that aggregate spending (MV) is equal to the nominal value of everything that is produced and sold (PY). It's like saying, "spending on GDP is equal to spending on GDP." To turn the truism into something more, economists made some behavioral assumptions about V and Y. Specifically, they assumed that V was stable enough to be treated as a constant and that Y tended to settle at full employment. If the entire equation is then set in motion—using calculus—then the rates of change of V and Y become zero (constants don't have a rate of change), leaving us with an equation that has only two variables that can move, M and P. To set the equation of exchange in motion, we apply some simple calculus. (The little dots indicate the rate of change [or growth rate] for each variable.) Since velocity (V) and real output (Y) are assumed to be constant, their growth rates are equal to zero. That leaves us with an equation that shows that the inflation rate is equal to the rate of growth of the money supply. To arrive at his famous claim that "inflation is always and everywhere a monetary phenomenon," Milton Friedman simply assumed that causality runs from money to inflation. Thus, if the central bank allows the money supply to grow twice as quickly as before, it would double the inflation rate.

5. The name derives from the famous British economist John Maynard Keynes, whose most well-known book, *The General Theory of Employment, Interest, and Money*, reshaped both the theory and practice of economics from the mid-1940s through the 1960s.

6. An economist named A. W. Phillips produced research showing a sta- tistical correlation between the unemployment rate and the rate of growth of money wages. The patterns in the data revealed an inverse relationship between the two variables, meaning a rise in one was associated with a fall in

the other. Over time, economists began to substitute price inflation for wage inflation and to depict the trade-off between inflation and unemployment visually in the form of a Phillips curve.

7. To keep inflation stable, Milton Friedman wanted the central bank to follow a strict rule. His rule dictated that the money supply (M) should be permitted to grow only as fast as the real economy (Y); that way, prices (P) would remain stable given (V), the assumption of constant income velocity of money.

8. For a further discussion of central bank independence, see L. Randall Wray, "Central Bank Independence: Myth and Misunderstanding," Working Paper No. 791, Levy Institute of Bard College, March 2014, www.levyinstitute .org/pubs/wp_791.pdf.

9. The Federal Reserve targets PCE. If it hits its target exactly, then the average price of the basket of goods used to construct the PCE will rise by 2 percent per year. For more on this, see Kristie Engemann, "The Fed's Inflation Target: Why 2 Percent?," Open Vault Blog, Federal Reserve Bank of St. Louis, January 16, 2019, www.stlouisfed.org/open-vault/2019/january/fed -inflation-target-2-percent.

10. See Dimitri B. Papadimitriou and L. Randall Wray, "Flying Blind: The Federal Reserve's Experiment with Unobservables," Working Paper No. 124, Levy Economics Institute of Bard College, September 1994, www.levy institute.org/pubs/wp124.pdf; and G. R. Krippner, *Capitalizing on Crisis: The Political Origins of the Rise of Finance* (Cambridge, MA: Harvard University Press, 2011).

11. Central banks also use other tools to influence prices, including savings policies, credit and banking regulations, exchange rate management, and market-structuring policies. However, interest rate adjustments remain the primary tool for day-to-day inflation management.

12. Given that the economics profession makes such a big deal of being scientific and data driven, it is hard not to find this approach a bit metaphysical.

13. William C. Dudley, "Important Choices for the Federal Reserve in the Future," speech delivered at Lehman College, Bronx, New York, April 18, 2018, www.newyorkfed.org/newsevents/speeches/2018/dud180418a.

14. Stephanie A. Kelton, "Behind Closed Doors: The Political Economy of Central Banking in the United States," Working Paper No. 47, University of Missouri–Kansas City, August 2005, www.cfeps.org/pubs/wp-pdf/WP47 -Kelton.pdf.

15. In fact, the mandates of most central banks around the world, including the Bank of Japan and the ECB, do not include unemployment. Instead, they are solely responsible for maintaining price stability.

16. The reason is simple. Businesses hire because they have to, not because they want to. Adding workers to the payroll is something that is done out of

necessity not benevolence for humanity. Capitalist economies, like the ones that dominate the world today, are what Keynes (and, before him, Marx) referred to as monetary production economies. Their raison d'etre is profit.

17. William Vickrey, "Fifteen Fatal Fallacies," chapter 15 in *Commitment to Full Employment: Macroeconomics and Social Policy in Memory of William S. Vickrey*, ed. Aaron W. Warner, Mathew Forstater, and Sumner M. Rosen (London: Routledge, 2015), first published by M.E. Sharpe, 2000.

18. Between 2008 and 2013, the Fed did three rounds of quantitative easing, buying trillions of dollars' worth of mortgage-backed securities and US Treasuries from private holders in exchange for digital dollar balances (bank reserves) at the Fed. This helped bring down longer-term interest rates, in the hope that homeowners would refinance mortgages, freeing up income to be spent in other ways, and businesses would borrow and invest in long-term capital goods like building new factories and buying new equipment.

19. Ben Bernanke, "Monetary Policy Is Not a Panacea," congressional testimony, House Financial Services Committee, July 18, 2012, posted by Stephanie Kelton, MMT, YouTube, September 23, 2012, 0:10, www.youtube.com /watch?v=eS7OYMIprSw.

20. Abba Ptachya Lerner, *The Economic Steering Wheel: The Story of the People's New Clothes* (New York: New York University Press, 1983).

21. Lerner also wanted the government to avoid borrowing—that is, selling US Treasuries—as a routine part of coordinating its fiscal operations. Since it was the currency issuer, it could just spend money into the economy and leave it there. Thinking back to our S(TAB) model, Lerner simply wanted the government to spend. It didn't necessarily need to follow that spending with taxes or borrowing. Taxes should go up only to remove inflationary pressure, and bonds should be sold only to support higher interest rates.

22. MMT economists, including Mathew Forstater, L. Randall Wray, and Pavlina R. Tcherneva, have recommended that the jobs be oriented around building a care economy. We will look more closely at the job guarantee in the final chapter of this book. For a detailed look at how the program would be administered, how much the jobs would pay, what kinds of jobs it would support, and how it would impact the economy as a whole, see L. Randall Wray, Flavia Dantas, Scott Fullwiler, Pavlina R. Tcherneva, and Stephanie A. Kelton, *Public Service Employment: A Path to Full Employment*, Levy Economics Institute of Bard College, April 2018, www.levyinstitute.org/pubs /rpr_4_18.pdf.

23. The job guarantee has its origins in the tradition of Franklin Delano Roosevelt, who wanted the government to guarantee employment as an economic right of all people. It was also an integral part of the civil rights movement led by Dr. Martin Luther King Jr., his wife, Coretta Scott King, and Reverend A. Philip Randolph. The influential economist Hyman Minsky

advocated such a program as a key pillar in his antipoverty work. It's important to note that the job guarantee doesn't require policy makers to try to divine the amount of slack in the labor market using something like a NAIRU. Instead, the government simply announces a wage and then hires everyone who turns up looking for a job. If no one shows up, it means the economy is already operating at full employment. But if fifteen million people show up, it reveals substantial slack. In a real sense, it's the only way to know for sure how substantially the economy is underutilizing available resources.

24. This means that the federal job guarantee becomes a new category of mandatory spending, much like Social Security or Medicare. The spending is nondiscretionary in the sense that lawmakers do not constrain funding for the job guarantee the way they set the budget for discretionary spending on infrastructure, defense, or education.

25. Pavlina R. Tcherneva, *The Case for a Job Guarantee* (Cambridge, UK: Polity Press, 2020).

26. Vickrey, "Fifteen Fatal Fallacies."

27. At the height of the Great Recession, some eight hundred thousand Americans were losing their jobs each month.

28. It might technically be possible for private employers to hire workers at a lower wage than the job guarantee program provides. If, for example, the job came with especially generous paid leave, more flexible work arrangements, better access to public transportation, or simply better options for career advancement, some people might be willing to work for lower pay. It is expected that this would be the exception to the rule, however.

29. Arjun Jayadev and J. W. Mason, "Loose Money, High Rates: Interest Rate Spreads in Historical Perspective," *Journal of Post Keynesian Economics* 38, no. 1 (Fall 2015): 93–130.

30. Despite protections against it, employers also discriminate on the basis of race, gender, sexual orientation, and physical disabilities and are prejudiced against the formerly incarcerated and the homeless. The federal job guarantee establishes a right to employment for all.

31. Top Democrats met with President Trump in 2019 to see if they could find a way to authorize $2 trillion for infrastructure.

32. MMT recognizes that inflation can increase for reasons that have little or nothing to do with excess demand pressures. Fighting inflation requires isolating the root cause(s) of the inflationary pressure and choosing targeted policies to attack the problem at its source. For more on this, see FT Alphaville, *Financial Times* (London), ftalphaville.ft.com/2019/03/01/1551434402000/An-MMT-response-on-what-causes-inflation/.

33. For a much more detailed discussion, please see Scott Fullwiler, "Replacing the Budget Constraint with an Inflation Constraint," New Economic

Perspectives, January 12, 2015, www.researchgate.net/publication/281853403
_Replacing_the_Budget_Constraint_with_an_Inflation_Constraint/citation
/download.

Chapter 3: The National Debt (That Isn't)

1. Funded by billionaire Peter G. Peterson, who has been actively supporting the privatization of Social Security for decades. The three members of
the committee who received awards were Independent senator Angus King
of Maine and Democratic senators Mark Warner and Tim Kaine, both of
Virginia.

2. Christina Hawley Anthony, Barry Blom, Daniel Fried, Charles Wha-
len, Megan Carroll, Avie Lerner, Amber Marcellino, Mark Booth, Pamela
Greene, Joshua Shakin et al., *The Budget and Economic Outlook: 2015 to 2025*,
Congressional Budget Office, 2015, www.cbo.gov/sites/default/files/114th
-congress-2015-2016/reports/49892-Outlook2015.pdf.

3. This is the subject of Chapter 6.

4. In June 2018, foreign governments and investors held $6.2 trillion or
about one-third of the US government bonds.

5. Edward Harrison, "Beijing Is Not Washington's Banker," Credit Writedowns, February 22, 2010, creditwritedowns.com/2010/02/beijing-is-not
-washingtons-banker.html.

6. Edward Harrison, "China Cannot Use Its Treasury Holdings as Leverage: Here's Why," Credit Writedowns, April 7, 2018, creditwritedowns.com
/2018/04/china-cannot-use-its-treasury-holdings-as-leverage-heres-why
.html.

7. Long-term rates reflect the expected path of future short-term interest
rates plus a term premium, which itself reflects the overall supply and demand for safe assets. The term premium can move around on its own, but
the future path of short-term rates is highly durable since the federal funds
futures market gives us the probabilities for what those rates will be, based on
collective market expectations about where the central bank will set short-
term rates going forward. (In the futures market, traders bet directly on how
the Fed will adjust the federal funds rate, and their winnings or losses are
directly tied to whether they guess right or wrong. Statistically, the federal
funds futures market is where the most accurate predictions are made.) This
gives central banks reasonably strong influence over long-term rates. To exercise even stronger control, central banks can effectively set rates across the
yield curve, as Japan has done.

8. The term *bond vigilantes* refers to the power of financial markets (or,
more accurately, investors in financial markets) to force sharp movements in

the price of a financial asset like government bonds so that the interest rate swings unexpectedly. Ultimately, the European Central Bank *did* keep the vigilantes at bay, but not without imposing painful austerity on the Greek people. See Yanis Varoufakis, *Adults in the Room: My Battle with Europe's Deep Establishment* (New York: Farrar, Straus and Giroux, 2017).

9. While criticizing President Obama's proposed budget, Senator Jeff Sessions said, "Next year, the United States could be like Greece." Congressman Paul Ryan made a similar argument, warning that "the President's budget ignores the drivers of our debt, bringing America perilously close to a European-style crisis." See Jennifer Bendery, "Paul Ryan, Jeff Sessions Warn Obama's Budget Could Spur Greek-Style Debt Crisis," Huffpost, February 13, 2012, www.huffpost.com/entry/paul-ryan-jeff-sessions-obama -budget-greece_n_1273809.

10. Alex Crippen, "Warren Buffett: Failure to Raise Debt Limit Would Be 'Most Asinine Act' Ever by Congress," CNBC, April 30, 2011, www.cnbc.com /id/42836791.

11. Warren Buffett, "We've Got the Right to Print Our Own Money So Our Credit Is Good," excerpt of *In the Loop* interview with Betty Liu, Bloomberg Television, July 8, 2011, posted by wonkmonk, YouTube, January 5, 2014, 0:31, www.youtube.com/watch?v=Q2om5yvXgLE.

12. US Treasuries have different life spans. The government issues long-dated bonds, those maturing in ten to thirty years; Treasury notes, with maturities between one and ten years; ten-year Treasury inflation-protected securities or TIPS; and T-bills with maturities of 13, 26, and 52 weeks. Most can be purchased in different denominations. The long-dated thirty-year bonds range from $1,000 to $1,000,000. See Investor Guide, "The 4 Types of U.S. Treasury Securities and How They Work" (webpage), investorguide .com, www.investorguide.com/article/11679/4-types-of-u-s-treasury-securities -and-how-they-work-igu/.

13. Laurence Kotlikoff, a firebrand economist who commonly refers to the national debt as a form of "fiscal child abuse," has characterized the US government's fiscal imbalances as a Ponzi scheme. I could not disagree more strongly with his views. See Joseph Lawler, "Economist Laurence Kotlikoff: U.S. $222 Trillion in Debt," RealClear Policy, November 20, 2012, www.real clearpolicy.com/blog/2012/12/01/economist_laurence_kotlikoff_us_222 _trillion_in_debt_363.html.

14. Patrick Allen, "No Chance of Default, US Can Print Money: Greenspan," CNBC, August 7, 2011, updated August 9, 2011, www.cnbc.com/id /44051683.

15. Niv Elis, "CBO Projects 'Unprecedented' Debt of 144 Percent of GDP by 2049," *The Hill*, June 25, 2019, thehill.com/policy/finance/450180-cbo -projects-unprecedented-debt-of-144-of-gdp-by-2049.

16. Jared Bernstein, "Mick Mulvaney Says 'Nobody Cares' About Deficits. I Do. Sometimes," *Washington Post*, February 6, 2019, www.washington post.com/outlook/2019/02/06/mick-mulvaney-says-nobody-cares-about -deficits-i-do-sometimes/.

17. "Dear Reader: You Owe $42,998.12," *Time* magazine cover, April 14, 2016, time.com/4293549/the-united-states-of-insolvency/.

18. James K. Galbraith, "Is the Federal Debt Unsustainable?," Policy Note, Levy Economic Institute of Bard College, February 2011, www.levyinstitute .org/pubs/pn_11_02.pdf.

19. Olivier Blanchard, "Public Debt and Low Interest Rates," Working Paper 19-4, PIIE, February 2019, www.piie.com/publications/working-papers /public-debt-and-low-interest-rates.

20. Greg Robb, "Leading Economist Says High Public Debt 'Might Not Be So Bad,'" MarketWatch, January 7, 2019, www.marketwatch.com/story /leading-economist-says-high-public-debt-might-not-be-so-bad-2019-01-07.

21. David Harrison and Kate Davidson, "Worry About Debt? Not So Fast, Some Economists Say," *Wall Street Journal*, February 17, 2019, www.wsj .com/articles/worry-about-debt-not-so-fast-some-economists-say-1155 0414860.

22. Scott T. Fullwiler, "Interest Rates and Fiscal Sustainability," Working Paper No. 53, Wartburg College and the Center for Full Employment and Price Stability, July 2006, www.cfeps.org/pubs/wp-pdf/WP53-Fullwiler.pdf.

23. Scott T. Fullwiler, "The Debt Ratio and Sustainable Macroeconomic Policy," *World Economic Review* (July 2016): 12–42, www.researchgate.net /publication/304999017_The_Debt_Ratio_and_Sustainable_Macroeconomic _Policy.

24. Ibid.

25. Ibid. This relates to interest rates paid by government.

26. Galbraith, "Is the Federal Debt Unsustainable?"

27. Japan Macro Advisors, "General Government Debt and Asset," December 20, 2019, www.japanmacroadvisors.com/page/category/economic -indicators/balancesheets/general-government/.

28. Fullwiler, "Interest Rates and Fiscal Sustainability."

29. Prior to the Treasury-Fed Accord, the Federal Reserve kept a tight grip on the long-term interest rate, refusing to let the rate climb above 2.5 percent. Taking control of the yield curve is impossible under a fixed exchange rate regime because interest rates become endogenous as government debt competes with the option to convert domestic currency into the reserve asset at the rate fixed by the government. For more on this, see Warren Mosler and Mathew Forstater, "A General Framework for the Analysis of Currencies and Commodities," in ed. Paul Davidson and Jan Kregel, *Full Employment and Price Stability in a Global Economy* (Cheltenham, UK: Edward

Elgar, 1999), cas2.umkc.edu/econ/economics/faculty/Forstater/papers/Book
ChaptersEnclopediaEntries/GeneralFrameworkAnalysisOfCurrencies
Commidities.pdf.

30. The Fed began targeting in 1942. See Jessie Romero, "Treasury-Fed Accord, March 1951" (webpage), Federal Reserve History, November 22, 2013, www.federalreservehistory.org/essays/treasury_fed_accord.

31. For an MMT description of what is meant by Fed independence, see L. Randall Wray, "Central Bank Independence: Myth and Misunderstanding," Working Paper No. 791, Levy Economics Institute of Bard College, March 2014, www.levyinstitute.org/pubs/wp_791.pdf.

32. Even some officials at the Federal Reserve are reportedly beginning to consider the possibility of explicitly targeting the longer end of the yield curve. See Leika Kihara, Howard Schneider, and Balazs Koranyi, "Groping for New Tools, Central Banks Look at Japan's Yield Controls," Reuters, July 15, 2019, www.reuters.com/article/us-usa-fed-ycc/groping-for-new-tools-central-banks-look-at-japans-yield-controls-idUSKCN1UA0E0.

33. Japan Macro Advisors, "Japan JGBs Held by BoJ" (webpage), Economic Indicators, www.japanmacroadvisors.com/page/category/economic-indicators/financial-markets/jgbs-held-by-boj/.

34. Eric Lonergan, Drobny Global Monitor (blog), Andres Drobny, Drobny Global LP, December 17, 2012, www.drobny.com/assets/_control/content/files/Drobny_121712_10_24_13.pdf.

35. Some bond market speculators believed that Japan was on a collision course with public debt well in excess of 200 percent of GDP. Believing that the government could not possibly sustain such high debt levels, some bond traders bet against Japanese government bonds by selling them short. Kyle Bass is notorious for losing vast sums with this trade, which is widely known as the widowmaker trade. See Wayne Arnold, "Japan's Widow-Maker Bond Trade Still Looks Lethal" (blog), Reuters, June 6, 2011, blogs.reuters.com/breakingviews/2011/06/06/japans-widow-maker-bond-trade-still-looks-lethal/.

36. The QTM was covered at some length in endnote 4 in Chapter 2.

37. Milton Friedman, "The Counter-Revolution in Monetary Theory," IEA Occasional Paper, no. 33, Institute of Economic Affairs, 1970, miltonfriedman.hoover.org/friedman_images/Collections/2016c21/IEA_1970.pdf.

38. As of July 2019, the Federal Reserve held about 13 percent of marketable US Treasuries. It could buy the remaining 87 percent the same way it bought the Treasuries it already holds—that is, by crediting bank reserves. See Kihara, Schneider, and Koranyi, "Groping for New Tools."

39. Interested readers might enjoy Carl Lane, *A Nation Wholly Free: The Elimination of the National Debt in the Age of Jackson* (Yardley, PA: Westholme, 2014).

40. The Federal Reserve System was created by the Federal Reserve Act in 1913.

41. Treasuries pay principal and interest. You might have purchased a ten-year Treasury with a 5 percent coupon (interest rate). The government takes your $1,000 and pays you $50 each year for ten years. At the end of the tenth year, the government returns the principal amount of $1,000 to you.

42. David A. Levy, Martin P. Farnham, and Samira Rajan, *Where Profits Come From* (Kisco, NY: Jerome Levy Forecasting Center, 2008), www.levy forecast.com/assets/Profits.pdf.

43. As we'll see in Chapter 5, countries that run trade surpluses are far less dependent on fiscal deficits. But countries like the United States—that is, those that run chronic trade deficits—are usually better off running fiscal deficits. Without them, growth becomes unsustainable. See Wynne Godley, "What If They Start Saving Again? Wynne Godley on the US Economy," *London Review of Books* 22, no. 13 (July 6, 2000), www.lrb.co.uk/v22/n13 /wynne-godley/what-if-they-start-saving-again.

44. Frederick C. Thayer, "Balanced Budgets and Depressions," *American Journal of Economics and Sociology* 55, no. 2 (1996): 211–212, JSTOR, www .jstor.org/stable/3487081.

45. Ibid.

46. I explore this in detail in Chapter 4. Also, see Scott Fullwiler, "The Sector Financial Balances Model of Aggregate Demand (Revised)," New Economic Perspectives, July 26, 2009, neweconomicperspectives.org/2009/07 /sector-financial-balances-model-of_26.html.

47. Apologies to Prince.

48. NPR gained access to a copy, which is now public, through a Freedom of Information Act (FOIA) request in 2011. You can read the backstory at David Kestenbaum, "What If We Paid Off the Debt? The Secret Government Report," *Planet Money*, NPR, October 20, 211, www.npr.org/sections /money/2011/10/21/141510617/what-if-we-paid-off-the-debt-the-secret -government-report.

49. The interest rate is known as the federal funds rate. It's the interest rate that banks charge one another when they lend reserves in the overnight market. When there is an abundance of reserves in the system, a bank that needs to borrow reserves doesn't have to pay very much to get them from banks that have more than they want to hold. They're cheap because they're easy to come by. To achieve a lower interest rate, all the Fed has to do is flood the banking system with enough reserves to bring the price down to its target rate. It does this by purchasing.

50. Kestenbaum, "What If We Paid Off the Debt?" Concern was that if the Fed had to buy other kinds of financial assets, it might look like it was picking winners and losers.

51. Before the recession hit, the US economy grew rapidly, pushing revenues up sharply. The boom was largely the result of a stock-market bubble,
which fueled the growth that moved the budget into surplus. As the bubble
began to collapse in January 2001, the economy moved into recession. The
fiscal surpluses didn't cause the recession, but they set the stage for the more
severe recession that began in 2007. For more on this, see Wynne Godley,
Seven Unsustainable Processes (Annandale-on-Hudson, NY: Jerome Levy
Economics Institute, 1999), www.levyinstitute.org/pubs/sevenproc.pdf.

52. In addition to buying US Treasuries, the Fed also purchased mortgage-
backed securities (MBS) and bonds issued by government-sponsored mortgage enterprises Fannie Mae and Freddie Mac.

53. The Fed officially ended its quantitative easing program in 2014. At
that point, the Fed held $2.8 trillion in US Treasuries on its balance sheet.
That was 22 percent of the $12.75 trillion in federal debt held by the public.

54. For a very detailed look at this, see Scott T. Fullwiler, "Paying Interest on Reserve Balances: It's More Significant than You Think," Social Science Research Network, December 1, 2004, papers.ssrn.com/sol3/papers.cfm
?abstract_id=1723589.

55. Although they were used to carry out quantitative easing, Fed chair
Janet Yellen said she hoped the Fed would never have to do it again. She also
said the Fed might need to consider buying a broader range of assets if it
ever had to do quantitative easing again.

56. This would require authorization to run overdraft, platinum coin, or a
new digital currency.

57. Some worry that this would lead to inflation. They think that bond-
financed deficits are less inflationary than money-financed deficits. MMT
shows that this is wrong. What matters is the spending, not whether the
government coordinates the spending with bond sales. See Stephanie Kelton
and Scott Fullwiler, "The Helicopter Can Drop Money, Gather Bonds or
Just Fly Away," *Financial Times*, December 12, 2013, ftalphaville.ft.com
/2013/12/12/1721592/guest-post-the-helicopter-can-drop-money-gather
-bonds-or-just-fly-away-3/.

58. Of course, there is no reason to tie this to the fiscal budget process.
It would be simple, for example, to establish a separate savings facility that
issued interest-earning debt instruments to eligible parties. Indeed, the Federal Reserve enacted such a program, the Term Deposit Facility, in 2008. See
The Federal Reserve, "Term Deposit Facility" (webpage), www.frbservices
.org/central-bank/reserves-central/term-deposit-facility/index.html.

59. The US Constitution was ratified in 1789, and the US federal government was formed.

Chapter 4: Their Red Ink Is Our Black Ink

1. Congressional Budget Office, *The 2019 Long-Term Budget Outlook* (Washington, DC: CBO, June 2019), www.cbo.gov/system/files/2019-06/55 331-LTBO-2.pdf.

2. Paul Krugman, "Deficits Matter Again," *New York Times*, January 9, 2017, www.nytimes.com/2017/01/09/opinion/deficits-matter-again.html.

3. George F. Will, "Fixing the Deficit Is a Limited-Time Offer," *Sun* (Lowell, Massachusetts), www.lowellsun.com/2019/03/12/george-f-will-fixing-the -deficit-is-a-limited-time-offer/.

4. Committee hearings are often carried live on C-SPAN 3. See Jason Furman, "Options to Close the Long-Run Fiscal Gap," testimony before the US Senate Committee on Budget, January 31, 2007, www.brookings.edu/wp -content/uploads/2016/06/furman20070131S-1.pdf.

5. Keynesian economists will often argue that there is a special circumstance under which crowding out doesn't happen. It's a situation—often described as a liquidity trap—where rising deficits don't push interest rates higher because rates are stuck at zero. In that situation, the government can safely add to the deficit without worrying that rising interest rates will crowd out private investment (since rates are stuck at zero). That gives the government a window of opportunity to boost spending without any kind of tradeoff. Once interest rates become unstuck, crowding out is immediately back in play. As we will see, MMT rejects the idea that crowding out is something that can only be avoided under highly unusual circumstances.

6. Jonathan Schlefer, "Embracing Wynne Godley, an Economist Who Modeled the Crisis," *New York Times*, September 10, 2013, www.nytimes .com/2013/09/11/business/economy/economists-embracing-ideas-of-wynne -godley-late-colleague-who-predicted-recession.html.

7. Ibid.

8. Post Editorial Board, "Locking in a Future of Trillion-Dollar Deficits," *New York Post*, July 23, 2019, nypost.com/2019/07/23/locking-in-a -future-of-trillion-dollar-deficits/.

9. Wynne Godley, *Seven Unsustainable Processes* (Annandale-on-Hudson, NY: Jerome Levy Economics Institute, 1999), www.levyinstitute.org/pubs /sevenproc.pdf.

10. "Life After Debt," second interagency draft, November 2, 2000, media .npr.org/assets/img/2011/10/20/LifeAfterDebt.pdf.

11. Godley coauthored some of his research with fellow Levy Institute economist and scholar L. Randall Wray. Both understood that the Clinton surpluses were possible only as long as the domestic private sector continued

to spend more than its income (i.e., to deficit spend). The problem, they explained, is that the private sector is a currency user, not a currency issuer, so it cannot remain in deficit forever. Another economist who understood all of this was James K. Galbraith, who tells an incredible story of being laughed at by his fellow economists when he dared to suggest that the Clinton surpluses weren't a champagne-popping accomplishment.

12. Katie Warren, "One Brutal Sentence Captures What a Disaster Money in America Has Become," Business Insider, May 23, 2019, www.business insider.com/bottom-half-of-americans-negative-net-worth-2019-5.

13. You might be tempted to think of a government surplus as a category of national savings. Don't! Remember, Uncle Sam isn't like the rest of us. He issues the US dollar, and the rest of us merely use it. He can spend dollars he doesn't have, and when he takes dollars away from the rest of us, it doesn't make *him* any richer. The government can run a fiscal surplus, like it did from 1998 until 2001, but what exactly is it "getting" when that (+) sign appears? The answer, really, is nothing. Like the referee who subtracts six points after reviewing a touchdown pass and determining that the receiver was out of bounds, our fiscal scorekeeper subtracts something from us, but he doesn't actually get anything in return. From the perspective of the currency issuer, a bucket of dollars is about as useful as a bucket of points in a football game. Politics aside, running a surplus today doesn't make it any easier for him to spend more in the future.

14. Much of standard macroeconomic theory continues to invoke this loanable funds theory of the rate of interest. John Maynard Keynes tried hard to demolish these ideas in his famous book, *The General Theory of Employment, Interest, and Money.* Unfortunately, the old (flawed) theories are still very much with us nearly a century later.

15. Scott Fullwiler, "CBO—Still Out of Paradigm After All These Years," New Economic Perspectives, July 20, 2014, neweconomicperspectives.org /2014/07/cbo-still-paradigm-years.html.

16. Net financial assets include currency in circulation, bank reserves, and outstanding government securities.

17. Here, we are talking about governments that operate with a sovereign currency, such as the US, Japan, the UK, and Australia. See L. Randall Wray, "Keynes after 75 Years: Rethinking Money as a Public Monopoly," Working Paper No. 658, Levy Economics Institute of Bard College, March 2011, www .levyinstitute.org/pubs/wp_658.pdf.

18. As defined in the Introduction.

19. Return to Chapter 1, where I discuss the role of bonds in MMT, if you need a refresher. If you feel especially ambitious, you can read MMT economist Eric Tymoigne for a detailed analysis of the US government's fiscal and monetary operations. See Tymoigne, "Government Monetary and Fiscal

Operations: Generalising the Endogenous Money Approach," *Cambridge Journal of Economics* 40, no. 5 (2018): 1317–1332, sci-hub.se/https://academic.oup.com/cje/article-abstract/40/5/1317/1987653.

20. For example, the Fed could be granted the authority to issue securities. For more on central bank issuance of securities, see Simon Gray and Runchana Pongsaparn, "Issuance of Central Bank Securities: International Experiences and Guidelines," IMF Working Paper, 2015, www.imf.org/external/pubs/ft/wp/2015/wp15106.pdf; and Garreth Rule, *Centre for Central Banking Studies: Issuing Central Bank Securities* (London: Bank of England, 2011), www.bankofengland.co.uk/-/media/boe/files/ccbs/resources/issuing-central-bank-securities.

21. Their special status as primary dealers requires them "to bid on a pro-rata basis in all Treasury auctions at reasonably competitive prices." That means that each primary dealer must tender bids for its fair share of the auction. Primary dealers can bid more aggressively or less aggressively, but they can't choose to sit out an auction. They have to offer to buy a portion of the debt at each auction. See "Primary Dealers" (webpage), Federal Reserve Bank of New York, www.newyorkfed.org/markets/primarydealers.

22. This was the actual, monthly deficit in August 2019. Jeffry Bartash, "U.S. Budget Deficit in August Totals $200 Billion, on Track to Post Nearly $1 Trillion Gap in 2019," MarketWatch, September 12, 2019, www.marketwatch.com/story/budget-deficit-in-august-totals-200-billion-us-on-track-to-post-nearly-1-trillion-gap-in-2019-2019-09-12.

23. A mix of short- and long-term securities is typical. Auctions generally include short-term securities known as T-bills that mature in a year or less, notes with two- to ten-year maturity, and thirty-year bonds. See more on auctions and timing at "General Auction Timing" (webpage), Treasury-Direct, www.treasurydirect.gov/instit/auctfund/work/auctime/auctime.htm.

24. Primary dealers (or their agent banks) purchase government securities using their reserve balances, essentially their "checking account" at the New York branch of the Federal Reserve.

25. One of the main risks of holding fixed-interest government bonds is inflation. If you're stuck earning 2 percent a year, but inflation is running at a consistent 2.5 percent annually, then your real (i.e., inflation-adjusted) return on this investment is minus 0.5 percent. Treasury sells inflation-protection securities (TIPS) for investors who want protection against inflation. See "Treasury Inflation-Protected Securities (TIPS)" (webpage), TreasuryDirect, www.treasurydirect.gov/instit/marketables/tips/tips.htm.

26. Stephanie Kelton, "Former Dept. Secretary of the U.S. Treasury Says Critics of MMT are 'Reaching,'" New Economic Perspectives, October 30, 2013, neweconomicperspectives.org/2013/10/former-dept-secretary-u-s-treasury-says-critics-mmt-reaching.html.

27. Following the Treasury-Fed Accord in 1951, the Fed was allowed to stop targeting the yield curve beyond the shortest maturity. It had long wanted to leave the interest rates on Treasuries (beyond the shortest maturities) to markets, and now it could finally do that. As it happened, though, an efficient private market for Treasuries required private financial institutions to trade them. The Fed designed a system of primary dealers for this, which were and are mostly subsidiaries of large banks. The primary dealers became the counterparties for the Fed's operations to hit an interest rate target in short-term interest rates, which became its official policy variable. In these operations, the Fed adds green dollars to the banking system by buying Treasuries—yellow dollars—from the dealers. To run its monetary policy, the Fed obviously needs an efficient and stable system of primary dealers. In essence, to do this, in order to leave the rates on Treasuries to markets and also do its own monetary policy at the same time, the Fed had to at the very least implicitly ensure dealers could finance their purchases of treasuries at or roughly at the Fed's interest rate target. This is what it means to say that the Fed "backstops" the primary dealers, who in turn "make the market" on behalf of the US Treasury.

28. The federal funds rate is the interest rate that banks charge one another to borrow reserves in the overnight market. A bank with reserve balances that it does not wish to hold can lend those reserves to another bank. It's an overnight loan, so the lending bank gets the reserves back—with interest—the following day. For more on this, see Scott Fullwiler, "Modern Central Bank Operations—The General Principles," chapter 2 in ed. Louis-Philippe Rochon and Sergio Rossi, *Advances in Endogenous Money Analysis* (Cheltenham, UK: Edward Elgar, 2017), 50–87.

29. There are basically two ways to support positive rates: (1) drain excess reserve balances by selling US Treasuries or (2) pay interest on reserves (IOR) at the Fed's target rate. For a detailed explanation, see Scott T. Fullwiler, "Setting Interest Rates in the Modern Money Era," Working Paper No. 34, Wartburg College and the Center for Full Employment and Price Stability, July 1, 2004, papers.ssrn.com/sol3/papers.cfm?abstract_id=1723591.

30. L. Randall Wray, "Deficits, Inflation, and Monetary Policy," *Journal of Post Keynesian Economics* 19, no. 4 (Summer 1997), 543.

31. The yield curve is a curve (or graph) that shows the interest rates on different debt instruments across a range of maturities.

32. Recall from the Introduction that we have defined monetary sovereignty to include countries that tax, borrow, and spend in a nontethered, that is, floating exchange rate currency that can only be issued by the government or its fiscal agents.

33. Today, it is standard operating procedure to coordinate deficit spending with bond sales. It doesn't have to be that way. Congress could always

rewrite its operating procedures to change this practice, especially now that the Federal Reserve no longer needs access to government bonds to hit its short-term interest rate target. A technical, but truly innovative alternative would have the Federal Reserve establish the rates it's willing to pay for short- or long-term bills, time deposits, or bonds and allow the private sector to buy in whatever quantities it desires while the rest of the deficit sits as zero-interest reserve balances.

34. Dan McCrum, "Mario Draghi's 'Whatever It Takes' Outcome in 3 Charts," *Financial Times* (London), July 25, 2017, www.ft.com/content/82c 95514-707d-11e7-93ff-99f383b09ff9.

35. Warren Mosler and Mathew Forstater, "The Natural Rate of Interest Is Zero," Center for Full Employment and Price Stability, University of Missouri–Kansas City, December 2004, www.cfeps.org/pubs/wp-pdf/WP37 -MoslerForstater.pdf.

36. Ibid.

37. Timothy P. Sharpe, "A Modern Money Perspective on Financial Crowding-out," *Review of Political Economy* 25, no. 4 (2013): 586–606.

38. William Vickrey, "Fifteen Fatal Fallacies," chapter 15 in *Commitment to Full Employment: Macroeconomics and Social Policy in Memory of William S. Vickrey*, ed. Aaron W. Warner, Mathew Forstater, and Sumner M. Rosen (London: Routledge, 2015), first published by M.E. Sharpe, 2000.

Chapter 5: "Winning" at Trade

1. Fox News, "Transcript of the 2015 GOP Debate," Cleveland, Ohio, August 7, 2015, CBS News website, www.cbsnews.com/news/transcript -of-the-2015-gop-debate-9-pm/.

2. Aimee Picchi, "Fact Check: Is Trump Right That the U.S. Loses $500 Billion in Trade to China?," CBS News, May 6, 2019, www.cbsnews.com /news/trump-china-trade-deal-causes-us-to-lose-500-billion-claim-review/.

3. Action News, "President Trump Visits Shell Cracker Plant in Beaver County," Pittsburgh's Action News, August 13, 2019, www.wtae.com/article /president-trump-shell-cracker-plant-beaver-county-pennsylvania/28689728#.

4. Ginger Adams Otis, "Clinton-Backing AFL-CIO Boss Trumka Visits President-elect Trump on Friday," *New York Daily News*, January 13, 2017, www.nydailynews.com/news/national/clinton-backing-afl-cio-boss-trumka -talks-trade-trump-article-1.2945620.

5. Robert E. Scott and Zane Mokhiber, "The China Toll Deepens," Economic Policy Institute, October 23, 2018, www.epi.org/publication/the-china -toll-deepens-growth-in-the-bilateral-trade-deficit-between-2001-and -2017-cost-3-4-million-u-s-jobs-with-losses-in-every-state-and-congressional -district/.

6. Mark Hensch, "Dems Selling 'America Is Already Great' Hat," *The Hill*, October 9, 2015, thehill.com/blogs/blog-briefing-room/news/256571-dems-selling-america-is-already-great-hat.

7. Jim Geraghty, "Chuck Schumer: Democrats Will Lose Blue-Collar Whites but Gain in the Suburbs," *National Review*, July 28, 2016, www.nationalreview.com/corner/chuck-schumer-democrats-will-lose-blue-collar-whites-gain-suburbs/.

8. Wynne Godley, "What If They Start Saving Again? Wynne Godley on the US Economy," *London Review of Books* 22, no. 13 (July 6, 2000), www.lrb.co.uk/v22/n13/wynne-godley/what-if-they-start-saving-again.

9. Strictly speaking, Uncle Sam's deficit must exceed the current account deficit (not merely the trade deficit) in order to keep the US private sector in surplus. The current amount is the trade balance plus some other international payments. The two are often used interchangeably, but the differences can be significant in some countries. For more on this, see William Mitchell, L. Randall Wray, and Martin Watts, *Macroeconomics* (London: Red Globe Press, 2019).

10. The US government can also add dollars directly to the foreign bucket. If it buys aircraft from the European corporation Airbus, instead of buying the planes from the US corporation Boeing, for example, that spending will add dollars to the foreign sector bucket instead of the US private sector bucket.

11. Donald J. Trump, Tweet, December 2, 2019, twitter.com/realDonaldTrump/status/1201455858636472320?s=20.

12. Mamta Badkar, "Watch How Germany Ate Everyone Else's Lunch After the Euro Was Created," *Business Insider*, July 18, 2012, https://www.businessinsider.com/presentation-german-current-account-balance-2012-7.

13. Pavlina R. Tcherneva, "Unemployment: The Silent Epidemic," Working Paper No. 895, Levy Economics Institute of Bard College, August 2017, www.levyinstitute.org/pubs/wp_895.pdf.

14. US Department of Labor, "Trade Adjustment Assistance for Workers" (webpage), www.doleta.gov/tradeact/.

15. Candy Woodall, "Harley-Davidson Workers Say Plant Closure after Tax Cut Is Like a Bad Dream," *USA Today*, May 27, 2018, updated May 28, 2018, www.usatoday.com/story/money/nation-now/2018/05/27/harley-davidson-layoffs/647199002/.

16. Committee on Decent Work in Global Supply Chains, "Resolution and Conclusions Submitted for Adoption by the Conference," International Labour Conference, ILO, 105th Session, Geneva, May–June 2016, www.ilo.org/wcmsp5/groups/public/---ed_norm/---relconf/documents/meetingdocument/wcms_489115.pdf.

17. Office of the Historian, "Nixon and the End of the Bretton Woods System, 1971–1973," Milestones: 1969–1976, history.state.gov/milestones /1969-1976/nixon-shock.

18. Kimberly Amadeo, "Why the US Dollar Is the Global Currency," The Balance, December 13, 2019, www.thebalance.com/world-currency-3305931.

19. Brian Reinbold and Yi Wen, "Understanding the Roots of the U.S. Trade Deficit," St. Louis Fed, August 16, 2019, medium.com/st-louis-fed /understanding-the-roots-of-the-u-s-trade-deficit-534b5cb0e0dd.

20. L. Randall Wray, "Does America Need Global Savings to Finance Its Fiscal and Trade Deficits?," *American Affairs* 3, no. 1 (Spring 2019), american affairsjournal.org/2019/02/does-america-need-global-savings-to-finance-its -fiscal-and-trade-deficits/.

21. L. Randall Wray, "Twin Deficits and Sustainability," Policy Note, Levy Economics Institute of Bard College, March 2006, www.levyinstitute.org /pubs/pn_3_06.pdf.

22. The 1997 Asian financial crisis, in particular, taught the world that pegging exchange rates is unwise if countries cannot maintain a stockpile of reserves, especially without capital controls. See Wray, "Twin Deficits and Sustainability."

23. Scott Ferguson, Maxximilian Seijo, and William Saas, "The New Post-colonial Economics with Fadhel Kaboub," MR Online, July 7, 2018, mronline .org/2018/07/07/the-new-postcolonial-economics-with-fadhel-kaboub/.

24. Noureddine Taboubi, "Strikes Overturn Wage Cuts, but IMF Blind-ness Risks Ruining Tunisia," Bretton Woods Project, April 4, 2019, www .brettonwoodsproject.org/2019/04/strikes overturn-wage-bill-but-imf -blindness-risks-ruining-tunisia/.

25. John T. Harvey, *Currencies, Capital Flows and Crises: A Post Keynesian Analysis of Exchange Rate Determination* (Abingdon, UK: Routledge, 2009).

26. Bill Mitchell, "Modern Monetary Theory in an Open Economy," Modern Monetary Theory, October 13, 2009, bilbo.economicoutlook.net /blog/?p–5402.

27. Predictably, the Volcker shock also devastated US workers, shutting down factories in the Midwest and ending manufacturing competitiveness with countries like Japan. Had the US established a job guarantee employ-ment policy to automatically stabilize the economy at full employment—as MMTers and our forebears would have recommended and as many US civil rights activists *were* recommending—perhaps people around the world could have avoided this catastrophe.

28. Jamee K. Moudud, "Free Trade Free for All: Market Romanticism versus Reality," Law and Political Economy (blog), March 26, 2018, lpeblog .org/2018/03/26/free-trade-for-all-market-romanticism-versus-reality /#more-620.

29. This is what happened in Turkey in 2018. Turkey's reliance on foreign borrowing—and accompanying budget deficits—hit a giant snag when North Atlantic countries started raising interest rates. Julius Probst, "Explainer: Why Some Current Account Imbalances Are Fine but Others Are Catastrophic," The Conversation, August 21, 2018, theconversation.com /explainer-why-some-current-account-imbalances-are-fine-but-others-are -catastrophic-101851.

30. Often this has meant importing nearly complete goods and merely finishing the manufacturing process. Kaboub and other economists refer to this as low-value-added content. See Scott Ferguson and Maxximilian Seijo, "The New Postcolonial Economics with Fadhel Kaboub," *Money on the Left* (podcast), Buzzsprout, July 7, 2018, 1:14:25, transcript of interview, www .buzzsprout.com/172776/745220.

31. James K. Galbraith, *The Predator State: How Conservatives Abandoned the Free Market and Why Liberals Should Too* (New York: Free Press, 2008).

32. Dean Baker is fond of pointing out that despite Trump's bluster, "General Electric, Boeing, Walmart and the rest did not lose from our trade deficit with China. In fact, the trade deficit was the result of their efforts to increase their profits." See Dean Baker, "Media Go Trumpian on Trade," Beat the Press, CEPR, August 24, 2019, cepr.net/blogs/beat-the-press/media -go-trumpian-on-trade.

33. Mitchell, "Modern Monetary Theory."

34. Pavlina R. Tcherneva and L. Randall Wray, "Employer of Last Resort Program: A Case Study of Argentina's *Jefes de Hogar* Program," Working Paper No. 41, CFEPS, April 2005, www.cfeps.org/pubs/wp-pdf/WP41 -Tcherneva-Wray-all.pdf.

35. Pavlina R. Tcherneva, "A Global Marshall Plan for Joblessness?" (blog), Institute for New Economic Thinking, May 11, 2016, www.ineteconomics.org /perspectives/blog/a-global-marshall-plan-for-joblessness.

36. "World Employment and Social Outlook 2017: Sustainable Enterprises and Jobs—Formal Enterprises and Decent Work," International Labour Organization report, October 9, 2017.

37. "Mexico Trade Surplus with the US Reach Record High US$81.5 Billion in 2018," *MexicoNow*, March 8, 2019, mexico-now.com/index.php /article/5232-mexico-trade-surplus-with-the-us-reach-record-high-us-81-5 -billion-in-2018.

38. Jeff Faux, "NAFTA's Impact on U.S. Workers," Working Economics Blog, Economic Policy Institute, December 9, 2013, www.epi.org/blog /naftas-impact-workers/.

39. Bill Mitchell, "Bad Luck if You Are Poor!," Modern Monetary Theory, June 25, 2009, bilbo.economicoutlook.net/blog/?p=3064.

Chapter 6: You're Entitled!

1. US Senate, "Glossary Term: Entitlement" (webpage), www.senate.gov /reference/glossary_term/entitlement.htm.

2. US Social Security Office of Retirement and Disability Policy, "Beneficiaries in Current-Payment Status," *Annual Statistical Report on the Social Security Disability Insurance Program, 2018*, Social Security Administration, released October 2019, www.ssa.gov/policy/docs/statcomps/di_asr/2018/sect 01.html.

3. Richard R. J. Eskow, host, *The Zero Hour with RJ Eskow*, "Shaun Castle on Social Security and Paralyzed Veterans of America," YouTube, April 22, 2019, 18:46, www.youtube.com/watch?v=avPbNku5Qoc&feature=youtu.be.

4. PVA, "Paralyzed Veterans of America Urges Preserving and Strengthening Social Security During Hearing on Capitol Hill," Paralyzed Veterans of America, April 10, 2019, pva.org/about-us/news-and-media-center /recent-news/paralyzed-veterans-of-america-urges-preserving-and/.

5. Confronting Poverty, "About the Project" (webpage), confronting poverty.org/about/.

6. Matt DeLong, "Groups Call for Alan Simpson's Resignation over 'Sexist' Letter," *Washington Post*, August 25, 2010, voices.washingtonpost .com/44/2010/08/group-calls-for-debt-commissio.html.

7. "The Insatiable Glutton" in *Puck* magazine, December 20, 1882, mentioned in James Marten, "Those Who Have Borne the Battle: Civil War Veterans, Pension Advocacy, and Politics," *Marquette Law Review* 93, no. 4 (Summer 2010): 1410, scholarship.law.marquette.edu/cgi/viewcontent.cgi ?article=5026&context=mulr.

8. EconoEdLink, Resource 6, Social Security: Visualizing the Debate, U.S. History: Lesson 3.1 in "The History of Social Security" in *Understanding Fiscal Responsibility*, Economics & Personal Finance Resources for K–12, www .econedlink.org/wp-content/uploads/legacy/1311_Social%20Security%206 .pdf.

9. Nancy J. Altman, *The Truth About Social Security: The Founders' Words Refute Revisionist History, Zombie Lies, and Common Misunderstandings* (Washington, DC: Strong Arm Press, 2018).

10. See, for example, "Polling Memo: Americans' Views on Social Security," Social Security Works, March 2019, socialsecurityworks.org/2019/03/26 /social-security-polling/.

11. Franklin D. Roosevelt, "President Franklin Roosevelt's 1943 State of the Union Address," January 7, 1943, History, Art & Archives, US House of Representatives, history.house.gov/Collection/Listing/PA2011/PA2011-07-0020/.

12. Altman, *The Truth About Social Security*, 7.

13. Ibid.

14. Board of Trustees of the Federal Old-Age and Survivors Insurance and Federal Disability Insurance Trust Funds, "Letter of Transmittal," Washington, DC, April 22, 2019, www.ssa.gov/OACT/TR/2019/tr2019.pdf.

15. Marc Goldwein, "Social Security Is Approaching Crisis Territory," *The Hill*, April 29, 2019, thehill.com/opinion/finance/441125-social-security-is -approaching-crisis-territory#.XMdbf0dTNXs.

16. Social Security Administration, *Summary of Provision That Would Change the Social Security Program*, Office of the Chief Actuary, SSA, December 30, 2019, www.ssa.gov/OACT/solvency/provisions/summary.pdf.

17. Laurence Kotlikoff, "Social Security Just Ran a $9 Trillion Deficit, and Nobody Noticed," *The Hill*, May 14, 2019, thehill.com/opinion/finance/443 465-social-security-just-ran-a-9-trillion-deficit-and-nobody-noticed.

18. NCPSSM, "Raising the Social Security Retirement Age: A Cut in Benefits for Future Retirees," National Committee to Preserve Social Security & Medicare, October 30, 2018, www.ncpssm.org/documents/social-security -policy-papers/raising-the-social-security-retirement-age-a-cut-in-benefits -for-future-retirees/.

19. Steven M. Gillon, *The Pact: Bill Clinton, Newt Gingrich, and the Rivalry That Defined a Generation* (New York: Oxford University Press, 2008).

20. Stephanie A. Kelton, "Entitled to Nothing: Why Americans Should Just Say 'No' to Personal Accounts," Working Paper No. 40, Center for Full Employment and Price Stability, University of Missouri–Kansas City, April 2005, www.cfeps.org/pubs/wp-pdf/WP40-Bell.pdf.

21. Nicole Woo and Alan Barber, "The Chained CPI: A Painful Cut in Social Security Benefits," Center for Economic and Policy Research, 2012, cepr .net/documents/publications/cpi-2012-12.pdf.

22. Dean Baker, "Statement on Using the Chained CPI for Social Security Cost of Living Adjustments," Center for Economic and Policy Research, July 8, 2011, cepr.net/press-center/press-releases//statement-on-using-the -chained-cpi-for-social-security-cost-of-living-adjustments.

23. "Consumer Price Index for the elderly," Bureau of Labor Statistics, US Department of Labor, March 2012.

24. 2011 OASID Trustees Report, Table V.C3: Legislated Changes in Normal Retirement Age and Delayed Retirement Credits, for Persons Reaching Age 62 in Each Year 1986 and Later, www.socialsecurity.gov/OACT/TR/2011 /V_C_prog.html#180548. See also US Bureau of Labor Statistics, "TED: The Economics Daily," Consumer Price Index for the Elderly, March 2, 2012, www.bls.gov/opub/ted/2012/ted_20120302.htm.

25. D. Rosnick and D. Baker, "The Impact on Inequality of Raising the Social Security Retirement Age," Center for Economic and Policy Research, April 2012, cepr.net/publications/reports/the-impact-on-inequality -of-raising-the-social-security-retirement-age.

26. Social Security and Medicare Boards of Trustees, "A Summary of the 2019 Annual Reports: A Message to the Public," US Social Security Administration, www.ssa.gov/oact/trsum/.

27. Ibid.

28. Transamerica Center for Retirement Studies, *18th Annual Transamerica Retirement Survey: A Compendium of Findings About American Workers*, Transamerica Institute, June 2018, www.transamericacenter.org /docs/default-source/retirement-survey-of-workers/tcrs2018_sr_18th _annual_worker_compendium.pdf.

29. Peter Whoriskey, "'I Hope I Can Quit Working in a Few Years': A Preview of the U.S. Without Pensions," *Washington Post*, December 23, 2017, www.washingtonpost.com/business/economy/i-hope-i-can-quit-working -in-a-few-years-a-preview-of-the-us-without-pensions/2017/12/22/5cc9fdf6 -cf09-11e7-81bc-c55a220c8cbe_story.html.

30. Teresa Ghilarducci, Michael Papadopoulos, and Anthony Webb, "40% of Older Workers and Their Spouses Will Experience Downward Mobility," Schwartz Center for Economic Policy Analysis Policy Note, The New School, 2018, www.economicpolicyresearch.org/resource-library/research /downward-mobility-in-retirement.

31. Alica H. Munnell, Kelly Haverstick, and Mauricio Soto, "Why Have Defined Benefit Plans Survived in the Public Sector?," Briefs, Center for Retirement Research, Boston College, December 2007, crr.bc.edu/briefs /why-have-defined-benefit-plans-survived-in-the-public-sector/.

32. Monique Morrissey, "The State of American Retirement: How 401(k)s Have Failed Most American Workers," Economic Policy Institute, March 3, 2016, www.epi.org/publication/retirement-in-america/.

33. Kathleen Romig, "Social Security Lifts More Americans Above Poverty Than Any Other Program," Center on Budget and Policy Priorities, www.cbpp.org/research/social-security/social-security-lifts-more-americans -above-poverty-than-any-other-program.

34. T. Skocpol, "America's First Social Security System: The Expansion of Benefits for Civil War Veterans," *Political Science Quarterly* 108, no. 1 (1993): 85–116.

35. "Oldest Civil War Pensioner Gets $73 a Month from VA," *Florida Today*, August 2017, www.floridatoday.com/story/news/2017/08/24/one-n-c -woman-still-receiving-civil-war-pension/594982001/.

36. Juan Williams, *Muzzled: The Assault on Honest Debate* (New York: Broadway, 2011).

37. John Light, "Déjà Vu: A Look Back at Some of the Tirades Against Social Security and Medicare," Moyers, October 1, 2013, updated August 14, 2014, billmoyers.com/content/deja-vu-all-over-a-look-back-at-some-of-the -tirades-against-social-security-and-medicare/4/.

38. John Nichols, *The "S" Word: A Short History of an American Tradition . . . Socialism* (London: Verso, 2012).

39. Sarah Kliff, "When Medicare Was Launched, Nobody Had Any Clue Whether It Would Work," *Washington Post*, May 17, 2013, www.washington post.com/news/wonk/wp/2013/05/17/when-medicare-launched-nobody -had-any-clue-whether-it-would-work/.

40. Bryan R. Lawrence, "The Illusion of Health-Care 'Trust Funds,'" *Washington Post*, October 18, 2012, www.washingtonpost.com/opinions/the -illusion-of-health-care-trust-funds/2012/10/18/844047d8-1897-11e2-9855 -71f2b202721b_story.html.

41. Gail Wilensky, "Medicare and Medicaid Are Unsustainable Without Quick Action," *New York Times*, January 11, 2016, www.nytimes.com /roomfordebate/2015/07/30/the-next-50-years-for-medicare-and-medicaid /medicare-and-medicaid-are-unsustainable-without-quick-action.

42. Philip Moeller, "Medicare and Social Security Stay on Unsustainable Financial Paths, Reports Show," PBS News Hour, April 22, 2019, www.pbs .org/newshour/health/medicare-and-social-security-stay-on-unsustainable -financial-paths-reports-show.

43. Diana Furchtgott-Roth, "Medicare Is Unsustainable in Current Form," MarketWatch, December 2012, www.marketwatch.com/story/medicare-is -unsustainable-in-current-form-2012-12-06.

44. J. Adamy and P. Overberg, "Growth in Retiring Baby Boomers Strains US Entitlement Programs," *Wall Street Journal*, June 21, 2018, www.wsj.com /articles/retiring-baby-boomers-leave-the-u-s-with-fewer-workers-to -support-the-elderly-1529553660.

45. Ibid.

46. Lenny Bernstein, "US Life Expectancy Declines Again, a Dismal Trend Not Seen Since World War I," *Washington Post*, WP Company, November 29, 2018, www.washingtonpost.com/national/health-science/us-life-expectancy -declines-again-a-dismal-trend-not-seen-since-world-war-i/2018/11/28 /ae58bc8c-f28c-11e8-bc79-68604ed88993_story.html.

47. Raj Chetty, Michael Stepner, Sarah Abraham, Shelby Lin, Benjamin Scuderi, Nicholas Turner, Augustin Bergeron, and David Cutler, "The Association Between Income and Life Expectancy in the United States, 2001–2014," *Journal of the American Medical Association* 315, no. 16 (April 2016): 1750–1766, jamanetwork.com/journals/jama/article-abstract/2513561.

48. Hendrik Hertzberg, "Senses of Entitlement," *The New Yorker*, April 1, 2013, www.newyorker.com/magazine/2013/04/08/senses-of-entitlement.

49. Richard R. J. Eskow, "'Entitlement Reform' Is a Euphemism for Letting Old People Get Sick and Die," Huffpost, February 25, 2011, www.huffpost .com/entry/entitlement-reform-is-a-e_b_828544.

50. John Harwood, "Spending $1 Billion to Restore Fiscal Sanity," *New York Times*, July 14, 2008, www.nytimes.com/2008/07/14/us/politics/14caucus .html.

51. Lori Montgomery, "Presidential Commission to Address Rising National Debt," *Washington Post*, April 27, 2010, www.washingtonpost.com /wp-dyn/content/article/2010/04/26/AR2010042604189_pf.html.

52. Between 2009 and 2011, the organization America Speaks received $4,048,073 from the Peterson Foundation; see the Center for Media Democracy, "America Speaks," SourceWatch, www.sourcewatch.org/index.php /America_Speaks.

53. Dan Eggen, "Many Deficit Commission Staffers Paid by Outside Groups," *Washington Post*, November 10, 2010, www.washingtonpost.com /wp-dyn/content/article/2010/11/10/AR2010111006850.html.

54. Peter G. Peterson, "Statement by Foundation Chairman Pete Peterson on Simpson-Bowles 'Bipartisan Path Forward to Securing America's Future,'" Peter G. Peterson Foundation, April 19, 2013, www.pgpf.org/press-release /statement-by-foundation-chairman-pete-peterson-on-simpson-bowles -bipartisan-path-forward-to-securing-america%E2%80%99s-future.

55. See, for example, Alan Simpson and Erskine Bowles, "A Moment of Truth for Our Country's Financial Future," *Washington Post*, November 29, 2017, www.washingtonpost.com/opinions/a-moment-of-truth -for-our-countrys-financial-future/2017/11/29/22963ce6-d475-11e7-a986-d0a 9770d9a3e_story.html; and Committee for a Responsible Federal Budget, "Bowles and Simpson Announce Campaign to Fix the Debt on CNBC's Squawkbox," The Bottom Line (blog), July 12, 2012, www.crfb.org/blogs /bowles-and-simpson-announce-campaign-fix-debt-cnbcs-squawkbox.

56. Peter G. Peterson Foundation, "Peterson Foundation to Convene 3rd Annual Fiscal Summit in Washington on May 15th" (press release), May 8, 2012, www.pgpf.org/event/peterson-foundation-to-convene-3rd-annual -fiscal-summit-in-washington-on-may-15th.

57. Michael Hiltzik, "'60 Minutes' Shameful Attack on the Disabled," *Los Angeles Times*, October 7, 2013, www.latimes.com/business/hiltzik/la-xpm -2013-oct-07-la-fi-mh-disabled-20131007-story.html.

58. Congresswoman Susan Wild, "Rep. Wild Secures Funding for Social Security Administration to Address Wait Times in House-Passed Government Funding" (press release), June 19, 2019, wild.house.gov/media/press -releases/rep-wild-secures-funding-social-security-administration-address -wait-times.

59. H. Luke Shaefer and Kathryn Edin, "Extreme Poverty in the United States, 1996 to 2011," Policy Brief no. 28, National Poverty Center, February 2012, npc.umich.edu/publications/policy_briefs/brief28/policybrief28.pdf.

60. Eduardo Porter, "The Myth of Welfare's Corrupting Influence on the Poor," *New York Times*, October 20, 2015, www.nytimes.com/2015/10/21/business/the-myth-of-welfares-corrupting-influence-on-the-poor.html.

61. Kyodo, Bloomberg, staff report, "Japan's Pension System Inadequate in Aging Society, Council Warns," *Japan Times*, June 4, 2019, www.japantimes.co.jp/news/2019/06/04/business/financial-markets/japans-pension-system-inadequate-aging-society-council-warns/#.XjQe1pNKjBI.

62. Alan Greenspan, "There is nothing to prevent government from creating as much money as it wants," Committee on the Budget, House of Representatives, March 2, 2005, posted by wonkmonk, YouTube, March 24, 2014, 1:35, www.youtube.com/watch?v=DNCZHAQnfGU.

63. C-SPAN, 2005 greenspan ryan, 02:42, March 2, 2005, www.c-span.org/video/?c3886511/user-clip-2005-greenspan-ryan-024200.

64. Ibid.

65. Robert Eisner, "Save Social Security from Its Saviors," *Journal of Post Keynesian Economics* 21, no. 1 (1998): 77–92.

66. Ibid., 80.

67. Eisner was not opposed to any of these particular changes, but he supported them on equity grounds, rather than viewing them as changes that were needed to help keep the system solvent.

68. "Policy Basics: Where Do Our Federal Tax Dollars Go?" Center on Budget and Policy Priorities, January 29, 2019, https://www.cbpp.org/research/federal-budget/policy-basics-where-do-our-federal-tax-dollars-go.

69. William E. Gibson, "Age 65+ Adults Are Projected to Outnumber Children by 2030," AARP, March 14, 2018, www.aarp.org/home-family/friends-family/info-2018/census-baby-boomers-fd.html.

Chapter 7: The Deficits That Matter

1. Rebecca Shabad, "Bernie Sanders Flips the Script with 'Deficit' Plan," *The Hill*, January 2015, thehill.com/policy/finance/230692-budget-ranking-member-lays-out-plan-to-eliminate-economic-deficits.

2. Sabrina Tavernise, "With His Job Gone, an Autoworker Wonders, What Am I as a Man?," *New York Times*, May 27, 2019, www.nytimes.com/2019/05/27/us/auto-worker-jobs-lost.html.

3. Robert McCoppin and Lolly Bowean, "Getting By with the Minimum," *Chicago Tribune*, February 2, 2014, www.chicagotribune.com/news/ct-xpm-2014-02-02-ct-minimum-wage-illinois-met-20140202-story.html.

4. Matthew Boesler, "Almost 40% of Americans Would Struggle to Cover a $400 Emergency," Bloomberg, May 23, 2019, www.bloomberg.com/news/articles/2019-05-23/almost-40-of-americans-would-struggle-to-cover-a-400-emergency.

5. Suresh Naidu, Eric Posner, and Glen Weyl, "More and More Companies Have Monopoly Power over Workers ‹Wages. That's Killing the Economy," Vox, April 6, 2018, www.vox.com/the-big-idea/2018/4/6/17204808/wages-employers-workers-monopsony-growth-stagnation-inequality.

6. Economic Innovation Group, *The New Map of Economic Growth and Recovery*, May 2016, eig.org/wp-content/uploads/2016/05/recoverygrowth report.pdf.

7. Chris Arnade, *Dignity: Seeking Respect in Back Row America* (New York: Sentinel, 2019).

8. Nicky Woolf, "Over 50 and Once Successful, Jobless Americans Seek Support Groups to Help Where Congress Has Failed," *Guardian* (Manchester, UK), November 7, 2014, www.theguardian.com/money/2014/nov/07/long-term-unemployed-support-groups-congress.

9. Jagdish Khubchandani and James H. Price, "Association of Job Insecurity with Health Risk Factors and Poorer Health in American Workers," *Journal of Community Health* 42, no. 2 (April 2017): 242–251.

10. David N. F. Bell and David G. Blanchflower, "Unemployment in the US and Europe," Department of Economics, Dartmouth College, August 7, 2018, www.dartmouth.edu/~blnchflr/papers/revised%20%20europe%20Underemployment%20paper%20august%207th%202018.pdf.

11. National Institute on Retirement Security, "New Report Finds Nation's Retirement Crisis Persists Despite Economic Recovery" (press release), September 17, 2018, www.nirsonline.org/2018/09/new-report-finds-nations-retirement-crisis-persists-despite-economic-recovery/.

12. Emmie Martin, "67% of Americans Say They'll Outlive Their Retirement Savings—Here's How Many Have Nothing Saved at All," Make It, CNBC, May 14, 2018, www.cnbc.com/2018/05/11/how-many-americans-have-no-retirement-savings.html.

13. Sean Dennison, "64% of Americans Aren't Prepared for Retirement—and 48% Don't Care," Yahoo Finance, September 23, 2019, finance.yahoo.com/news/survey-finds-42-americans-retire-100701878.html.

14. Emmie Martin, "Here's How Much More Expensive It Is for You to Go to College Than It Was for Your Parents," Make It, CNBC, November 2017, www.cnbc.com/2018/05/11/how-many-americans-have-no-retirement-savings.html.

15. FRED, "Working Age Population: Aged 15–64; All Persons for the United States" (chart), Federal Reserve Bank of Saint Louis, updated October 9, 2019, fred.stlouisfed.org/series/LFWA64TTUSM647S.

16. Alessandro Malito, "The Retirement Crisis Is Bad for Everyone—Especially These People," MarketWatch, August 2019, www.marketwatch.com/story/the-retirement-crisis-is-bad-for-everyone-especially-these-people-2019-04-12.

17. Associated Press, "Nearly One-Quarter of Americans Say They'll Never Retire, According to a New Poll," CBS News, July 2019, www.cbsnews.com /news/nearly-one-quarter-of-americans-say-theyll-never-retire-according -to-new-poll/.

18. AnnaMaria Andriotis, Ken Brown, and Shane Shifflett, "Families Go Deep into Debt to Stay in the Middle Class," *Wall Street Journal*, August 1, 2019.

19. Sarah Jane Glynn, "Breadwinning Mothers are Increasingly the US Norm," Center for American Progress, December 19, 2016, www.american progress.org/issues/women/reports/2016/12/19/295203/breadwinning -mothers-are-increasingly-the-u-s-norm/.

20. Steve Dubb, "Baltimore Confronts Enduring Racial Health Disparities," NonProfit Quarterly, November 22, 2017, nonprofitquarterly.org/baltimore -confronts-enduring-racial-health-disparities/.

21. Gaby Galvin, "87M Adults Were Uninsured or Underinsured in 2018, Survey Says," *U.S. News & World Report*, February 7, 2019, www.usnews .com/news/healthiest-communities/articles/2019-02-07/lack-of-health -insurance-coverage-leads-people-to-avoid-seeking-care.

22. Tami Luhby, "Is Obamacare Really Affordable? Not for the Middle Class," CNN, November 2016, money.cnn.com/2016/11/04/news/economy /obamacare-affordable/index.html.

23. Boesler, "Almost 40% of Americans Would Struggle to Cover a $400 Emergency."

24. Bob Herman, "Medical Costs Are Driving Millions of People into Poverty," Axios, September 2019, www.axios.com/medical-expenses-poverty -deductibles-540e2c09-417a-4936-97aa-c241fd5396d2.html.

25. Lori Konish, "137 Million Americans Are Struggling with Medical Debt. Here's What to Know if You Need Some Relief," CNBC, November 12, 2019, ww.cnbc.com/2019/11/10/americans-are-drowning-in-medical-debt-what -to-know-if-you-need-help.html.

26. Matt Bruenig, "How Many People will Obamacare and AHCA Kill?" (blog), MattBruenig Politics, mattbruenig.com/2017/06/22/how-many -people-will-obamacare-and-ahca-kill/.

27. Catherine Rampell, "It Takes a B.A. to Find a Job as a File Clerk," *New York Times*, February 19, 2013, www.nytimes.com/2013/02/20/business /college-degree-required-by-increasing-number-of-companies.html.

28. Leslie Brody, "New York City Plans to Give More 3-Year-Olds Free Early Childhood Education," *Wall Street Journal*, January 10, 2019, www .wsj.com/articles/new-york-city-plans-to-give-more-3-year-olds-free-early -childhood-education-11547165926?mod=article_inline).

29. US Department of Education, "Obama Administration Investments in Early Learning Have Led to Thousands More Children Enrolled in

High-Quality Preschool," September 2016, www.ed.gov/news/press-releases /obama-administration-investments-early-learning-have-led-thousands -more-children-enrolled-high-quality-preschool.

30. US Department of Education, "Every Student Succeeds Act (ESSA)," www.ed.gov/essa.

31. Timothy Williams, "Poor Schools Keep Getting Crushed in the Football. Is it Time to Level the Playing Field?" *New York Times*, September 2019, www.nytimes.com/2019/09/22/us/school-football-poverty.html.

32. Martin, "Here's How Much More Expensive It Is for You to Go to College Than It Was for Your Parents."

33. Demos, "African Americans, Student Debt, and Financial Security," 2016, www.demos.org/sites/default/files/publications/African%20Americans %20and%20Student%20Debt%5B7%5D.pdf.

34. Alexandre Tanzi, "U.S. Student-Loan Delinquencies Hit Record," Bloomberg Businessweek, February 22, 2019, www.bloomberg.com/news /articles/2019-02-22/u-s-student-loan-delinquencies-hit-record.

35. Elise Gould, "Higher Returns on Education Can't Explain Growing Wage Inequality," Economic Policy Institute, March 15, 2019, www.epi.org /blog/higher-returns-on-education-cant-explain-growing-wage-inequality/.

36. Scott Fullwiler, Stephanie Kelton, Catherine Ruetschlin, and Marshall Steinbaum, *The Macroeconomic Effects of Student Debt Cancellation*, Levy Economics Institute of Bard College, February 2018, www.levyinstitute.org /pubs/rpr_2_6.pdf.

37. Patrick McGeehan, "Your Tales of La Guardia Airport Hell," *New York Times*, August 29, 2019, www.nytimes.com/interactive/2019/08/29/nyregion /la-guardia-airport.html?smid=tw-nytimes&smtyp=cur.

38. Irwin Redlener, "The Deadly Cost of Failing Infrastructure," *The Hill*, April 2019, thehill.com/opinion/energy-environment/437550-ignoring -warning-signs-made-historic-midwest-floods-more-dangerous.

39. ASCE, "2017 Infrastructure Report Card: Dams," Infrastructure Report Card, 2017, www.infrastructurereportcard.org/wp-content/uploads/2017/01 /Dams-Final.pdf.

40. ASCE, Infrastructure Report Card, www.infrastructurereportcard.org/.

41. Lauren Aratani, "'Damage Has Been Done': Newark Water Crisis Echoes Flint," *Guardian* (Manchester, UK), August 2019, www.theguardian .com/us-news/2019/aug/25/newark-lead-water-crisis-flint.

42. Peter Gowan and Ryan Cooper, *Social Housing in the United States*, People's Policy Project, 2018, www.peoplespolicyproject.org/wp-content /uploads/2018/04/SocialHousing.pdf.

43. Richard "Skip" Bronson, "Homeless and Empty Homes—an American Travesty," Huffpost, May 25, 2011, www.huffpost.com/entry/post_733 _b_692546.

44. IPCC, *Global Warming of 1.5° C*, Special Report, United Nations Inter-governmental Panel on Climate Change, 2018, www.ipcc.ch/sr15/.

45. Nathan Hultman, "We're Almost Out of Time: The Alarming IPCC Climate Report and What to Do Next," Brookings Institution, Octo-ber 16, 2018, www.brookings.edu/opinions/were-almost-out-of-time-the-alarming-ipcc-climate-report-and-what-to-do-next/.

46. Umair Irfan, "Report: We Have Just 12 Years to Limit Devastating Global Warming," Vox, October 8, 2018, www.vox.com/2018/10/8/17948832/climate-change-global-warming-un-ipcc-report.

47. Brandon Miller and Jay Croft, "Planet Has Only Until 2030 to Stem Catastrophic Climate Change, Experts Warn," CNN, October 8, 2018, www.cnn.com/2018/10/07/world/climate-change-new-ipcc-report-wxc/index.html.

48. Union of Concerned Scientists, "Underwater: Rising Seas, Chronic Floods, and the Implications for US Coastal Real Estate," 2018, www.ucsusa.org/global-warming/global-warming-impacts/sea-level-rise-chronic-floods-and-us-coastal-real-estate-implications.

49. Doyle Rice, "Hundreds Flee as Record Rainfall Swamps North-ern California, but Thousands Refuse to Leave," *USA Today*, Febru-ary 27, 2019, www.usatoday.com/story/news/nation/2019/02/27/california-floods-hundreds-flee-their-homes-thousands-refuse/3004836002/.

50. Dana Goodyear, "Waking Up from the California Dream in the Age of Wildfires," *The New Yorker*, November 11, 2019, www.newyorker.com/news/daily-comment/waking-up-from-the-california-dream.

51. Umair Irfan, Eliza Barclay, and Kavya Sukumar, "Weather 2050," Vox, July 19, 2019, www.vox.com/a/weather-climate-change-us-cities-global-warming.

52. Sebastien Malo, "U.S. Faces Fresh Water Shortages Due to Climate Change, Research Says," Reuters, February 28, 2019, www.reuters.com/article/us-usa-climatechange-water/u-s-faces-fresh-water-shortages-due-to-climate-change-research-says-idUSKCN1QI36L.

53. Josie Garthwaite, "Stanford Researchers Explore the Effects of Climate Change on Water Shortages," Stanford News, March 22, 2019, news.stanford.edu/2019/03/22/effects-climate-change-water-shortages/.

54. Robin Meyer, "This Land Is the Only Land There Is," *The Atlantic*, August 8, 2019, www.theatlantic.com/science/archive/2019/08/how-think-about-dire-new-ipcc-climate-report/595705/.

55. Hultman, "We're Almost Out of Time."

56. Callum Roberts, "Our Seas Are Being Degraded, Fish Are Dying—but Humanity Is Threatened Too," *Guardian* (Manchester, UK), Septem-ber 19, 2015, www.theguardian.com/environment/2015/sep/20/fish-are-dying-but-human-life-is-threatened-too.

57. Damian Carrington, "Plummeting Insect Numbers 'Threaten Collapse of Nature,'" *Guardian* (Manchester, UK), February 10, 2019, www.the guardian.com/environment/2019/feb/10/plummeting-insect-numbers -threaten-collapse-of-nature.

58. Union of Concerned Scientists, "Vehicles, Air Pollution, and Human Health" (webpage), July 18, 2014, www.ucsusa.org/resources/vehicles -air-pollution-human-health.

59. Drew Shindell, Greg Faluvegi, Karl Seltzer, and Cary Shindell, "Quantified, Localized Health Benefits of Accelerated Carbon Dioxide Emissions Reductions," Nature Climate Change, March 19, 2018, www.nature.com /articles/s41558-018-0108-y.

60. World Economic and Social Survey, "Report: Inequalities Exacerbate Climate Impacts on Poor," Sustainable Development Goals, United Nations, 2016, www.un.org/sustainabledevelopment/blog/2016/10/report-inequalities -exacerbate-climate-impacts-on-poor/.

61. Kelsey Piper, "Is Climate Change an 'Existential Threat'—or Just a Catastrophic One?," Vox, June 28, 2019, www.vox.com/future-perfect /2019/6/13/18660548/climate-change-human-civilization-existential-risk.

62. University of Adelaide, "IPCC Is Underselling Climate Change," Science Daily, March 20, 2019, www.sciencedaily.com/releases/2019/03/190320102010 .htm.

63. Irfan, "Report: We Have Just 12 Years to Limit Devastating Global Warming."

64. David Roberts, "What Genuine, No-Bullshit Ambition on Climate Change Would Look Like," Vox, October 8, 2018, www.vox.com /energy-and-environment/2018/5/7/17306008/climate-change-global -warming-scenarios-ambition.

65. MCC, "That's How Fast the Carbon Clock Is Ticking," Mercator Research Institute on Global Commons and Climate Change, December 2018, www.mcc-berlin.net/en/research/co2-budget.html.

66. Kimberly Amadeo, "The US National Debt Clock and Its Warning," The Balance, February 13, 2019, www.thebalance.com/u-s-national -debt-clock-definition-and-history-3306297.

67. WEF, *The Inclusive Development Index 2018: Summary and Data Highlights* (Geneva, Switzerland: World Economic Forum, 2018), www3.weforum .org/docs/WEF_Forum_IncGrwth_2018.pdf.

68. Quentin Fottrell, "Alone," MarketWatch, October 10, 2018, www .marketwatch.com/story/america-has-a-big-loneliness-problem-2018-05-02.

69. Children's Defense Fund, "Child Poverty" (webpage), www.childrens defense.org/policy/policy-priorities/child-poverty/.

70. Sheri Marino, "The Effects of Poverty on Children," Focus for Health, April 1, 2019, www.focusforhealth.org/effects-poverty-on-children/.

71. Christopher Ingraham, "Wealth Concentration Returning to 'Levels Last Seen During the Roaring Twenties,' According to New Research," *Washington Post*, February 8, 2019, www.washingtonpost.com/us-policy/2019/02/08 /wealth-concentration-returning-levels-last-seen-during-roaring-twenties -according-new-research/.

72. Sean McElwee, "The Income Gap at the Polls," *Politico Magazine*, January 7, 2015, www.politico.com/magazine/story/2015/01/income-gap-at-the -polls-113997.

73. Sabrina Tavernise, "Many in Milwaukee Neighborhood Didn't Vote— and Don't Regret It," *New York Times*, November 20, 2016, www.nytimes .com/2016/11/21/us/many-in-milwaukee-neighborhood-didnt-vote-and -dont-regret-it.html.

74. Jake Bittle, "The 'Hidden' Crisis of Rural Homelessness," *The Nation*, March 28, 2019, www.thenation.com/article/rural-homelessness-housing/.

75. Chris Arnade, "Outside Coastal Cities an 'Other America' Has Different Values and Challenges," *Guardian* (Manchester, UK), February 21, 2017, www.theguardian.com/society/2017/feb/21/outside-coastal-bubbles-to-say -america-is-already-great-rings-hollow.

76. Chris Arnade, *Dignity: Seeking Respect in Back Row America* (New York: Sentinel, 2019).

77. Martin Gilens and Benjamin I. Page, "Testing Theories of American Politics: Elites, Interest Groups, and Average Citizens," *Perspectives on Politics* 12, no. 3 (September 2014): 564–581, www.cambridge.org/core/journals /perspectives-on-politics/article/testing-theories-of-american-politics -elites-interest-groups-and-average-citizens/62327F513959D0A304D4893 B382B992B/core-reader.

78. Facundo Alvaredo, Lucas Chancel, Thomas Piketty, Emmanuel Saez, and Gabriel Zucman, *World Inequality Report 2018: Executive Summary*, World Inequality Lab, 2017, wir2018.wid.world/files/download/wir2018 -summary-english.pdf.

79. "Federal Individual Income Tax Rates History" (chart), 1913–2013, files .taxfoundation.org/legacy/docs/fed_individual_rate_history_adjusted.pdf.

80. Robert B. Reich, *Saving Capitalism: For the Many, Not the Few* (New York: Alfred A. Knopf, 2015).

81. Robert Reich, Tweet, March 12, 2019, 5:22 p.m., available at Meme, me.me/i/robert-reich-rbreich-the-concentration-of-wealth-in-america-has -408c58b6e98d4dcf9f4969d237dd3442.

82. Era Dabla-Norris, Kalpana Kochnar, Nujin Suphaphiphat, Frantisek Ricka, and Evridiki Tsounta, *Causes and Consequences of Income Inequality: A Global Perspective*, International Monetary Fund, June 2015, www.imf.org /external/pubs/ft/sdn/2015/sdn1513.pdf.

83. Josh Bivens and Lawrence Mishel, "Understanding the Historic Divergence Between Productivity and a Typical Worker's Pay," Briefing Paper No. 406, Economic Policy Institute, September 2, 2015, www.epi.org/publication/understanding-the-historic-divergence-between-productivity-and-a-typical-workers-pay-why-it-matters-and-why-its-real/.

84. Ibid.

85. Reuters, "CEOs Earn 361 Times More Than the Average U.S. Worker—Union Report," May 22, 2018, www.reuters.com/article/us-usa-compensation-ceos/ceos-earn-361-times-more-than-the-average-u-s-worker-union-report-idUSKCN1IN2FU.

86. Alvaredo et al., *World Inequality Report 2018*.

87. Chuck Collins and Josh Hoxie, *Billionaire Bonanza 2017: The Forbes 400 and the Rest of Us*, Institute for Policy Studies, November 2017, inequality.org/wp-content/uploads/2017/11/BILLIONAIRE-BONANZA-2017-Embargoed.pdf.

Chapter 8: Building an Economy for the People

1. The meeting was arranged by former city councilman Troy Nash, who joined us for the meeting.

2. He also had an ambitious plan to reform the banking system, which is where the seeds of the crisis were sown.

3. Congressional Budget Office, *The Long-Term Budget Outlook* (Washington, DC: CBO, June 2010, revised August 2010), www.cbo.gov/sites/default/files/111th-congress-2009-2010/reports/06-30-ltbo.pdf.

4. Ibid.

5. Warren Mosler recounts a number of similar experiences in his book. See Mosler, *The 7 Deadly Innocent Frauds of Economic Policy* (Christiansted, USVI: Valance, 2010).

6. There are many excellent books that deal with one or more of these issues. See, for example, Robert B. Reich, *Saving Capitalism* (New York: Alfred A. Knopf, 2015); David Cay Johnston, *Free Lunch* (London: Penguin, 2007); Thomas Frank, *Listen, Liberal* (New York: Metropolitan Books/Henry Holt, 2015); Richard Florida, *The New Urban Crisis* (New York: Basic Books/Hachette, 2017); Chris Arnade, *Dignity* (New York: Sentinel, 2019); Anand Giridharadas, *Winners Take All* (New York: Vintage, 2019); and David Dayen, *Chain of Title* (New York: New Press, 2016).

7. Center on Budget and Policy Priorities, "Policy Basics: Introduction to the Federal Budget Process," updated July 8, 2019, www.cbpp.org/research/policy-basics-introduction-to-the-federal-budget-process.

8. Of course, Congress could change the mandatory side of the budget as well. For example, there are calls to increase in Social Security benefits and

to lower the eligibility age from sixty-five to zero to provide health care to all
people under a single-payer, Medicare-for-all system.

9. For more on this see A. G. Hart, "Monetary Policy for Income Stabiliza-
tion" in *Income Stabilization for a Developing Democracy*, ed. Max F. Millikan
(New Haven, CT: Yale University Press, 1953); Simon Gray and Runchana
Pongsaparn, *Issuance of Central Securities: International Experiences and
Guidelines*, IMF Working Paper, WP/15/106, May 2015, www.imf.org
/external/pubs/ft/wp/2015/wp15106.pdf; and Rohan Grey, "Banking in a Digi-
tal Fiat Currency Regime," in *Regulating Blockchain: Techno-Social and Legal
Challenges*, ed. Philipp Hacker, Ioannis Lianos, Georgios Dimitropoulos, and
Stefan Eich (Oxford, UK: Oxford University Press, 2019), 169–180, rohangrey
.net/files/banking.pdf.

10. The CBO estimates that net interest expenditure will rise from 1.8
percent of GDP in 2019 to 3.0 percent by 2029, climbing all the way to 5.7
percent by 2049. See Congressional Budget Office, *The 2019 Long-Term Budget Outlook* (Washington, DC: CBO, 2019), www.cbo.gov/system/files/2019
-06/55331-LTBO-2.pdf. This line item in the federal budget could be eliminated by abandoning the current practice of coordinating fiscal deficits with
bond sales. Instead of selling bonds, Congress could simply leave any resulting reserve balances in the system, where they would earn interest at the Fed's
target rate. Most if not all MMT economists would prefer to see the interest
rate paid on overnight reserve balances permanently maintained at (or very
near) zero, but this is not essential to carrying out the other prescriptive ele-
ments of MMT.

11. Charles Blahous, "The Costs of a National Single-Payer Healthcare
System," Mercatus Working Paper, Mercatus Center, George Mason University, 2018, www.mercatus.org/system/files/blahous-costs-medicare-mercatus
-working-paper-v1_1.pdf.

12. Both were created under the Congressional Budget and Impoundment
Control Act of 1974. See "History" (webpage), Congressional Budget Office,
www.cbo.gov/about/history.

13. The other way to offset new spending is by carving money out of some
other area of the budget. For example, you might see legislation that proposes
to pay for new spending by reducing the defense budget.

14. Of course, there's no guarantee that a "clean bill" would have passed.
Would it have garnered more votes? Who knows? There is not much bipar-
tisanship in Congress these days. But one thing is for sure—the practice of
insisting that every proposed dollar of spending must be *fully* offset by a new
dollar of revenue (or care out) is both economically unnecessary and politically inept. The latest report calls for $4.59 trillion over a ten-year period.

15. Sheryl Gay Stolberg, "Senate Passes $700 Billion Pentagon Bill, More Money Than Trump Sought," *New York Times*, September 18, 2017, www .nytimes.com/2017/09/18/us/politics/senate-pentagon-spending-bill.html.

16. Christal Hayes, "Alexandria Ocasio-Cortez: Why Does GOP Fund 'Unlimited War' but Not Medicare Program?," *USA Today*, August 9, 2018, www .usatoday.com/story/news/politics/onpolitics/2018/08/09/alexandria -ocasio-cortez-republicans-finance-war-not-healthcare-tuition/946511002/.

17. Calvin H. Johnson, "Fifty Ways to Raise a Trillion," in *Tax Reform: Lessons from the Tax Reform Act of 1986*, Hearing Before the Committee on Finance, US Senate (Washington, DC: US GPO, 2010), 76, books.google.com /books?id=e4jnhl_AkLgC&pg=PA76&lpg=PA76&dq=calvin+johnson +shelf+project&source=bl&ots=yeBPKBOXV1&sig=ACfU3U3OXXYvNQ grroi7ZBFI8jrStMJJBg&hl=en&sa=X&ved=2ahUKEwiTqekg6blAhVK 11kKHXiwAtkQ6AEwEHoECAkQAQ#v=onepage&q=calvin%20 johnson%20shelf%20project&f=false.

18. Ibid.

19. Keith Hennessey, "What Is a Vote-a-Rama?" (blog), March 25, 2010, keithhennessey.com/2010/03/25/vote-a-rama/.

20. Paul Krugman, "Deficits Saved the World," *New York Times*, July 15, 2009, krugman.blogs.nytimes.com/2009/07/15/deficits-saved-the-world/.

21. Jeff Spross, "You're Hired!," *Democracy: A Journal of Ideas* 44 (Spring 2019), democracyjournal.org/magazine/44/youre-hired/.

22. Bureau of Labor Statistics, "Most Unemployed People in 2018 Did Not Apply for Unemployment Insurance Benefits," econintersect.com, econ intersect.com/pages/contributors/contributor.php?post=201910220659.

23. In the version of the federal job guarantee developed by MMT economists, anyone who is legally eligible to work—age sixteen and over and a US citizen or noncitizens who are legally permitted to work in the US—would automatically qualify for employment. See L. Randall Wray, Flavia Dantas, Scott Fullwiler, Pavlina R. Tcherneva, and Stephanie A. Kelton, *Public Service Employment: A Path to Full Employment*, Levy Economics Institute of Bard College, April 2018, www.levyinstitute.org/pubs/rpr_4_18.pdf.

24. Economists have proposed different versions of a job guarantee. This chapter features the version put forward by leading MMT economists. Workers would be paid $15/hr along with benefits (health care, childcare, and paid leave). For an alternative version that incorporates differential compensation based on experience and other considerations, see Mark Paul, William Darity Jr., and Darrick Hamilton, "The Federal Job Guarantee—A Policy to Achieve Permanent Full Employment," Center on Budget and Policy Priorities, March 9, 2018, https://www.cbpp.org/research/full-employment /the-federal-job-guarantee-a-policy-to-achieve-permanent-full-employment.

25. It is not a make-work scheme. Many of the jobs could resemble those created under the New Deal programs of the 1930s. For example, many public works projects were undertaken through the Works Progress Administration, a lot of environmental work was performed under the Civilian Conservation Corps, and part-time jobs were created for 1.5 million high school students and 600,000 college students under the National Youth Administration. In contrast to many of the Roosevelt-era New Deal programs, which excluded blacks and other minority groups from participating, the job guarantee would ensure universal access to all.

26. The job guarantee is not meant to replace any of the existing safety net programs. All of them, including unemployment insurance, can be maintained alongside the federal job guarantee. Of course, spending on food stamps, Medicaid, and other means-tested programs will naturally decline as many people who take public service jobs will become ineligible once their incomes are lifted sufficiently above poverty.

27. Remember, households (and businesses) are currency users. Once consumers decide that they've taken on too much debt—credit cards, mortgages, auto loans, student loans—they typically retrench. When that happens, the credit cycle reverses, and businesses experience a decline in sales.

28. See, for example, Michael J. Murray and Mathew Forstater, eds., *Full Employment and Social Justice* (New York: Palgrave Macmillan, 2018); Michael J. Murray and Mathew Forstater, eds., *The Job Guarantee* (New York: Palgrave Macmillan, 2013); Pavlina R. Tcherneva, *The Case for a Job Guarantee* (Cambridge, UK: Polity Press, 2020); and William S. Vickrey, *Full Employment and Price Stability* (Cheltenham, UK: Edward Elgar, 2004).

29. Wray et al., *Public Service Employment: A Path to Full Employment*.

30. For a more thorough discussion of how this would work, see Pavlina R. Tcherneva, "The Job Guarantee: Design, Jobs, and Implementation," Working Paper No. 902, Levy Economics Institute of Bard College, April 2018, www.levyinstitute.org/pubs/wp_902.pdf.

31. At $15 per hour, a full-time participant will earn an annual income of $31,200, calculated as $15/hour x 40 hours x 52 weeks = $31,200. Using current (2019) guidelines from the US Department of Health & Human Services, that is enough to lift a family of five above the poverty line. See US Department of Health & Human Services, "Poverty Guidelines," ASPE, aspe.hhs.gov/poverty-guidelines.

32. 8 hours per day x 5 days per week x 50 weeks x 12 million = 24,000,000,000.

33. The Civilian Conservation Corps was established by FDR in 1933. The program was not open to all. It was available only to unemployed, unmarried male citizens between the ages of eighteen and twenty-six. Blacks could

participate, but they were placed in what amounted to segregated camps. Any modern-day revival must be available to all who wish to participate.

34. Racial minorities are more likely to experience unemployment. They tend to be the first to lose jobs when the economy softens and the last to be hired when businesses are staffing up. They suffer both higher rates of unemployment and longer bouts of joblessness. The black unemployment rate, for example, is persistently double that of whites.

35. Pavlina R. Tcherneva, "Beyond Full Employment: The Employer of Last Resort as an Institution for Change," Working Paper No. 732, Levy Economics Institute of Bard College, September 2012, www.levyinstitute.org/pubs /wp_732.pdf.

36. Ibid.

37. After three years, the program was phased out and replaced with conventional unemployment insurance along with a more traditional welfare reform program that provided cash assistance instead of employment. Interestingly, Tcherneva discovered that income was among the least valued aspects of the Jefes de Hogar plan. Indeed, participants ranked income fifth (second to last) on the list of things they valued about working in the program. Ahead of income, they ranked: (1) doing something useful, (2) working in a good environment, (3) helping the community, (4) learning a valuable skill. Other benefits included: short commutes, proximity to day care, a feeling of connectedness to neighborhoods, gained respect, and a sense of empowerment. See Pavlina R. Tcherneva, "Modern Money and the Job Guarantee," posted by Jacobin, Vimeo, January 9, 2014, 14:02, vimeo .com/83813741.

38. Public Works & Infrastructure, "Welcome to EPWP" (webpage), Department: Public Works and Infrastructure, Republic of South Africa, www .epwp.gov.za/.

39. Ibid.

40. Klaus Deininger and Yanyan Liu, "Heterogeneous Welfare Impacts of National Rural Employment Guarantee Scheme: Evidence from Andhra Pradesh, India," *World Development* 117 (May 2019): 98–111, www.science direct.com/science/article/pii/S0305750X18304480?via%3Dihub.

41. Peter-Christian Aigner and Michael Brenes, "The Long, Tortured History of the Job Guarantee," *The New Republic*, May 11, 2018, newrepublic .com/article/148388/long-tortured-history-job-guarantee.

42. The Economic Bill of Rights would also have guaranteed the right to an education, the right to housing, the right to health care, and the right to a secure retirement. Franklin D. Roosevelt, "State of the Union Message to Congress: January 11, 1944," Franklin D. Roosevelt Presidential Library and Museum, www.fdrlibrary.marist.edu/archives/address_text.html.

43. Martin Luther King Jr., "The 50th Anniversary of Martin Luther King, Jr.'s 'All Labor Has Dignity,'" Beacon Broadside, Beacon Press, March 18, 2018, www.beaconbroadside.com/broadside/2018/03/the-50th-anniversary-of-martin-luther-king-jrs-all-labor-has-dignity.html.

44. We could augment the job guarantee with other new automatic stabilizers. The more driverless features we attach to the budget mechanism, the smoother our economic ride will become. Indexing wages (or other spending) in the job guarantee program to the inflation target—as opposed to the actual inflation rate—would provide an automatic boost to expenditures when actual inflation was running below, say, 2 percent.

45. Council of Economic Advisers: Walter Heller, Kermit Gordon, James Tobin, Gardner Ackley, and Paul Samuelson, recorded interview by Joseph Pechman, August 1, 1964, John F. Kennedy Library Oral History Program, www.jfklibrary.org/sites/default/files/archives/JFKOH/Council%20of%20Economic%20Advisers/JFKOH-CEA-01/JFKOH-CEA-01-TR.pdf.

46. Space.com staff, "May 25, 1961: JFK's Moon Shot Speech to Congress," Space.com, May 25, 2011, www.space.com/11772-president-kennedy-historic-speech-moon-space.html.

47. Inflation rose after President Johnson committed troops to Vietnam in July 1965.

48. Mariana Mazzucato, *The Entrepreneurial State: Debunking Public vs. Private Sector Myths* (Cambridge, MA: Anthem Press, 2014).

49. Mariana Mazzucato, "Mobilizing for a Climate Moonshot," Project Syndicate, October 8, 2019, www.project-syndicate.org/onpoint/climate-moonshot-government-innovation-by-mariana-mazzucato-2019-10.

Index

Stephanie Kelton, a professor of economics and public policy at Stony Brook University, is a leading expert on Modern Monetary Theory and a former chief economist on the US Senate Budget Committee (Democratic staff). She was named by Politico as one of the fifty people most influencing the policy debate in America.

Dr. Kelton advises policy makers, consults with investment banks and portfolio managers across the globe, and is a regular commentator on national radio and broadcast television. In addition to her many academic publications, she has been a contributor at Bloomberg Opinion and has written for the *New York Times*, *Los Angeles Times*, *U.S. News & World Reports*, and CNN.

Dr. Kelton is Executive Director of the MMT Project, holds a PhD in economics from the New School for Social Research, and was chair of the Department of Economics at the University of Missouri, Kansas City, before joining Stony Brook University.

PublicAffairs is a publishing house founded in 1997. It is a tribute to the standards, values, and flair of three persons who have served as mentors to countless reporters, writers, editors, and book people of all kinds, including me.

I. F. STONE, proprietor of *I. F. Stone's Weekly*, combined a commitment to the First Amendment with entrepreneurial zeal and reporting skill and became one of the great independent journalists in American history. At the age of eighty, Izzy published *The Trial of Socrates*, which was a national bestseller. He wrote the book after he taught himself ancient Greek.

BENJAMIN C. BRADLEE was for nearly thirty years the charismatic editorial leader of *The Washington Post*. It was Ben who gave the *Post* the range and courage to pursue such historic issues as Watergate. He supported his reporters with a tenacity that made them fearless and it is no accident that so many became authors of influential, best-selling books.

ROBERT L. BERNSTEIN, the chief executive of Random House for more than a quarter century, guided one of the nation's premier publishing houses. Bob was personally responsible for many books of political dissent and argument that challenged tyranny around the globe. He is also the founder and longtime chair of Human Rights Watch, one of the most respected human rights organizations in the world.

·   ·   ·

For fifty years, the banner of Public Affairs Press was carried by its owner Morris B. Schnapper, who published Gandhi, Nasser, Toynbee, Truman, and about 1,500 other authors. In 1983, Schnapper was described by *The Washington Post* as "a redoubtable gadfly." His legacy will endure in the books to come.

Peter Osnos, *Founder*